T0223694

Lecture Notes in Computer Science 1002

Edited by G. Goos, J. Hartmanis and J. van Leeuwen

Advisory Board: W. Brauer   D. Gries   J. Stoer

Springer

Berlin
Heidelberg
New York
Barcelona
Budapest
Hong Kong
London
Milan
Paris
Santa Clara
Singapore
Tokyo

James Jay Kistler

Disconnected Operation in a Distributed File System

Springer

Series Editors

Gerhard Goos
Universität Karlsruhe
Vincenz-Priessnitz-Straße 3, D-76128 Karlsruhe, Germany

Juris Hartmanis
Department of Computer Science, Cornell University
4130 Upson Hall, Ithaca, NY 14853, USA

Jan van Leeuwen
Department of Computer Science,Utrecht University
Padualaan 14, 3584 CH Utrecht, The Netherlands

Author

James Jay Kistler
Systems Research Center, Digital Equipment Corporation
130 Lytton Avenue, Palo Alto, CA 94301, USA

Cataloging-in-Publication data applied for

Die Deutsche Bibliothek - CIP-Einheitsaufnahme

Kistler, James Jay:
Disconnected operation in a distributed file sytem / James Jay Kistler. - Berlin ;
Heidelberg ; New York ; Barcelona ; Budapest ; Hong Kong ; London ; Milan ; Paris ;
Tokyo : Springer, 1996
  (Lecture notes in computer science ; 1002)
  ISBN 3-540-60627-0

NE: GT

CR Subject Classification (1991): D.4, C.2.4, E.5, F.2.2

ISBN 3-540-60627-0 Springer-Verlag Berlin Heidelberg New York

Typesetting: Camera-ready by author
SPIN 10486054   06/3142 – 5 4 3 2 1 0   Printed on acid-free paper

For Chris

Foreword

Tension between *autonomy* and *interdependence* lies at the heart of every distributed system. The ability to use remote resources enhances the storage capacity and computational power of a client. But there is a price to be paid: reliance on remote resources renders the client vulnerable to failures of the network or servers. In the worst case, a client can be totally crippled by the unavailability of a remote resource. This problem is already serious today, and will only worsen with further growth in the size and complexity of distributed systems.

How can one alleviate this problem? The traditional approach has been to use *replication* at servers. Unfortunately, there are limits to the value of this approach. It comes at significant hardware cost. Worse, it is useless if a network failure isolates a client from all server replicas. The latter scenario is especially common in *mobile computing*, where intermittent connectivity is an unfortunate fact of life.

In this doctoral dissertation, Jay Kistler describes a radically different solution. His approach, called *disconnected operation*, calls upon a client to mask failures from users and applications by emulating the functionality of a server. For distributed file systems, Kistler observes that this emulation can efficiently and cheaply be performed by exploiting the file cache already maintained by the client for performance reasons. This leads to a tantalizingly simple design: it just requires pre-loading the cache with critical data, continuing normal operation until disconnection, logging all changes made while disconnected, and replaying them upon reconnection.

Of course, reality is never that simple. There are many conceptual and implementation problems that arise when one tries to implement this functionality. For example:

- How does one arrange to have the right files in the cache at disconnection?
- How does the client conserve scarce cache space while disconnected?
- How can the process of reintegrating changes be made efficient and transparent?
- What are the security implications of disconnected operation?
- How can one reconcile the conflicting demands of availability and performance on caching?

- How can disconnected operation be seamlessly integrated with server replication?
- How likely are update conflicts, and how does one detect and cope with them?

Kistler answers these and many related questions in this work. The implementation he describes is of such high quality that it has been in serious use for over four years. The evaluation of the system is thorough and it sheds much light on the above questions. In addition, the work describes a new model of computation called the "inferred transaction model" that cleanly captures the semantics of disconnected operation. This model serves as an excellent conceptual foundation for reasoning about the consistency properties of disconnected operation.

This research has had substantial impact on industry. Many software companies have efforts under way to exploit these results commercially. There is now broad consensus that disconnected operation is a key enabling technology for mobile computing.

In closing, it is a pleasure to read a dissertation that is such a model of clarity and lucid exposition. The subtleties of the subproblems are brought out with great skill, and the specific solutions adopted are convincingly substantiated. The document is indeed worthy of the research it describes. I would expect no less of my friend, colleague, and former graduate student, Jay Kistler.

M. Satyanarayanan
Professor of Computer Science
Carnegie Mellon University
Pittsburgh, Pennsylvania
August 1995

Preface

Disconnected operation refers to the ability of a distributed system client to operate despite server inaccessibility by emulating services locally. The capability to operate disconnected is already valuable in many systems, and its importance is growing with two major trends: the increasing scale of distributed systems, and the proliferation of powerful mobile computers. The former makes clients vulnerable to more frequent and less controllable system failures, and the latter introduces an important class of clients which are disconnected frequently and for long durations – often as a matter of choice.

This dissertation shows that it is practical to support disconnected operation for a fundamental system service: general purpose file management. It describes the architecture, implementation, and evaluation of disconnected file service in the Coda file system. The architecture is centered on the idea that the disconnected service agent should be one and the same with the client cache manager. The Coda cache manager prepares for disconnection by pre-fetching and *hoarding* copies of critical files; while disconnected it logs all update activity and otherwise *emulates* server behavior; upon reconnection it *reintegrates* by sending its log to the server for replay. This design achieves the goal of high data availability – users can access many of their files while disconnected – but it does not sacrifice the other positive properties of contemporary distributed file systems: scalability, performance, security, and transparency.

Disconnected operation in Coda was designed and implemented during the period of 1989 to 1993. At the time this dissertation was completed, the system had been actively used by more than 20 people over the course of two years. Both stationary and mobile workstations had been employed as clients, and disconnections had ranged up to about ten days in length. Usage experience was extremely positive. The hoarding strategy sufficed to avoid most disconnected cache misses, and partitioned data sharing was rare enough to cause very few reintegration failures. Measurements and simulation results indicated that disconnected operation in Coda should be equally transparent and successful at much larger scale.

Since 1993 the system has continued to be used as a research vehicle at Carnegie Mellon University. The number of local users has grown significantly and the code has been made available for distribution outside of CMU.

Coda researchers have extended the system with important new functionality, including weakly-connected operation, advanced hoarding support, and transactional file system semantics. Reports of this progress are beginning to appear and to generate discussion in the academic literature.

Disconnected file service is also beginning to make its mark in the commercial world, driven by the tremendous success of mobile computers in the marketplace. Products offering limited forms of disconnected file support have been available from small companies for several years, and industry heavyweights such as IBM, DEC, and Microsoft are beginning to weigh-in with efforts of their own. These initial products are all hampered to some degree by the legacy of PC operating systems, but the obstacles are rapidly being overcome. I am certain that we will see more – and better – products of this type in the near future. Indeed, I am as confident today about the future of disconnected operation as I was two years ago when I wrote the final sentence of this dissertation: *The advantages of disconnected file service are so compelling that its support will – in my opinion – be a standard feature of all widely-used operating environments of the future.*

Acknowledgments

Performing the thesis research and writing this dissertation turned out to be a larger undertaking than I ever imagined. I could not have completed it without the care and support of many wonderful people, and I'm delighted to be able to acknowledge them here.

First, I would like to thank my advisor, Satya. I couldn't have had a better mentor. He always made time to see me, no matter how busy his schedule. He was a constant source of good ideas and an infallible detector of bad ones. He challenged me when I needed to be challenged and boosted my confidence when it needed to be boosted. He taught me the importance of critical thinking and of validating one's ideas through experimentation. More than anything, though, he has been a true and steady friend.

The other members of my thesis committee were helpful throughout my career at CMU. Early on, Rick Rashid and Eric Cooper co-advised me and made me feel comfortable as I was finding my way. Later, they gave sound advice on my topic and on research in general. Mike Schroeder helped to expose and formulate the problem that my work addresses, and his careful reading and critiquing of the dissertation made it a much better document. I thank all three of them for their efforts.

I warmly thank my colleagues in the Coda group: Maria Ebling, Puneet Kumar, Qi Lu, Hank Mashburn, Lily Mummert, Brian Noble, Josh Raiff, Ellen Siegel, and David Steere. They are all very talented individuals and it was a pleasure to work with them. Their help in the design, implementation, and usage phases of my work was invaluable. Many of them also read the dissertation and gave useful feedback on it, and I thank them for that extra effort. Special thanks go to Puneet, who never failed to help with a problem or to put a happy face on a discouraging development. I have never known anyone as cheerful or as generous as he.

I thank all of the people who used my software, who persevered through the rough stages of development and who gave me their feedback on what was good and what was bad. My users included all of the members of the Coda group, plus these other folks: Anurag Acharya, Adam Beguelin, Avrim Blum, David Eckhardt, Garth Gibson, Tammy Green, Tom Mitchell, Hugo Patterson, Henry Rowley, Karen Shay, Peter Stout, Manuela Veloso, and Matt Zekauskus.

A number of people on the CMU facilities staff helped me in setting up the Coda testbed environment, in collecting measurements, and in troubleshooting various problems. Special thanks go to Mike Accetta, Paul Parker, Mark Puskar, and Dimitris Varotsis. Bob Baron, Mike Jones, and Mary Thompson of the Mach group also assisted in these respects, and I thank them as well.

I also wish to thank the CMU-SCS faculty and administration for providing such a stimulating – and yet humane – environment in which to conduct research. I know of no other place that meets both of those objectives so well. Special thanks go to Sharon Burks as the cutter of all red-tape and to Catherine Copetas as the junk-food angel of mercy.

A large and wonderful circle of friends made my family's stay in Pittsburgh very special. In addition to the people mentioned already, I'd like to thank Robert and Edie, Harry, Linda and Phil, Claire and Craig, Rhoda and Julian, Geli and Bernd, Dave and Gretchen, Dave and Ann, Deborah, Wendy and Craig, Brian and Debbie, and Wayne and the rest of the "brew crew" for their friendship and for all of the good times.

My parents, Jim and Rita, instilled in me the desire to learn and the value of hard work. Without that grounding and their love I never could have come this far. My pal, Rigsby, took me on countless rejuvenating trips to the park and returned my affection manyfold. I thank the three of them for always being there.

My first daughter, Hannah, was born part way through my thesis research, and she gave me added incentive to finish. More importantly, she made me realize that, although I couldn't write the perfect dissertation, I couldn't be such a bad guy because I'd helped to bring her into the world. My second daughter, Nora, was born after I'd finished, and she continues to help put my work in perspective. My love and thanks go out to both of them.

Finally, my wife, Chris, deserves greater thanks than I can possibly give. For more than a dozen years she has stayed with me, patiently allowing me to pursue my dreams. She didn't complain when I asked her to move from Berkeley to England to continue my studies. Unbelievably, she didn't object when I asked her to leave London for Pittsburgh so that I could enter graduate school. In the course of almost seven years at CMU she never once complained that I was taking too long. During the really grim periods of dissertation writing, when I doubted everything I'd done and believed I could do no more, she comforted me and gave me the strength to keep going. Without her there for me I surely would have quit. I will always be grateful to her.

James Jay Kistler
Palo Alto, California
August 1995

Table of Contents

List of Figures

List of Tables

1. Introduction

This dissertation is concerned with the availability of data in distributed file systems. It argues that conventional system designs seriously limit availability, and that this limitation will become much more severe as computing environments expand in size and evolve in form to incorporate new technologies. It advocates the extension of *client caching* to support *disconnected operation* as a solution to this problem, and describes a working system built around this idea.

This chapter begins with context – about client/server computing in general, and distributed file access in particular. It then introduces the problem of disconnected clients and the proposed solution of disconnected operation. The chapter concludes with a statement of the thesis and an outline of the remainder of the document.

1.1 Distributed Computing

Distributed computing represents the convergence of the personal and time-shared computing paradigms. Personal computing is desirable because it gives users control over resources, allowing them to compute where, when and how they want. Time-shared or centralized computing is desirable because it permits efficient sharing – sharing of physical resources and sharing of information. Distributed computing attempts to provide the best of both worlds.

Collections of computers are formed into *distributed systems* by connecting them via communications networks and operating systems software. Sharing is achieved by exchanging messages which distribute data or request computation involving remote resources. The usual framework for organizing this activity is the *client/server* paradigm. In this model a client process invokes a service by sending a message to a server process, which performs the requested operation and sends back appropriate results. The client and server processes may be running on the same node (requiring only local communication), or they may be running on separate nodes (requiring remote communication). This distinction is conveniently hidden from programmers and users by layers of system software.

The client/server model is very flexible. In theory, a service can be located at any machine that has appropriate physical resources. Client processes at that site can use the service, as well as processes located throughout the network. Services can be relocated to match changing usage patterns, and new services introduced as sites acquire more resources.

In practice, however, most systems are organized around a nucleus of dedicated server machines, operated by a central authority, which provide service to a much larger community of independently owned client workstations. The motivations for this structure are twofold. One is to preserve the autonomy users expect from personal computing. Exporting a service from a personal machine means that a user's resources may be consumed by others – perhaps uncontrollably. Moreover, the exporter may incur unwanted obligations to back-up data, repair broken hardware promptly, refrain from turning the machine off, and so on. Neither of these situations is consistent with the expectations of personal computing.

The other motivation for physically separating clients and servers is to cope with the effects of scale. Beyond small scale, system security and operability become paramount concerns. Spreading services across many machines multiplies the burden and cost of keeping the system operational. Worse, it reduces security to the level of the least secure machine in the system – an intolerable situation. Centralizing services makes it possible to administer the system and provide reasonable security in a cost effective way.

1.2 Distributed File Systems

Distributed file systems are the bedrock of distributed computing in office/engineering environments. Their utility is obvious: they enhance information sharing among users, decouple users from particular hosts, facilitate parallel processing, and simplify the administration of large numbers of machines. The popularity of distributed file systems such as NFS [78] and AFS [83] attests to the compelling nature of these considerations. In many cases, other services such as electronic mail delivery and printing are layered on top of the distributed file system, furthering its importance.

The basic principles of distributed file systems are well understood. Server processes which export an interface allowing clients to read and write objects are located at nodes with non-volatile storage. Support for naming, authentication, and synchronization may be provided as well. Most often the programming interface is the same as or very similar to that of a non-distributed file system. This provides the major benefit of a ready body of applications that can use the system. Several excellent surveys [52, 82, 95] provide background on the field and compare contemporary distributed file systems across various criteria.

Client Caching. By far the most important architectural feature of distributed file systems is the caching of data at clients. Caching keeps copies of information where it will be used so that expensive communication can be avoided. Most distributed file systems cache file data in the main memory of client machines. Some, such as AFS and Cedar [90], employ a further level of file caching on the client's local disk.

Caching improves client performance and the scalability of the distributed file system, often dramatically. Performance is improved because the average latency to read data is lowered by requests that hit in the cache. Scalability benefits from the fact that servers handle fewer requests and transfer fewer bytes of data per client. Performance and scalability are enhanced even further if writes are delayed and sent in batch rather than immediately written through to the server.

Caching is so effective in distributed file systems because of the way files are used. Numerous studies of file usage patterns [24, 23, 65, 79, 93] have confirmed the following:

− *spatial locality* is high; most files are read and written sequentially, and in their entirety.
− *temporal locality* is high; a file accessed once is likely to be accessed again by the same user, probably soon, and probably multiple times.
− most files are small, less than a few tens of kilobytes.
− *write-sharing* is rare, particularly within short time intervals.

The first three points mean that relatively small caches can capture typical *working sets* [19] and adapt quickly to changes in them. The last point means that *cache coherence* – mutual consistency of cached data – can be maintained with modest effort.[1]

Caching alters the structure of the client/server model by adding a level of indirection. Without caching, user processes make direct requests of file servers. The local operating system is involved only inasmuch as it may provide underlying message support. With caching, user processes are no longer clients of the file service per se, but clients of a local "file-cache service" instead. The file-cache server is a client – and in fact the only local client – of the file service proper. This indirection is hidden from user processes by machinery below the operating system interface. The file-cache server, or *cache manager*, may be implemented as a module inside the operating system, or as a separate user-level process, or as some combination of the two. Figure 1.1 illustrates the distinction between generic caching and non-caching organizations.

---

[1] The latest study by Baker et al [5] notes the occurrence of more "access-once" activity on large files (such as images and simulation data). The implication is that caching will not be useful for these objects. However, a significant core of "conventional usage" remains, for which caching will continue to be effective.

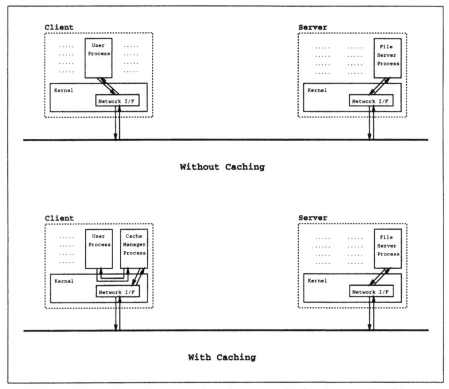

The top figure shows the processing of a request in the absence of caching. The bottom figure illustrates request processing with caching, where the cache manager services some requests on its own and passes others on to remote servers. The cache manager and file server are depicted as user-level processes running on top of a lightweight kernel, but alternatively could be modules inside a conventional, monolithic operating system.

Fig. 1.1. Effect of Caching on Service Structure

1.3 Disconnected Clients

The Achilles' heel of distributed computing is service availability. In non-distributed systems all services are provided locally, so whenever a user's process is running it can obtain any of the services supported by the host machine. If the operating system crashes or the hardware fails then this is immediately apparent, and the machine can be rebooted or repaired as necessary. Service availability is determined solely by the reliability of the local hardware and system software.

In contrast, a distributed system client obtains many services remotely, exchanging messages over a network with various server machines. Service availability is contingent upon more than just the local machine being up: the server machine, the server process, and all intervening network components must be operational as well. A client which is functioning normally, but which cannot obtain a service due to remote failure is said to be *disconnected* with respect to that service. A disconnected client will not in general know the cause of disconnection – the only sure evidence is a message sent to the server process which is not acknowledged in a reasonable period of time.

Disconnections are bad because they impede computation. Typically, a process which invokes a service from which it is disconnected will block indefinitely or abort. Either result is likely to frustrate the user. This is particularly true when the service is within the capabilities of the local machine, but remote access has been configured for the purpose of sharing. In such circumstances the autonomy gained by decentralizing computation is lost; the user does indeed have control over local resources, but they are not sufficient to get real work done.

Disconnections are a real-life problem – they are not hypothetical. Every serious user of a distributed system has faced situations in which critical work has been impeded by remote failure. Leslie Lamport noted this long ago with his wry definition of a distributed system as "one where I can't get my work done because of some computer that I've never heard of." The severity of the problem varies from system to system, but, in general, the larger and more heterogeneous the system the more acute it is likely to be.

It is tempting to hope that improvements in hardware technology (such as Autonet [89]) will render disconnections insignificant over time. While such developments may alleviate aspects of the problem, I do not believe that they will completely solve it. On the contrary, I believe that disconnections will increase rather than decrease in significance in the future, for at least two reasons:

1. the increasing scale of distributed systems will result in more frequent *involuntary* disconnections (i.e., unplanned entry into disconnected state).
2. the proliferation of mobile computers will dramatically increase the importance of disconnections. Mobile clients that are networked by conventional wired technologies will experience frequent *voluntary* disconnection (i.e., intentional entry into disconnected state), while those networked by newer wireless technologies will suffer many more involuntary disconnections per-capita than their stationary counterparts.

These two issues are explored further in the following subsections.

1.3.1 Impact of Large Scale

Successful distributed systems tend to grow in size. Large scale increases the likelihood of disconnection in two ways. First, it encourages the splitting of complementary services and the partitioning of single services across multiple machines. For example, locating authentication and file servers on different hosts, or distributing the namespace supported by a name service across multiple machines. This makes any given client dependent on more machines and network paths than at smaller scale. Assuming somewhat independent failure behavior, the client will be disconnected from at least some service a higher percentage of the time. Moreover, a partial disconnection is often as damaging as a total one, since many tasks require multiple services in order to complete.

Second, large scale necessarily results in much larger interconnects. Unfortunately, large networks often turn out to be rather fragile and unreliable. They are typically constructed by piecing together many smaller, heterogeneous sub-networks using active elements such as bridges and routers. These components are very sensitive to the rate and patterns of traffic flowing across them. A traffic change which overflows or saturates a router, for example, can have a cascading effect throughout the network – initially lost packets, then retransmission storms, then further saturations, and so on. Confinement of damage becomes very difficult, and the overall reliability of the network tends to degrade to that of its least reliable component.

Compounding the problem is the fact that parts of the network are likely to be owned and administered by separate organizations or administrative units. Fault diagnosis, load balancing, component upgrade, and even routine maintenance are all problematic when network authority and control are distributed. Independent budgets and political issues may block even obvious problem remedies, and make network policy consensus impossible to achieve.

1.3.2 Impact of Mobile Computers

Mobile computers are one of the fastest-growing segments of the computer industry. In 1991, they accounted for 14% of total personal computer sales, and it's predicted that by 1995 over half of all PCs sold will be of this class [100]. Many current units are as powerful as desktop workstations, can easily be connected to standard networks such as ethernet, and could well benefit from shared access to resources and data.

Yet mobile computers are seldom used in distributed systems today. This is because few of the places that users want to take their computers to are within reach of conventional, high-bandwidth networks. Few airplanes, lecture halls, or shady oak trees have ethernet taps, for example. Use of a mobile computer in current distributed systems is therefore futile, since it implies frequent voluntary disconnections – which occur just when the machine should be most useful. So although the number of actual disconnections involving mobile computers is currently low, the opportunity cost – measured in foregone voluntary disconnections – is exceedingly high.

High-bandwidth wireless networks, based on packet radio, infrared, or other still-developing technologies, would mitigate the problem of voluntary disconnection. However, these technologies typically have intrinsic limitations such as short-range, dead zones, or line-of-sight constraints. These shortcomings imply that mobile clients will continue to be limited by disconnections even if wireless communication becomes widespread in the future. The only difference is that a greater fraction of the disconnections will be involuntary than if wired network technologies continue to dominate.

1.4 Disconnected Operation

There are two basic approaches to the problem of disconnected clients, avoidance and accommodation. Avoidance treats causes rather than symptoms. The last section argued that avoidance based solely on highly reliable hardware is insufficient, at least for the foreseeable future.

Replicating servers is a second technique for avoiding disconnections. A client in contact with an appropriate subset of servers is still logically "connected" to the service. Server replication is often effectively used to mask site failures, since small replication factors suffice to cover independent failures. Unfortunately, it is far less effective in combating network failures, as the degree of replication needed to avoid all or even most disconnections rises quickly. In the case of mobile computers no degree of server replication is adequate, as voluntary disconnections are unavoidable by definition. Server replication is also vulnerable to dependent failures, such as replicated bugs.

The alternative to avoidance is to build enough resiliency into the system to allow work to continue in spite of disconnections. *Disconnected operation* refers to the ability of a client to continue computing during disconnections by *emulating* services it would otherwise obtain remotely. Emulation typically requires a local agent to act as a representative of the disconnected service, although for simple services it may suffice just to alter the libraries which invoke it. In some cases additional hardware may be needed at the client – for example, to emulate a printing service.

Disconnected operation is neither a specific technique nor a radically new idea.[2] Rather, it is a general philosophy which holds that it is often better to receive an approximation to something than it is to receive nothing at all. Client emulation yields an approximation to the service that would have been provided absent disconnection In the best case, the approximation will be so good that the user or application will not notice the difference; that is, the emulation will be fully *transparent*. But even when full transparency is not feasible, an emulation which offers a known approximation to the service may be far preferable to blocking or aborting a computation.

Many simple network services have long and effectively supported disconnected operation. For example, the hostname lookup library of BSD Unix[3] systems will fall-back on search through a local host file if the name server is inaccessible. The host database changes very slowly, so this approach almost

---

[2] Disconnected operation is identical to *stashing*, as defined by Birrell [7] and Schroeder [88]. Disconnected operation seems a more general term, as "stashing" connotes emulation techniques which are not always applicable.

[3] Unix is a trademark of Unix System Laboratories. BSD refers to the family of Berkeley Software Distributions of Unix.

always yields correct results. Similarly, time-of-day queries often continue to be serviced using a local clock during disconnection, even though uncorrected drift may cause readings to differ significantly from the "true" network time. In practice, drift is small over the length of most disconnections, so this emulation is almost always transparent.

Disconnected operation for some services is inherently much harder than for others. Those which involve shared access to mutable data are particularly difficult to handle. Emulation in such cases necessarily involves data replication, and must be concerned with partitioned accesses to the same logical data items. At risk is the mutual consistency of the replicas and the semantics of computation involving the data. In general, availability and consistency cannot both be maximized in the presence of sharing and partitionings. Hence, disconnected service may involve a compromise between unrestricted access and strong semantics for sharing data. In cases where sharing is pervasive and the strongest possible semantics are required, disconnected operation may be severely restricted or simply not practical.

1.5 The Thesis

But we do not yet understand whether [disconnected operation] is feasible.

Andrew Birrell [7]

[Disconnected operation for] files, for example, may be hard – but is worth exploring.

Mike Schroeder [88]

Past research into distributed file system availability has focused almost entirely on *server-side* remedies; i.e., flavors of server replication (see, for example, [27, 69, 99, 55, 73, 25]). Scant attention has been given to *client-side* approaches to the problem. I claim that this inattention has been costly, and that it is now appropriate to redirect efforts towards the client end of the system. My claim is based on the following observations:

– large system scale introduces failure modes for which server replication is not cost effective.
– server replication is inadequate to address the needs of mobile computing.
– file usage patterns – high locality and low write-sharing – make file service an excellent candidate for emulation at disconnected clients.
– modern distributed file systems already have a sophisticated subsystem – caching – for emulating service at connected clients.

These observations lead directly to the thesis statement:

Disconnected operation at distributed file system clients can be supported effectively using caching, such that availability is significantly increased without undue sacrifice of scalability, performance, semantics, usability or overall system utility. The technique also permits the graceful integration of mobile clients into the system.

1.5.1 Requirements for Masking Disconnection

Client cache managers currently emulate file server actions in the interest of performance and scalability. Emulation is constrained by certain events and service guarantees which require communication with servers. These vary somewhat from system to system, but communication generally results from the following:

- references to uncached data or naming information.
- validation/invalidation of the currency of cached data, and propagation of changes to make them visible to other processes.
- propagation of changes to free cache space.
- propagation of changes to guarantee persistence.
- verification of user identity or access rights.

The thesis postulates that caching can be overloaded to increase availability. For this to be successful, the system must eliminate the need for client/server communication during disconnections. *Masking* disconnection requires the system to address a set of issues corresponding directly to the above list of communication-inducing events:

- *cache miss avoidance*: the probability that a disconnected reference will miss in the cache must be minimized. Naming information must be cached with file data to support disconnected path expansion.
- *replica control*: a policy and algorithm for partitioned replica control must be designed. The resulting impact on the semantics of user computation must be carefully considered and specified.
- *update buffering*: updates must be buffered at the client until connection is reestablished. Use of buffer space must be optimized to avoid early exhaustion of resources.
- *persistence*: the state of a disconnected client must be persistent, i.e., it must survive restarts. Data must be *recoverable* even in the face of unclean shutdown and asynchronous update of non-volatile store.
- *security*: the legality of disconnected operations, particularly updates, must be ensured. Disconnected operation should not allow the security model of the system to be circumvented.

In addition to these masking requirements, the system must also make disconnected operation convenient and usable. It should appear as much like connected operation as possible, and make minimal extra demands on users to work well. Finally, it should not reduce the utility of connected operation in any significant way.

1.5.2 Establishing the Thesis

The thesis was investigated by incorporating disconnected support into the caching subsystem of an existing distributed file system, *Coda* [86]. Coda is a descendant of AFS whose goal is to improve data availability within the framework of large, distributed computing environments. A complete design and implementation of disconnected file service was produced, and about two dozen individuals were recruited to use the system in their everyday work. Versions of the system were actively used for a period of about two years, and both stationary and mobile workstations were employed as clients. The system was evaluated both qualitatively and quantitatively, with the results providing strong validation of the thesis statement.

1.6 Organization of this Document

The rest of this document is organized as follows. Chapter 2 provides rationale for the design of disconnected operation in Coda. It presents the system model of AFS, and explains why the bulk of it is preserved in Coda. Chapter 2 also contains in-depth treatment of the replica control issues involved in disconnected operation, and motivates the replica control strategy employed in Coda. Chapter 3 contains an overview of the Coda architecture for disconnected operation. It introduces the three states of cache manager operation, as well as the key mechanisms for masking client/server communication during disconnection.

Chapters 4, 5, 6, and 7 cover the design and implementation of the system in depth. Each of the latter three chapters is devoted to one of the states of cache manager operation: hoarding, server emulation, and reintegration, respectively. Chapter 4 presents material on the internal structuring of Coda that is useful in understanding the chapters which follow.

Chapter 8 evaluates the design and implementation of disconnected operation in Coda. The evaluation is based on actual usage experience gained by a moderately-sized user community over a period of several years. Chapter 8 also reports the results of experiments which characterize system behavior quantitatively, and which extrapolate it to conditions beyond those of the testbed environment. Chapter 9 discusses related work, and Chapter 10 concludes with a summary of the thesis work and its contributions and a discussion of interesting future work.[4]

---

[4] Three earlier papers have focused on disconnected operation in Coda [44, 43, 45]. The last of these is the most in-depth, and serves as an extended abstract of this entire document.

2. Design Rationale

Coda is a distributed file system with the goal of providing scalable, secure, and highly available file service to a community of users with personal workstations. Disconnected operation and server replication are the two mechanisms used in Coda to support high availability. This chapter provides background and rationale for the design of Coda in general, and for disconnected operation in particular.

2.1 AFS Heritage

Coda is a descendant of the Andrew file system (AFS) [85, 39, 83]. Three distinct versions of AFS, known as AFS-1, AFS-2, and AFS-3, were developed at Carnegie Mellon University (CMU) from 1983 to 1989. A fourth version, AFS-4, has been developed and is being marketed by Transarc Corporation. Coda was cleaved from the family tree at the time of AFS-2, and although development of the two branches has proceeded independently, Coda retains much of the original AFS model and mechanisms. Hence, it is appropriate to begin the discussion of Coda with an overview of AFS.[1]

2.1.1 Vice/Virtue

AFS was designed to serve the filing needs of the entire CMU community. Each member of the community was expected to eventually have their own workstation, implying a scale of nearly 10,000 nodes. This was at least one order of magnitude larger than any distributed file system built or conceived of at that time. Not surprisingly, the scale of the system became the dominant consideration in its design.

The AFS designers addressed scale at the structural level by partitioning the nodes into two sets. *Vice* consists of a relatively small collection of dedicated server machines, owned and administered by a central authority. *Virtue* consists of a much larger set of Unix workstations which are owned and operated by independent groups or individuals. User computation is performed only at workstations, never at server machines. A conceptual view of the system is shown in Figure 2.1.

---

[1] Unqualified use of the term "AFS" should henceforth be taken to mean AFS-2.

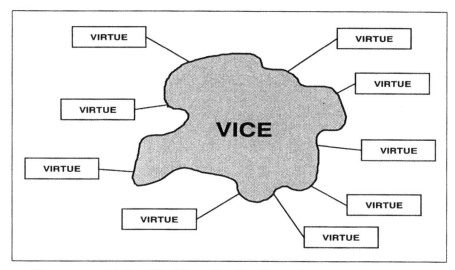

The structure labeled "Vice" is a collection of trusted servers and untrusted
networks. The nodes labeled "Virtue" are private or public workstations
(or occasionally time-sharing systems). Vice is reputed to stand for "Vast
Integrated Computing Environment," and Virtue for "Virtue is Realized
through Unix and Emacs." This figure is courtesy of M. Satyanarayanan.

Fig. 2.1. Vice and Virtue

A process called *Venus* runs on each Virtue workstation and acts as the
principal client interface to Vice. Venus makes the shared files in Vice appear
as a single large subtree of the workstation file system. *Name* and *location
transparency* are provided within the Vice portion of the namespace. That
is, Vice files have the same name at each workstation, and the particular
server for a Vice file is not apparent from its name. Each workstation also
has a non-shared area of the namespace which is used for temporary files, files
essential for booting the machine, local devices, and virtual memory paging.
The file system view seen by a workstation user is depicted in Figure 2.2.

The Vice/Virtue separation is crucial to the usability of the system at
scale. It pervades each of the following issues.

Security. The distributed control of machines, widespread access to the network, and relative anonymity of users make security a major concern at large
scale. The "goodwill of one's colleagues" no longer suffices to protect one's
data. AFS addresses this concern in three ways: physically securing shared
machines (i.e., those in Vice), conducting all Vice/Virtue communication over
secure connections, and providing a powerful protection specification mechanism. Physical security is ensured by keeping servers in locked rooms and
running only trusted system software on them. Secure connections are arranged through a variant of the Needham and Schroeder private key authen-

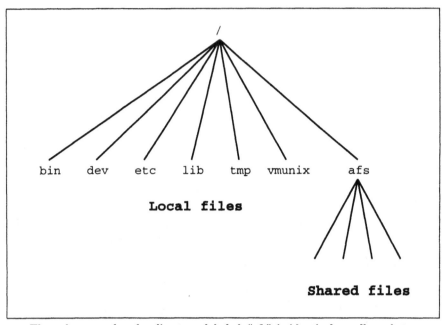

The subtree under the directory labeled "afs" is identical at all workstations. The other files and directories are local to each workstation.

Fig. 2.2. File System View at a Virtue Workstation

tication protocol [62]. Protection is specified via per-directory access-control lists containing the names of groups and users and their particular rights on all objects in the directory.

The system places no reliance on the integrity of client workstations. It is assumed that workstations can have their hardware and software tampered with in arbitrary ways. Any other assumption would be naïve and perilous in a large system. Consequently, AFS is geared towards confining damage which results from such activity rather than preventing its occurrence. An attacker which subverts a workstation gains access only to objects for which the user of the workstation had legitimate rights. The protection and authentication mechanisms of the system prevent the spread of damage to arbitrary regions of the namespace. Hence, a user may protect his or her own data by using only "clean" workstations, but this responsibility is his or her own and not that of the system at large.[2]

System administration. A central operations staff can focus effort and resources on the relatively small number of servers, and delegate responsibility

---

[2] In reality, even a careful AFS user is vulnerable to network attacks which intercept or modify unencrypted data packets. Encryption is an option of the system, but it is typically not enabled for data packets because software encryption is too slow and hardware encryption is too expensive. The advent of fast, cheap encryption hardware would close this security loophole.

for clients to the cost centers that own them. New clients can be added to the system simply by attaching them to the network and assigning them addresses.

Client autonomy. A Virtue workstation has no responsibility for the overall functioning of the system. In particular, no other client depends on it for service. Hence, it can be turned off or relocated at any time without inconveniencing other users. Such flexibility allows the machine to be viewed as a genuine "personal computer," which also happens to benefit from shared file service.

Satyanarayanan [84] summarizes the AFS approach as "[decomposing] a large distributed system into a small nucleus that changes relatively slowly, and a much larger and less static periphery. From the perspectives of security and operability, the scale of the system appears to be that of the nucleus." He notes further that physical separation of clients and servers is essential to this approach, and argues that no system ignoring this distinction can scale beyond moderate size.

2.1.2 Client Caching

AFS makes heavy use of client caching to reduce the amount of client/server communication and the server load imposed by each client. This has both local and global benefits. Locally, it results in better performance, as average latency decreases due to accesses which hit in the cache. Globally, it results in better scalability, as more clients can be supported by each server.

The AFS cache manager, Venus, intercepts file system calls made on Vice objects and services them locally whenever possible. When necessary, it communicates with servers in Vice using a remote procedure call (RPC) interface. The following characteristics are central to the client-caching architecture of AFS:

- whole files are transferred and cached rather than individual blocks.
- files are cached in non-volatile store, on a disk local to each client.
- naming information – directories and symbolic links – is cached in addition to plain files.
- an object's status (attributes, etc) is cached separately from its contents.
- cache coherence is maintained at the granularity of *sessions* rather than individual reads and writes.
- the coherence protocol is invalidation-based rather than validate-on-use.

These characteristics are discussed further below.

Cache Structure. Whole-file caching is motivated chiefly by considerations of scale. It permits the use of bulk-transfer protocols which impose much less overhead per-byte than do page or other block-oriented schemes. Cache management is also simplified, since there is less state to keep track of. Of course, the whole-file approach is effective only if most applications access entire objects rather than small pieces of them. Although this is the typical access pattern in Unix environments, certain applications, particularly databases, do not match it well. AFS effectively requires that such applications be supported by some other mechanism.

On-disk caching also contributes to system scalability. It allows much larger – and therefore more effective – caches to be used than does a main-memory caching architecture. Disk caches of several hundred megabytes are not at all unreasonable. Disk caching also means that the cache does not have to be re-loaded on machine reboot, a surprisingly frequent occurrence in many environments. Moreover, a local disk obviates any need for cross-network paging, which can be a serious impediment to scalability.

The caching of naming information is beneficial in two ways. First, for applications which directly read such information, the benefit is the same as for plain files. That is, repeated accesses to such objects incur less latency and impose less system overhead than if they were not cached. Second, and perhaps more importantly, it permits pathname resolution to be done by Venus rather than by servers. Name resolution maps high-level, multi-component string names to the low-level identifiers required to access physical storage. It entails repeated lookups of path components within directories, and expansion of symbolic links as they are encountered. Having this information cached saves at least one server interaction per pathname, which reduces latency and server load considerably.

Venus keeps separate caches of object status descriptors and object contents. An object's status can be cached without its contents, but not vice-versa. Status-only caching is useful when an object's attributes are read via a stat call but the object is not subsequently open'ed at the workstation. Such behavior is very common in practice, arising from "namespace exploration" and the use of tools such as make. In these cases status-only caching conserves precious cache space and avoids the latency and server load due to fetching unneeded information.

Cache Coherence. Cache coherence in AFS is based on the notion of *sessions*. In most cases, a session is the same as a system call. The most important exception concerns open and close calls, and the events that can occur between them. A session is defined to be one of the following:

– the sequence of calls on a file or directory bracketed by open and close calls. When there are overlapping opens, the session is delineated by the first open and the last close.
– a readlink call.
– an attribute reading call: access, stat.
– an attribute setting call: chmod, chown, truncate, utimes.
– a mutating directory call: create, link, mkdir, rename, rmdir, symlink, unlink.

The first type is known as a *compound* session, and the others are all known as *simple* sessions.[3]

AFS ensures that caches are coherent at the start of all sessions and the end of mutating sessions, but not when mutating sessions are in progress. At the start of a compound session – that is, when handling an open call – Venus checks to see whether it has the latest copy of the object cached. If it does not, it fetches fresh data from Vice. Operations on the open object are performed only on the cache copy – they involve no remote communication. At session end, Venus stores the entire file back to Vice if any part of it was updated. In the case of a simple session, the system call is coincident with both session start and end, but the same basic approach applies: cache copies are made coherent, updates are written back to Vice if appropriate, and the operation is performed locally.

The use of session rather than read/write coherence is beneficial because it reduces the frequency of client/server interaction. However, it also affects the accuracy of Unix emulation. Processes which expect to write-share open files must be running on the same client to receive precise Unix semantics. Processes on different clients see changes only at the granularity of open and close events. This limitation has proved acceptable in the AFS world because most such sharing occurs between system daemons and user processes – which naturally do run on the same client, or is associated with database applications – which are already presumed outside the domain of the system.

Cache coherence is enforced in AFS via a simple *callback* scheme [41]. Each server keeps a table identifying which clients have which objects in their caches. When one client updates an object, the server sends invalidation messages to other clients which have entries in its table for the object. Invalidation causes the client to discard its now stale copy and the server to remove the corresponding table entry. A table entry is known as a *callback promise*, and an invalidation is known as a *callback break*.[4]

The value of a callback scheme is that it avoids communication at session start time. The "currency check" made by Venus simply tests whether the object is cached and has a callback promise outstanding. If both conditions are true, then Venus need not contact Vice to verify currency. Since write-sharing is rare and temporal locality high in Unix usage patterns, this situation very often holds. Scalability is much improved and latency much reduced over the alternative of checking with the server on each open or other session-starting call.

---

[3] The earliest reference to file sessions is in Maloney and Black [54]. Their definition encompasses only the compound type of session described here.

[4] Callback schemes are referred to as *directory-based* protocols in the multi-processer caching literature.

2.1.3 Volumes

AFS uses a data-structuring primitive known as a *volume* [92] to make administration of the system efficient at large scale. A volume is a collection of files located on one server and forming a partial subtree of the Vice namespace. Volumes are conceptually similar to mountable Unix file systems, but are considerably more flexible. Typically, one volume is assigned to each user, with additional system and group volumes deployed as necessary. A volume may grow or shrink in size, and may be transparently moved from one server to another. Movement may occur even when objects in the volume are being fetched or updated. Disk storage quotas may be specified and enforced for individual volumes. Backup is performed by making a read-only clone of a volume in machine-independent format. The clone can later be restored on any available server.

The complete Vice namespace is formed by gluing volumes together at *mount points*. A mount point is a leaf node of a volume which identifies another volume whose root directory is attached at that node. Mount points are represented as special symbolic links, whose contents are the name of the target volume and whose mode bits are a reserved value. Venus recognizes mount points during name resolution and crosses them automatically. This scheme ensures name transparency, since the composition of volumes is determined globally by state in the file system itself, rather than locally by actions taken at each client (as with the NFS mount mechanism, for example).

Volumes are pivotal to location as well as name transparency. Neither high- nor low-level names contain direct location information. The low-level name of each object is its *file identifier* (fid), a 96-bit quantity consisting of a 32-bit *volume identifier* and a 64-bit *vnode number*. An object is located by mapping its volume identifier to the server which is the current *custodian* of the volume. These mappings are contained in the volume location database (VLDB), which is replicated at each server. Venus obtains VLDB mappings as it crosses mount points, and caches them for future use. The movement of a volume from one server to another changes its VLDB entry, meaning that cached location information at some Veni is no longer valid. Those Veni will discover this the next time they approach the "old" server about an object in the volume, and they will re-query the VLDB to get the new information.

2.2 Coda Charter

AFS succeeded to a very large degree in meeting its design goals. The scalability of the architecture has been convincingly demonstrated; several installations have exceeded 1000 nodes, and the *cellular* extensions of AFS-3 [102] have been used to link more than 50 installations worldwide into a single namespace. AFS performance has been generally competitive with other distributed file systems, though systems which employ true *copy-back* of mutations can do somewhat better.[5]

2.2.1 High Availability in an AFS-Like Environment

The most serious limitation of AFS has been data availability. As AFS installations have gotten bigger, involving more and more servers and spanning more and more network segments, failures have had a significant effect on data availability. In addition, integration of mobile computers has been thwarted because the system requires constant, reliable network connectivity between clients and servers.

Coda was chartered to address these limitations, without sacrificing any of the positive characteristics of AFS. This meant preserving the basic architectural elements discussed in the last section: the Vice/Virtue model, client caching, and volumes. Coda also makes essentially the same environmental assumptions as AFS:

- medium to large scale of the system – on the order of thousands to tens of thousands of nodes.
- a typical office/engineering workload – text editing, program development, electronic mail, data analysis, etc. Highly concurrent, fine-grained access typified by database applications is specifically not assumed.
- a client hardware base of engineering workstations and high-end personal computers. Each client has a high-bandwidth, low-latency network connection, and a moderate amount of non-volatile storage (tens to a few hundreds of megabytes).
- a *primary-user* model of client operation. The primary-user controls the console, and remote users are allowed at his or her discretion. The workstation may be private, public, or shared among the members of a small group.
- the Unix application program interface (API).[6]

The important additional assumption made by Coda is that the client base includes significant numbers of mobile computers. These machines may be networked using wired or wireless technologies and, in either case, are often used outside the limits of the network.

---

[5] AFS-4 [42] does employ true copy-back, using a token scheme similar to that of Echo [38].

[6] There are actually many distinct "Unix APIs," as that system has evolved in many directions over the years. However, the differences in the APIs matter little for the purposes of this thesis. Unless otherwise noted, the specific API referred to is that of 4.3 BSD [51].

2.2.2 First- versus Second-Class Replication

High data availability obviously requires replication. We – the designers of Coda – chose to explore both server- and client-based replication strategies. We felt that each would have advantages over the other in certain situations, and that the two could be used in tandem to provide the highest possible availability. But we also considered it important that each mechanism be usable by itself, so that solutions could be tailored to specific environmental conditions.

The two availability-enhancing mechanisms we designed and implemented are known as *server replication* and *disconnected operation*. The former replicates data at servers and allows computation to continue at a client when it is connected to only a subset of the permanent replication sites. The latter makes use of cached data to allow clients which are disconnected from all permanent replication sites to continue computing.

A basic tenet of Coda is that server replication and disconnected operation should work together to increase data availability. Neither mechanism alone is optimal in all situations. Server replication increases the availability of all shared data, but it is expensive and does not help if all servers fail or if all of them are inaccessible due to a network failure adjacent to a client. Voluntary disconnection of a mobile computer is a special case of the latter. On the other hand, disconnected operation is limited by the fact that client storage capacity is small in relation to the total amount of shared data, and because future accesses cannot be predicted with complete certainty. In addition, certain kinds of clients, such as public workstations and large, multi-user machines, are not comfortable with all of the consequences of disconnected operation.

A useful distinction to make is between *first-class* replicas on servers, and *second-class* replicas on clients. This dichotomy follows directly from the Vice/Virtue organization inherited from AFS. First-class replicas are of higher quality: they are more persistent, widely known, secure, and complete. Second-class replicas, in contrast, are inferior along all these dimensions. The system's efforts in supporting disconnected operation can be seen as masking the "quality gap" between first- and second-class replicas.[7]

In this new terminology, first-class replication is synonymous with server replication and second-class replication with disconnected operation. These terms will be used interchangeably throughout the rest of this document.

The Coda strategy is to rely on first-class replication as long as it is cost-effective, and to turn to disconnected operation only as a last resort. The degree of server replication that is appropriate is a function of how well the system can mask the quality gap, and of the marginal contribution to availability of each additional first-class replica. In environments where

---

[7] The terms first- and second-class were used by Purdin in [72] to make a similar distinction between replication sites.

disconnected operation is very successful, server replication may not be cost-effective even at replication factor two. In other situations, for example a clientele of low-capacity portable computers with wireless network capability, server replication to degree three or four may be appropriate. Coda offers the flexibility to vary replication factors over time and across the namespace. Figure 2.3 depicts a scenario in which server replication and disconnected operation are used together to improve availability.

2.3 Partitioned Replica Control

Replica control refers to the mapping of requests to read and write logical data items onto physical copies of objects. It may also include activity which occurs independent of any specific request, such as the background propagation of the value at one replica to another.

Replica control is made difficult by the fact that the network can partition the sites storing replicas into disjoint sets. Partitioning forces the system to trade-off consistency of data versus availability. Fundamentally, a trade-off is required because updates made in one partition cannot be seen in others until the partitioning is healed. Unrestricted access to partitioned physical copies can therefore lead to inconsistencies and incorrect computations. Maintaining strict consistency, on the other hand, requires severe restrictions on the accesses that can be allowed during partitionings. Although consistency and availability cannot both be maximized, numerous trade-offs are possible. The design task is to identify the compromise which best matches the requirements of the system at hand.

Partitionings are a critical issue for both server replication and disconnected operation in Coda. In the former case, network failure partitions first-class replicas with disjoint sets of clients. In the latter case, network failure or voluntary disconnection partitions a client's second-class replica from the first-class replica at the server. If an installation is using both server replication and disconnected operation, then combinations of these scenarios can occur.

Coda applies a common philosophy and model of replica control to disconnected operation and server replication. This provides a consistent semantics when the two are used together in the same system. The implementations of the mechanisms are somewhat different, however, reflecting the fundamental distinction between clients and servers in the AFS/Coda model. Most of the rest of this section discusses issues common to both mechanisms, and the term "replica" need not be qualified by server or client (or first- or second-class). Subsection 2.3.4 is the only place where rationale specific to one mechanism – disconnected operation – is given.

Replica control in Coda is optimized for availability, scalability, and performance. Consistency, or, more accurately, faithfulness to BSD Unix seman-

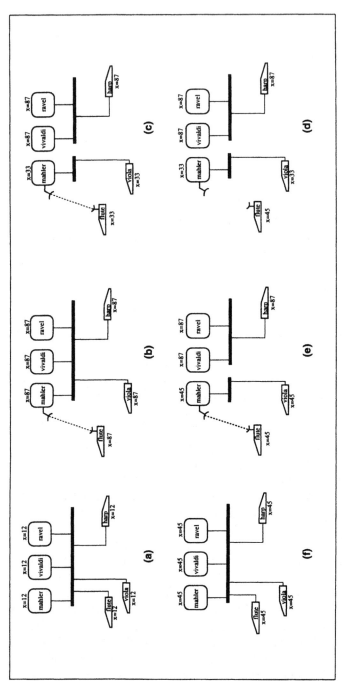

Three servers (*mahler, vivaldi,* and *ravel*) have replicas of file x. This file is potentially of interest to users at three clients (*flute, viola,* and *harp*). *Flute* is capable of wireless communication (indicated by a dotted line) as well as regular network communication. Proceeding clockwise, the steps above show the value of x seen by each node as the connectivity of the system changes. Note that in step (d), *flute* is operating disconnected.

Fig. 2.3. Integration of Server Replication and Disconnected Operation

tics, is relaxed in certain controlled ways to achieve this. Four features are of primary importance in characterizing the Coda approach:

- the use of the *transaction* model of computation.
- having the system *infer* transactional boundaries in order to provide compatibility with existing software.
- the use of a transaction specification that is optimized for availability.
- the use of *optimistic* algorithms for regulating partitioned access.

The first three features essentially define the combinations of partitioned operations that are legal, while the fourth determines how legality is enforced. Each feature is discussed in its own subsection in the following.

2.3.1 Transaction Model of Computation

Coda employs a computation model based on transactions in order to achieve high data availability while also providing useful sharing semantics. This model allows many more operations to be executed under partitionings than does the traditional Unix file system model. Primarily, this is because transactions expose the dependencies between computations whereas the Unix interface does not.[8]

The Limitation of Shared Memory. The traditional model of computation in the Unix file system domain is processes accessing shared memory. Essentially, the file system is a block of common store which processes may read and write without otherwise revealing the structure of their computations. The system cannot tell whether two data accesses are part of the same computation or completely unrelated ones. Similarly, it does not know which accesses are for the purpose of synchronization and which represent normal computation. All it sees is a linear stream of requests to read and write specific memory locations.

The Unix model can be retained for partitioned operation, but only at a heavy cost in availability. To understand why, let's begin with a firmer definition of what it actually means to retain the model:

> A distributed file system is *one-copy Unix equivalent* (1UE) if for every set of computations the final file system state generated by any partitioned execution is the same as that resulting from some execution of the same computations on a single Unix host.

Two simple, alternative disciplines can be employed to guarantee 1UE. The first restricts read and write access to a logical data item to a single partition. Post-partitioning propagation of updated values to other replicas

---

[8] The rest of this document assumes some familiarity with the concepts and terminology of transactions and serializability theory. The book by Bernstein et al [6] is an excellent reference on the subject.

restores mutual consistency. Correctness is obvious because the final state generated by a partitioned execution is the same as that of any one-copy execution in which partition-order is preserved (i.e., in which every operation has the same ordering relative to all other operations from its partition). The second discipline allows a logical data item to be read in multiple partitions, but it permits updating only in the absence of partitioning. Post-partitioning propagation is not an issue in this case, since updates are required to write into each copy of an object. 1UE is again obvious from the fact that a partitioned execution generates a final state that is the same as any one-copy execution that preserves partition-order.

Both of the preceding disciplines work by confining *conflicting* accesses to the same partition. Two operations are said to conflict if they access the same logical data item and at least one of them is a write. A *read/write conflict* occurs when exactly one of the two accesses is a write; a *write/write conflict* occurs when both are.

Confining conflicting accesses to the same partition is a sufficient but not a necessary condition for 1UE. In fact, there are many cases in which partitioned read/write conflicts do not preclude equivalence with a one-copy execution of the same computations. Suppose, for example, that a source file is edited in one partition and read for the purposes of printing it in another. The final, post-partitioning state of that execution is clearly the same as if the printing and the editing had occurred (in that order) at a single Unix host. Unfortunately, because of the opaqueness of the shared memory interface, it is impractical to discriminate between benign cases of partitioned read/write conflict such as this and cases which do preclude one-copy equivalence, such as that illustrated in Figure 2.4. Hence, the system has no real choice with the shared memory model other than to assume the worst and to prohibit all partitioned read/write conflicts. The reduction in data availability that results is substantial and most unfortunate.

Initially,   W == X == Y == Z == 0.

Partition 1	Partition 2
W = 1	X = 1
if (X == 0) Y = 1	if (W == 0) Z = 1

Propagating updates at partitioning heal yields   W == X == Y == Z == 1.

The code in this example is written in pidgin-C. Assume that W, X, Y, and Z correspond to individual files, and that file open, read, write, and close calls are inserted as necessary. Failure to restrict read/write conflicts to the same partition results in a final state (following update propagation) different from that following every possible one-copy execution. (The 1UE final states have (W, X, Y, Z) equal to (1, 1, 1, 0), (1, 1, 0, 1), or (1, 1, 0, 0).) This example is adapted from one in Adve and Hill [3].

Fig. 2.4. A Non-1UE Execution Resulting from Partitioned Read/Write Conflict

Availability Advantages of the Transaction Model. Transactions are a well-known concept whose origins are in the database world. A transaction is a set of data accesses and logical operations which represent an indivisible piece of work. The requirements of a transaction processing system are three-fold: *failure atomicity*, *persistence*, and *serializability*. Serializability serves the same role for transactions as one-copy Unix equivalence does in the shared memory model. In the case of replicated data, serializability generalizes to *one-copy serializability* (1SR). This criterion is satisfied if:

> the concurrent [possibly partitioned] execution of transactions is equivalent to a serial execution on non-replicated data [18].

As with 1UE, equivalence means that the final system state is identical following both executions.

Admissibility of Partitioned Read/Write Conflicts. From the viewpoint of partitioned data access, the transaction model is superior to shared memory because the boundaries of computations are visible at the system interface. In this model a computation is one and the same with a transaction, and each data access carries the identity of its associated transaction/computation. This information can be exploited to recognize more partitioned executions as being correct – i.e., as being equivalent to some non-partitioned execution. In particular, it allows many correct executions which contain partitioned read/write conflicts to be recognized. Of course, not all executions containing partitioned read/write conflicts have one-copy equivalents. Some do and some don't. The key point is that the transaction model allows at least some of the correct subset of such executions to be efficiently recognized, whereas the shared memory model does not.

The question of exactly which partitioned executions have one-copy equivalents – whether or not they involve read/write conflicts – does not have a simple answer. In general, the correctness of a given execution depends on the intra-partition ordering of all the transactions and the specific accesses that each one makes. In some cases it may also depend on the pre-partitioning state of the system and the logic of the individual computations. Indeed, there are many partitioned executions which are 1SR, but which can only be recognized as such by computing the final state reached by every possible one-copy execution of the transactions and comparing each one to the state represented by the partitioned execution. Figure 2.5 illustrates one such case where 1SR-ness is dependent on pre-partitioning state.

Because of the obvious intractability of recognizing all 1SR executions, it is common to focus on subsets which are feasible to recognize. These subsets are normally defined strictly by *syntactic* properties of executions. That is, they make no use of the internal logic of any transaction nor of the pre-partitioning state of the system. The syntactic representation of an execution is called a *history*. The information in a history typically consists of the names

Partition 1	Partition 2
T1: if (Y % 2 == 0) X++	T2: if (X % 2 == 0) Y++

As in Figure 2.4, the code in this example is written in pidgin-C. Assume again that X and Y correspond to individual files, and that file open, read, write, and close calls are inserted as necessary. The 1SR-ness of partitioned execution of T1 and T2 depends upon the pre-partitioning state of the system. If either X or Y (or both) are odd, then the partitioned execution is 1SR. If both data items are even at the time of the partitioning, however, the partitioned execution is not 1SR.

Fig. 2.5. Partitioned Transaction Example where 1SR-ness is Data-Dependent

of the data items that each transaction has accessed, along with the nature of each access (i.e., read or write). In addition, there is a partial ordering of the data accesses which – at the least – orders every pair of conflicting accesses of the same physical copy of a data item.

A particularly important, syntactically-defined 1SR subset is the *one-copy view serializable* (1VSR) histories [6]. A multi-copy history is 1VSR if it is *view equivalent* to some serial, one-copy history over the same transactions. The essential condition for view equivalence is that the multi-copy history, H, and the one-copy history, H_{1C}, must have the same *reads-from* relationships on logical data items. That is, transaction T_j must read the value written for data item x by transaction T_i in H if and only if it does in H_{1C}. What this condition ensures is that every transaction reads the same values in both the multi-copy and the one-copy histories. Given that property, it must then be true that every transaction writes the same values in both executions, and consequently that the final system state is identical in both cases.[9]

The transaction model and 1VSR correctness criterion admit many histories that involve partitioned read/write conflicts. Figure 2.6 provides a simple example. But, are there efficient replica control algorithms which can recognize such histories, or at least a useful subset of them? In fact, many common algorithms do not recognize any of these histories. They rely on the partitioned read/write conflict exclusion rule to ensure that they admit no non-1VSR histories (and thereby prohibit many other histories that are 1VSR). The availability offered by these algorithms is thus no better than that which is possible with the shared memory model. Fortunately, there are also efficient replica control algorithms which do admit many, if not all,

---

[9] A second condition on view equivalence is needed to guarantee that the final system states are indeed identical. That condition requires that every *final write* in H_{1C} is also a final write in H for at least one copy of the data item. This is satisfied automatically in most cases by the reads-from condition, but there are a few obscure situations that necessitate the final writes requirement. Note that the "final state" of the multi-copy history is technically not reached until final writes have been propagated to previously partitioned copies. Bernstein et al contains a proof that the histories defined by the view equivalence conditions are indeed 1SR.

1VSR histories containing partitioned read/write conflicts. The availability characteristics of particular types of replica control algorithms are discussed later in Subsection 2.3.4.

Partition 1	Partition 2
T1: `read W`	T3: `read X`
`write W`	`write X`
T2: `read X`	T4: `read W`
`read Y`	`read Z`
`write Y`	`write Z`

There are partitioned read/write conflicts in this history on data items W and X. The history is 1VSR because it is view equivalent to the serial, one-copy execution T4 · T1 · T2 · T3 (among others).

Fig. 2.6. A 1VSR Partitioned History with Read/Write Conflicts

Query Processing. A special case of partitioned read/write conflict admissibility concerns the handling of read-only transactions or *queries*. An algorithm based on the transaction model can exploit queries to provide higher availability than any based on the shared memory model. This is true even if the algorithm is conservative and applies the partitioned read/write conflict exclusion rule to update transactions. Two sub-cases of this phenomenon can be distinguished.

In the first sub-case, a query which accesses only one logical data item can be legally executed in any partition regardless of whether the item is updated in another. This is because in any partitioned transaction history which is 1SR without the query, the history with the query is also guaranteed to be 1SR. This can be intuitively understood by noting that the query can always be "serialized before" any conflicting, partitioned update transaction. That is, the query can be inserted into the original, one-copy equivalent history at any point prior to the first update transaction that accesses the queried data item, and the resulting history is guaranteed to be equivalent to the augmented multi-copy history. Note that a shared memory model algorithm cannot take advantage of this special case because it cannot distinguish a read-only computation from one that also makes updates. A read access looks the same to it in either case.

The other sub-case concerns queries that read more than one data item. Such a query cannot always be serialized before partitioned transactions that update items it reads, even if read/write conflicts are prevented between partitioned update transactions. Figure 2.7 illustrates how this can happen. Garcia-Molina and Wiederhold [26] argue that in many cases it is preferable to allow the partitioned processing of multi-item queries than to restrict them merely to avoid situations like that in the figure. They term such queries *weakly-consistent* because, although they each see a consistent system state –

the result of a 1SR execution of update transactions – they may not be 1SR with respect to each other.

The view taken in Coda is that – for a file system at least – weak-consistency for queries is an acceptable price to pay in return for the availability it permits. It is a slight, controlled departure from the correctness criterion, and one that is fairly intuitive. One-copy serializability is still enforced with respect to all update transactions. Moreover, it is possible to admit weak-consistency selectively, and enforce strong-consistency (i.e., 1SR) for only those queries that need it. Finally, queries are a large fraction of the workload in a typical filing environment, so the payoff of being able to execute a higher percentage of them partitioned is likely to be very high.

Partition 1	Partition 2

T1: read A
    write A
	T3: read B
	    write B

T2: read A
    read B
	T4: read A
	    read B

This execution is not 1SR because T2 requires an ordering where T1 precedes T3, and T4 requires one where T3 precedes T1. Such precedence conditions are derivable using two simple rules; Tx must precede Ty in an equivalent one-copy history if either:

- Tx and Ty are in the same partition, Tx preceded Ty in the partition sub-history, and Tx wrote a data item that was later read by Ty or it read a data item that was later written by Ty; or
- Tx and Ty are in different partitions and Tx read a data item that Ty wrote.

Fig. 2.7. Multi-Item Queries Violating One-Copy Serializability

As a final point, it may seem odd that the example in Figure 2.7 is claimed to be non-1SR, or, indeed, that any query could cause an otherwise 1SR history to be non-1SR. According to the definition, a partitioned history is 1SR if it generates a final system state identical to a one-copy execution of the transactions. So, since queries do not write any data items, how can they possibly affect the 1SR-ness of a partitioned transaction history? The answer is that there are very few "pure" or "blind" queries in most systems, where the results of such a query are completely unseen. In almost all cases the results of a query are sent to some output device, such as a video terminal or a printer. Such cases are more properly viewed as a special kind of update transaction than as a pure query, where the data items written – lines on a video typescript or roll of printer paper – have the property that they are written only once. Given this interpretation, it should be clear that multi-item queries can lead to non-1SR executions, and also that these types of executions are appreciably "less incorrect" than non-1SR executions involving general update transactions.

2.3.2 System-Inferred Transactions

The transaction model admits higher data availability than the shared memory model because the system has more information about the structure of computations. This information is normally specified directly in the programming interface. Programmers bracket individual computations with begin- and end-transaction statements, and they access data items via routines which identify the enclosing transaction. The system then takes care of concurrency and replica control issues transparently to the application.

The Unix programming interface, however, has no transactional support built into it. Adding the necessary calls to the interface would be a relatively straightforward task, but modifying the existing set of applications to use the calls most certainly would not. The number of useful Unix programs is prohibitively large, and in many cases the source code is not generally available.

Coda is able to realize many of the benefits of the transaction model without augmenting the system interface and forcing applications to be modified. The approach is to internally map sequences of system calls onto transactions according to a simple heuristic. This amounts to *inferring* transactions by the system rather than having them explicitly identified by the programmer. Since the programming interface has not changed there is no requirement to modify applications. The only user-visible effect of inferring transactions is to expand the set of partitioned operations that can be allowed as compared to a shared memory implementation.

Inferring AFS-2 Sessions as Transactions. The transaction-inferring heuristic used in Coda is to regard each AFS-2 session as a separate transaction. Recalling the definition of sessions from earlier in this chapter, this means that most Unix file system calls constitute their own, independent transaction. The key exception concerns compound sessions, which aggregate all of the reads and writes on an open file into a single transaction. Like all heuristics, this one is sometimes incorrect. However, for many common types of Unix file activity it is entirely appropriate.

The actual mapping of system call sequences to transaction types is mostly straightforward. Table 2.1 describes the calls that make up the BSD Unix file interface and Table 2.2 lists the set of inferred Coda transactions. The latter contains one line for each transaction type which gives its name and key arguments, and a second line which describes the system call sequences that map to it. A few clarifications to the mappings are needed:

- only ioctl calls which get (set) access-rights map to the readstatus (setrights) transactions. Other types of ioctl do not map to any Coda transaction type.
- an unlink system call applied to a plain file maps to either the rmfile or unlink transaction type, depending on whether the object is also removed or not (i.e., on whether its link-count falls to 0 as a result of the unlinking).

An unlink system call applied to a symbolic link maps to the rmsymlink transaction type.

- a creat system call is split into two parts which map to different transactions types. The first part is the creation of the file, and it maps to the mkfile transaction type. The second part is the opening of the file for update, and it maps to the store transaction type. This same splitting applies to an open system call which has specified the O_CREAT option.
- a rename system call in which the "to name" is already bound is also split into two parts. The first part is the removal of the bound name, and it maps to either an unlink or an rmfile/rmdir/rmsymlink transaction. The second part is the renaming itself, and it maps to a rename transaction.
- the resolution of pathnames to objects is assumed to occur outside the scope of Coda transactions. Pathname expansion could be specified to occur within transactions, but doing so would add little strength to the model.

Finally, certain system calls only manipulate state which is not part of Coda - for example mknod and mount - and therefore do not map to any Coda transaction type.

Limitation of the Inferencing Approach. The key limitation of the inferred transaction approach is that sessions are only an approximation to the "true" transactions implicit in the minds of programmers and users. When a true transaction spans multiple sessions, partitioned execution in Coda can produce incorrect results. That is, the resulting executions may not be 1SR with respect to the true transactions. The example in Figure 2.4 is a trivial instance of this. More serious examples involve programs like make, which may read and write hundreds of objects while assuming isolation from other file system activity.

In practice, the availability and compatibility benefits of the inferred transaction approach have easily outweighed the cost of non-1SR executions. There are several reasons for this:

- the session heuristic is pretty good. It matches the assumptions of many typical distributed file system activities (text editing, electronic mail, etc).
- the likelihood of partitioned activity leading to non-1SR behavior is small in practice. Most partitionings are fairly short - a few minutes to perhaps a day - and the amount of sharing over this interval is typically small. Even when partitionings are longer, as might be expected with voluntary disconnected operation, the chance of incorrect execution is still usually small.
- partition state is not hidden from users; a monitoring tool is available which displays the local topology view. Users can modify their behavior during partitionings to avoid higher-risk activities, for example complex makes, or make use of external synchronization channels such as email or the telephone to minimize the risk of interference.

access	Check access permissions for the specified object.
chmod	Set mode bits for the specified object.
chown	Set ownership for the specified object.
close	Terminate access to an open object via the specified descriptor.
fsync	Synchronize the specified object's in-core state with that on disk.
ioctl	Perform a control function on the specified object.
link	Make a hard link to the specified file.
lseek	Move the read/write pointer for the specified descriptor.
mkdir	Make a directory with the specified path.
mknod	Make a block or character device node with the specified path.
mount	Mount the specified file system on the specified directory.
open, creat	Open the specified file for reading or writing, or create a new file.
read, readv	Read input from the specified descriptor.
readlink	Read contents of the specified symbolic link.
rename	Change the name of the specified object.
rmdir	Remove the specified directory.
stat	Read status of the specified object.
statfs	Read status of the specified file system.
symlink	Make a symbolic link with the specified path and contents.
sync	Schedule all dirty in-core data for writing to disk.
truncate	Truncate the specified file to the specified length.
umount	Unmount the file system mounted at the specified path.
unlink	Remove the specified directory entry.
utimes	Set accessed and updated times for the specified object.
write, writev	Write output to the specified descriptor.

Table 2.1. 4.3 BSD File System Interface

– Unix itself provides no formal support for concurrency control. Hence, transaction-assuming applications like make are exposed to non-serializable behavior even without replication. Partitioned operation increases the risk of such behavior, because the window of vulnerability is the duration of the partitioning rather than the duration of the transaction. But no new class of (mis)behavior is introduced.

The problem of incorrect inferences could be eliminated, of course, by making transactions explicit in the programming interface. This would serve to strengthen the semantics of both partitioned and non-partitioned operation. A transactional interface to the file system is, in fact, being designed and implemented by another member of the Coda project. When this new interface is in place, the inferred transaction behavior will serve as the default for applications that have not been re-coded to use the new calls. This will

```
readstatus[object, user]
     access | ioctl | stat
readdata[object, user]
     (open read* close) | readlink
chown[object, user]
     chown
chmod[object, user]
     chmod
utimes[object, user]
     utimes
setrights[object, user]
     ioctl
store[file, user]
     ((creat | open) (read | write)* close) | truncate
link[directory, name, file, user]
     link
unlink[directory, name, file, user]
     rename | unlink
rename[directory1, name1, directory2, name2, object, user]
     rename
mkfile[directory, name, file, user]
     creat | open
mkdir[directory1, name, directory2, user]
     mkdir
mksymlink[directory, name, symlink, user]
     symlink
rmfile[directory, name, file, user]
     rename | unlink
rmdir[directory1, name, directory2, user]
     rename | rmdir
rmsymlink[directory, name, symlink, user]
     rename | unlink
```

The notation used in the second line of each description is that of regular expressions; i.e., juxtaposition represents succession, "*" represents repetition, and "|" represents selection.

Table 2.2. Coda Transaction Types and System Call Mapping

allow an incremental upgrade path, with conversion effort spent earliest and most heavily on those (relatively few) applications that really need it. The future work section of Chapter 10 discusses the explicit transaction extension in greater detail.

2.3.3 High Availability Transaction Specification

The mapping of system calls to transaction types in Table 2.2 forms the basis for characterizing the availability afforded by the Coda model. In theory, any partitioned execution of instances of those transactions types is permissible as long as it is equivalent to some non-partitioned execution of the same transactions – i.e., as long as it is 1SR. In reality, of course, any efficient algorithm must rely on the syntax of transactions, and thus will only be able to recognize a subset of the 1SR histories For the time being, the target subset may be assumed to be the 1VSR histories. The key replica control task, then, is to devise an algorithm that can recognize as large and as useful a subset of the 1VSR histories as possible.

Before discussing particular algorithms, however, it is necessary to focus more closely on the transaction specification. Perhaps surprisingly, the details of the specification can have significant effect on the availability that is eventually realized by the algorithm. Three specification issues in particular contribute to increased availability in Coda:

- the avoidance of under-specification errors which obscure the true data accesses of computations.
- the redefinition of certain system call semantics to eliminate non-critical side-effects.
- the exploitation of type-specific information to enlarge the subset of the 1SR histories that can be efficiently recognized.

Each of these issues is discussed in a subsection below. A fourth subsection, 2.3.3, combines these factors to characterize the potential availability of the Coda model in more specific terms.

Avoiding Under-Specification Problems. Because practical algorithms for regulating partitioned transaction processing must rely on syntactic information to ensure correctness, it is essential that a transaction's specification accurately reflect its true access behavior. Otherwise, the replica control algorithm may unknowingly permit incorrect executions or prevent correct ones. The former type of error arises from omission of an accessed data item in the specification, the latter from inclusion of an unaccessed one.

The chief danger in deriving a transaction specification from the system call to transaction mapping of Table 2.2 is *under-specifying* data accesses. Under-specification is a variant of the unnecessary inclusion type of error which results from specifying data accesses at too coarse of a granularity. That is, an under-specified data access does name the actual item that is referenced, but it names some neighboring set of unaccessed items as well. Under-specification results in *false conflicts* when two transactions access a data item in a conflicting way and one or both of the accesses is false.

False conflicts reduce availability because they make it appear that certain partitioned histories do not have one-copy equivalents when in fact they do. Consider specifically the task of determining whether a given multi-copy history is 1VSR. If two partitioned transactions in the history are in read/write conflict, then that effectively removes a degree of freedom in finding a one-copy history with the same reads-from relationship. This is because only one-copy histories in which the reader appears before the writer have a chance of being a match. Partitioned read/write conflicts therefore make it more likely that the entire history will be judged incorrect. Partitioned write/write conflicts, on the other hand, normally guarantee that the history will be considered incorrect. This is because write/write conflicts almost always represent reciprocal read/write conflicts between the same transactions.[10] Thus, when partitioned conflicts are false they can make a legal history appear illegal – with virtual certainty in the write/write case, and with increased probability in the read/write case.

The Coda specification takes care to avoid under-specification and false conflicts in three distinct ways.

Sub-Object Level Data Description. The most intuitive level at which to specify Coda transactions is that of entire Unix objects (i.e., whole files, directories, and symbolic links). However, this is not the level at which data items are actually accessed by system calls. Hence, specifying transactions in terms of objects would introduce a substantial number of false conflicts. For example, chmod and chown transactions on the same object would appear to be write/write conflict with each other, but the conflict would in fact be false.

The proper granularity for specification is the sub-object level. At this level each attribute field and each element of an object's body is viewed as an independent data item. Figure 2.8 contains a description of Coda objects at the sub-object level in C++ syntax. The three object types – plain files, directories, symbolic links – share a common base structure called a *vnode* (for Vice-inode). This structure contains the attributes and other meta-data of an object and corresponds to a Unix inode. The body or data portion of an object is specific to its type. In all three cases the data is specified as a fixed-size array, with each element potentially an independent data item.

Access Control. The model of protection in Unix is roughly that of a classic *access matrix*. In such a model each cell of the matrix represents the rights that a particular user has for a particular object. The file system consults the matrix to make sure that a user is authorized to perform a given request.

In Unix, however, the access matrix is very tightly encoded. Three fields in an object's inode – owner, group, mode – encode the access vector that is associated with the object. The mode field has components which represent the rights for three classes of user: the object's owner, the members of the object's group, and everybody else. A separate, system-wide database identifies the members of every group.

The Unix encoding of protection information would make a transaction specification very vulnerable to false conflicts. It would mean that a protection change intended to affect one user could falsely conflict with – and thus unnecessarily inhibit – a transaction invoked by another user in a different partition. For instance, suppose that a file were chmod'ed in one partition

---

[10] The exception is when a transaction writes a data item without first reading it. Such "blind" writes are uncommon in practice.

```
const int MAXUIDS = 2^{32} ;
const int MAXFILELEN = 2^{32} ;
const int MAXDIRENTRIES = 256^{256} ;
const int MAXSYMLINKLEN = 2^{10} ;

struct vnode {
    fid_t fid;
    uid_t owner;
    time_t modifytime;
    short mode;
    short linkcount;
    unsigned int length;
    rights_t rights[MAXUIDS];              /* implemented as access-control
                                              list */
};

struct file : vnode {
    unsigned char data[MAXFILELEN];        /* implemented as list of blocks
                                              covering [0..length - 1] */
};

struct directory : vnode {
    fid_t data[MAXDIRENTRIES];             /* implemented as hash table con-
                                              taining only bound names */
};

struct symlink : vnode {
    unsigned char data[MAXSYMLINKLEN];    /* implemented as list of blocks
                                              covering [0..length - 1] */
};
```

Fig. 2.8. Coda Data Item Description

with the intention of restricting the rights of the users in the file's group. Then that transaction would falsely conflict with many transactions in other partitions that attempted to access the file on behalf of other users (e.g., a store submitted by the file's owner).

The Coda specification avoids the foregoing type of false conflict by using an explicit representation of the access matrix rather than the Unix encoding. The rights array in a Coda vnode is precisely the object's access vector, and it is consulted for protection-checking purposes rather than the owner, group, and mode attributes. Similarly, protection changes are accomplished via the setrights transaction rather than by the chown and chmod transactions.[11]

---

[11] The actual implementation of access vectors is via access-control lists (acls) rather than MAXUID-size arrays. Groups may have entries on acls as well as specific users, and individual access rights must be computed by "joining" the system's group database with acls (the procedure is described fully in [81]). In addition, only directories contain acls; the acl governing a file or symbolic link

If the traditional Unix attributes are irrelevant for protection in Coda, then why do they still appear in the vnode and why are there still transactions for manipulating them? The answer to this is that certain important programs encode non-protection information in the owner and mode attributes, and break badly if they are not allowed to do so. Hence, those two fields are maintained for backward-compatibility purposes, essentially as a form of private storage. The group attribute is not similarly abused and therefore has been eliminated from the vnode. Attempts to change it are rejected, and the value that is read for it in the readstatus transaction is a manifest constant.

Directory Contents. A Unix directory is essentially a set of <name, fid> bindings, with the restriction that any name can be bound at most once. The intuitive view held by Unix users and programmers is that bindings are basically independent of each other. For example, a computation which adds a new binding to a directory normally does not care what the complete set of extant bindings is. All it needs to know is that there is no existing binding which has the same name component as the one it proposes to add.

The Coda specification supports this independent directory entry view by modeling directory contents as a fixed-size array. Each element represents the current state of one name in the universe of legal names. If that name is currently "bound," then the array element contains the fid that it is bound to. If it is currently "unbound," then the array element contains the special fid-value $\perp$. The universe of names – and hence the size of the array – is equal to $\mathcal{A}^m$, where $\mathcal{A}$ is the size of the alphabet and m is the maximum length of any name. Of course, in any real directory the fraction of elements with non-$\perp$ values will be exceedingly small.

The modeling of directory contents in this way is essential to admitting a reasonable degree of partitioned file system activity. Consider the alternative of modeling contents as a list of actual bindings (which is basically how they are implemented). Then any pair of transactions which inserted bindings or removed them from a directory would be in write/write conflict with each other because they both write "the bindings list." As a result they could not be legally executed in different partitions, even though they might well involve bindings with different names. This would be yet another case of false conflicts unnecessarily restricting partitioned activity. With the Coda array model, in contrast, the transactions would conflict over directory contents only if the names in the respective bindings were the same. Such conflicts are real, not false, because the same logical data item is accessed in both cases.

Eliminating Non-Critical Side-Effects. BSD Unix semantics require that certain "time" attributes be maintained for each file system object. These attributes – access-time, change-time, modify-time – are kept in the object's inode, and are updated as side-effects of particular system calls. Roughly-speaking, the access-time is supposed to reflect the last time a plain

---

is that of its parent directory. None of these implementation issues are relevant for specification purposes, however.

file was read or written, the change-time is supposed to reflect the last time an object of any type was updated, and the modify-time is supposed to reflect the last time the body of an object of any type was updated. Change-time is updated whenever modify-time is, plus whenever the status part of the object is changed (e.g., as the result of a chmod or chown operation). Access-time and modify-time may also be set directly via the utimes system call.

Maintaining time attributes as per BSD semantics severely restricts the amount of partitioned activity that can be allowed. Consider what it would mean in terms of the Coda transaction model:

- the readdata transaction type would not be read-only since it would be required to update the access-time attribute. Two readdata transactions on the same object would therefore be in write/write conflict with each other, and hence could not be executed in different partitions.
- every pair of transactions which updated any part of the body of an object would be in write/write conflict because of each one's need to update the change-time and modify-time. In the case of two store transactions a write/write conflict is inevitable, because the model assumes whole-file update. But in cases of directory contents update a write/write conflict is not otherwise inevitable, as each name in a directory is considered to be independent. Maintaining change-time and modify-time thus would introduce many new write/write conflicts between directory-contents updating transactions, and thereby inhibit a great deal of useful partitioned activity.
- the need to update change-time as a result of attribute-setting transactions (e.g., chown, chmod) would introduce write/write conflicts between pairs of those transactions, and also between a transaction of that type and one which updates the data part of an object (e.g., a store or rmdir). These conflicts would further reduce the set of allowable partitioned transactions.

The net effect of these restrictions would be to limit access to an object for either read or write to a single partition.

Rather than restrict partitioned access so severely just to support time attribute maintenance, the Coda model simply re-defines certain operational semantics to eliminate the offending side-effects. Two changes are involved:

- no system call – and thus no Coda transaction – updates the modify-time for a directory object, except for the utimes system call/transaction. The modify-time for plain files and symbolic links is maintained as per the BSD specification.
- no system call – and thus no Coda transaction – updates access-time or change-time. Since these two attributes are never updated, the vnode does not even store a copy of them. The value returned for each in a readstatus transaction is simply the current value of the object's modify-time.

These changes have two extremely positive effects on availability. First, the readdata transaction is truly read-only, allowing it to be executed unrestricted in any partition. Second, naming operations involving distinct names and attribute setting operations that update different attributes are not automatically in write/write conflict, and hence can potentially be executed in different partitions.

While the availability impact of these changes is substantial, their semantic impact is small in practice. This basically reflects the limited informational content of most of the time attributes. As an illustration, consider that most distributed Unix file systems do not maintain access-time accurately (since doing so severely limits the effectiveness of caching), and yet few users are even aware of this. Few programs or users also seem to care either whether change-time is maintained accurately or not. Modify-time for files is relied upon by some programs, notably make, and is important to users in organizing and identifying their data. Modify-time for directories, however, is not nearly so critical in practice. Usage experience has shown that virtually all of the utility of time-stamping objects can be achieved by stamping updated files at the time they are closed.

Exploiting Type-Specific Semantics. The specification techniques for avoiding false conflicts and the elimination of the time attribute side-effects are essential to realizing high availability with the Coda model. However, there is one remaining specification issue that poses a problem for partitioned operation. That issue is the requirement to update object link-count and directory length attributes as side-effects of certain operations. Link-count represents the number of directory bindings that refer to an object. It is updated by system calls which insert or remove bindings, such as link and rmdir. Directory length is the cumulative length of all the names that are currently bound in the directory contents. It is also updated by system calls which insert or remove directory bindings. The maintenance of these attributes thus would appear to cancel much of the availability advantage claimed earlier. For example, it appears to put naming transactions that involve the same directory but different names in write/write conflict with each other, and therefore to prohibit their partitioned execution. Note that unlike most of the time attributes, link-count and directory length are fairly important quantities. Thus, it is not possible to get around this problem simply by omitting the offending side-effects from the operational semantics.

The key to solving this problem is to look more closely at the semantics of the two data items. Both link-count and directory length function essentially as *counter* data types. Counters have two primitive operations in addition to read and write: *increment* and *decrement*. The former adds some specified number to the counter and the latter subtracts some specified number from it. The key property of the data type is that any transaction which invokes the increment or decrement operation is indifferent to the exact initial and final values of the counter. All that matters to it is that the final value is greater or less than the initial value by the specified amount.

Intuitively, it's not hard to see how the semantics of counters can be exploited to improve availability. Consider the simple case of two partitioned transactions which each increment the same counter and do not access any other common data item. The corresponding history is not 1VSR because – using the standard read/write framework – both transactions read and write the same logical data item. Consequently, neither of the two possible one-copy histories of the transactions has the same reads-from relationship as the multi-copy history does. However, it's obvious that the final state resulting from propagation of the final writes of the updated non-counter data-items plus the propagation of the "missing" increments/decrements to each copy is the same as that resulting from either one-copy execution.

Counter semantics can be exploited in the general case by making the increment and decrement operations explicit in the transaction syntax. Transactions which formerly specified read and write operations to represent a logical increment or decrement now contain the latter operations directly in their specification. View equivalence for histories using the expanded syntax is defined almost identically as before. The only differences are (1) that the reads-from relation now refers to the last writer, incrementer, or decrementer of a data item, and (2) that final writes now refer to increments and decrements as well. As a practical matter, the procedure for making copies mutually consistent following partition must be somewhat different as well. Increments and decrements must not be propagated blindly as final writes are; instead, the "net change" value for every partition must be computed, exchanged, and added or subtracted as appropriate.[12]

Characterizing Potential Availability. The specification and other transaction issues discussed so far can be brought together to give a clearer picture of the potential availability of the Coda model. Two different characterizations are useful. The first clarifies the relationships between the various classes of transaction histories that have been discussed. Figure 2.9 depicts a superset of the 1VSR histories denoted 1VSR'. This syntactically-recognizable set extends the 1VSR histories to take advantage of weakly-consistent queries and the special semantics of counter operations. It represents a new target recognition set for the Coda replica control algorithms.

The second characterization focuses on the particular types of transactions in the Coda specification. Table 2.3 lists each transaction type again along with its read, write, increment, and decrement set. Data items are identified as fields of the Coda object structures defined in Figure 2.8. The object designations come from the argument templates introduced in Table 2.2. The argument names are abbreviations of those given in the earlier table ("o" stands for "object," "d1" stands for "directory1," and so on). The

---

[12] I do not give a proof here that the histories satisfying this extended notion of view equivalence are all 1SR. Such a proof could be given fairly easily using the graph formalism of Bernstein et al, but doing so would require an extended discussion of the formalism (which is non-essential to this thesis). Chapter 7, anyway, proves the point which really is of relevance to this thesis, that the exploitation of counter semantics by the specific replica control algorithm of disconnected operation does not cause non-1SR histories to be admitted.

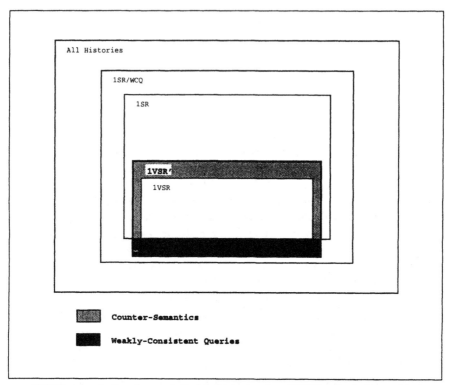

1VSR' extends the view serializable histories (set 1VSR) to include two history sub-classes: (1) histories which become view serializable once counter
operations are added to the syntax, and (2) histories which become view
serializable once queries are allowed to be weakly-consistent. (In the diagram, "1SR/WCQ" stands for "1SR with Weakly-Consistent Queries.")

Fig. 2.9. Composition of the 1VSR' History Class

symbol "*" is used as a wildcard, to represent either all of the elements of an
array or all of the components of a structure. Note that for compactness of
representation, the types for making and removing the three kinds of objects
have been combined into generic mkobject and rmobject transaction types.
This is possible because the transactions access essentially the same data
items regardless of the object type.[13] Hereafter, any reference to a mkobject
or rmobject transaction should be taken to mean a transaction of any of the
corresponding sub-types.

Table 2.3 makes plain all of the allusions to partitioned transaction compatibility or incompatibility made earlier. To recap, the key facts derivable
from the specification are the following:

---

[13] The only exception is that mkdir (rmdir) increments (decrements) the parent
directory's link-count, while the transactions for files and symbolic links do
not.

Transaction Type	Read Set	Write Set	Incr. Set	Decr. Set
readstatus[o, u]	o.fid, o.owner, o.modifytime, o.mode, o.linkcount, o.length, o.rights[u]			
readdata[o, u]	o.fid, o.rights[u], o.length, o.data[*]			
chown[o, u]	o.fid, o.rights[u], o.owner	o.owner		
chmod[o, u]	o.fid, o.rights[u], o.mode	o.mode		
utimes[o, u]	o.fid, o.rights[u], o.modifytime	o.modifytime		
setrights[o, u]	o.fid, o.rights[u]	o.rights[u]		
store[f, u]	f.fid, f.rights[u], f.modifytime, f.length, f.data[*]	f.modifytime, f.length, f.data[*]		
link[d, n, f, u]	d.fid, d.rights[u], d.data[n], f.fid	d.data[n]	d.length, f.linkcount	
unlink[d, n, f, u]	d.fid, d.rights[u], d.data[n], f.fid	d.data[n]		d.length, f.linkcount
rename[d1, n1, d2, n2, o, u]	d1.fid, d1.rights[u], d1.data[n1], d2.fid, d2.rights[u], d2.data[n2], o.fid, o.data[".."]	d1.data[n1], d2.data[n2], o.data[".."]	d2.linkcount, d2.length	d1.linkcount, d1.length
mkobject[d, n, o, u]	d.fid, d.rights[u], d.data[n], o.*	d.data[n], o.*	d.linkcount, d.length	
rmobject[d, n, o, u]	d.fid, d.rights[u], d.data[n], o.*	d.data[n], o.*		d.linkcount, d.length

Note that in the rename transaction o.data[''..''] is relevant only when the renamed object is a directory.

Table 2.3. Coda Transaction Specification

- readstatus and readdata are multi-item queries. Because the model admits weakly-consistent queries, it is always legal to execute transactions of these types in any partition.
- update transactions are generally in write/write conflict only when they write the same attribute, write the contents of the same plain file, or write the same directory entries. The rmobject transaction type is an exception. An rmobject is in write/write conflict with every transaction that updates any field of the removed object.
- transactions which mutate different names in the same directory are not in write/write conflict because they increment or decrement the linkcount and length fields rather than reading and writing them.
- read/write conflicts are rare; most transactions are either in write/write conflict or access disjoint sets of data items. The notable exception involves the setrights transaction type. A setrights is in read/write conflict with every update transaction on the same object made on behalf of the same user.

The last item means that it is unlikely that a history will be non-1VSR' unless there are write/write conflicts between partitioned transactions. It is possible, however, for a history to be incorrect due solely to combinations of read/write conflicts. Figure 2.10 illustrates how this can occur.

Partition 1	Partition 2
T1: setrights[*d1*, *u*]	T3: setrights[*d2*, *u*]
T2: rename[*d1*, *"foo"*, *d2*, *"bar"*, *f1*, *u*]	T4: rename[*d2*, *"foo"*, *d1*, *"bar"*, *f2*, *u*]

This history is not in 1VSR' even though there are no write/write conflicts because T2 requires a partial ordering of T1 < T2 < T3 and T4 requires a partial ordering of T3 < T4 < T1. (N.B. It is assumed that "bar" is not a bound name in either d1 or d2 at the start of the partitioning.)

Fig. 2.10. A Non-1VSR' History without Write/Write Conflicts

2.3.4 Optimistic Enforcement of Correctness

The model of computation is only a partial determinant of the availability offered by a given system. The other major determining factor is the particular replica control algorithm that is used. Essentially, the model defines the set of partitioned histories that are legal, and the algorithm refines that set into an efficiently recognizable subset.

Davidson et al [18] have classified partitioned replica control algorithms into two types, *pessimistic* and *optimistic*. Pessimistic algorithms make worst-case assumptions about the transactions that will be submitted during partitionings. They assume that if an incorrect execution can occur, it will occur.

Hence, they *a priori* define the operations that are permitted in any partition such that no partitioned conflict – and thus no incorrect execution – is ever possible. Unfortunately, any such assignment disallows many correct executions as well as all of the incorrect ones. Weighted voting [27] is a common example of the pessimistic type of approach.

Optimistic algorithms, in contrast, make best-case assumptions about partitioned activity. They assume that conflicting, partitioned requests are rare. Consequently, any restriction of partitioned processing is almost always unnecessary, and only serves to reduce availability. The essence of the optimistic approach is to permit any operation in any partition that has physical copies of the data, and sometime after the partitioning ends *detect* and *resolve* the few violations of correctness that may have occurred. Logging or other recording of partitioned operations is required to support this. Resolution typically consists of *undoing* conflicting transactions until the remaining set no longer violates correctness. Undone transactions can either be *redone* in the merged system state, or they can be *compensated* for in a system- or transaction-dependent way. Davidson's optimistic protocol [17] and the version-vector protocol of the Locus distributed system [67, 69] are the best-known examples of the optimistic type of approach.

Coda uses optimistic replica control for both first- and second-class replicas because of the much higher availability it affords. In addition, optimistic management has significant practical advantages that are specific to disconnected operation. This rationale is developed further in the following two subsections. Chapters 3, 6, and 7 give the details of the replica control algorithm used for disconnected operation.

Common Rationale. Optimistic algorithms offer three types of availability benefits over pessimistic algorithms:

1. optimistic algorithms can recognize many 1SR histories that involve partitioned read/write conflict. Indeed, an optimistic algorithm can theoretically recognize all histories in the set 1VSR', although there may be other factors (e.g., efficiency) which limit recognition to a smaller set. Nonetheless, the recognized set is almost certain to be larger than that of any pessimistic algorithm, since no such algorithm can recognize any history that embodies partitioned read/write conflict.

2. optimistic algorithms avoid the need to assign the rights for partitioned access to physical copies of data items. All pessimistic algorithms must make such assignments – for example the assignment of votes in a weighted voting scheme – to avoid partitioned, conflicting accesses. In general, these assignments must be made prior to the advent of actual partitionings, and without full knowledge of the transactions that will be submitted in each partition. This can result in situations not unlike false conflicts, in which *assignment errors* cause partitioned transactions to be refused despite the fact that their execution would not actually violate correctness. For example, suppose that read and write rights are assigned

to copy A of a data item, a partitioning separates copies A and B, no transaction attempts to access copy A, and transaction T1 attempts – unsuccessfully – to access copy B. Then T1's access will have been denied when it need not have been; an assignment which allocated access rights to copy B rather than A would have let T1 continue.[14]

3. optimistic algorithms offer the potential to automatically re-perform transactions that must be undone to ensure that the remainder of a non-1SR history is correct. This requires that the system have a *static* representation of transactions – i.e., a piece of code and an environment that can be automatically invoked to re-perform the computation. If this is feasible then, from the user's point of view, it's as if his or her partitioned transactions are always accepted (though the final results may not be the same as in the original execution).

The second of these advantages is the one that is currently most important to Coda. The effect of rights assignment in pessimistic algorithms is to establish a "binding" of allowable operations to partitions. Unfortunately, this binding must be done very early, at a point before partitioning has even occurred. In practice, there is little information to guide the construction of such bindings, so they are mostly arbitrary. Hence, they often don't match the actual pattern of partitioned requests, and result in assignment error situations like that described above. Optimistic algorithms avoid this problem by effectively delaying binding to the latest possible instant – i.e., to the point where requests are actually submitted. Note that late binding is particularly advantageous for naming operations, because early binding at the granularity of individual directory entries is even more tedious and more random than at the level of whole objects. For example, how would a user or administrator know to allocate rights for directory names beginning with "a" and "b" to one physical copy, and names beginning with "c" and "d" to another? In practice, therefore, a system using a pessimistic algorithm would almost certainly bind operations to entire directories, and thus forego the possibility of partitioned updates to different entries.

With inferred rather than explicit transactions, the first and third of the optimistic advantages contribute little real availability. The fact that correct histories with partitioned read/write conflicts can be admitted is of marginal utility because, as pointed out in Section 2.3.3, there are very few Coda transactions which are in read/write but not write/write conflict with each other. The only such cases involve setrights transactions, which are relatively rare in practice anyway. Similarly, the third potential advantage of the optimistic approach, automatic re-performance of undone transactions, cannot be exploited because the system does not have the necessary static representation of transactions. Of course, if and when an explicit transaction interface is in

---

[14] Note that "access rights" used in this context are different from those used in the context of security. In this case access rights confer privileges on physical copies of data items. In the security case they confer privileges on users.

place, both the read/write conflict and the automatic re-performance issues could become very significant.

Optimistic algorithms have two disadvantages in comparison with pessimistic approaches. One is conceptual, and refers to the fact that the system is "correct" only at equilibrium points, when all violations of correctness have been detected and resolved. A corollary of this is that the notion of transaction commitment is weakened. A transaction that is "committed" during a partitioning may later be aborted in the course of resolution. Pessimistic strategies have the more attractive properties that correctness holds at all times and that transaction commitment is irreversible. The other potential disadvantage of optimistic replication is that the system may not be powerful enough to re-perform undone transactions on its own. This is indeed a problem in the current version of Coda since transactions are inferred rather than being programmer-supplied. As a result, manual intervention is needed to recover from the effects of incorrect partitioned computations. Manual intervention is unpleasant for users, as it tends to be tedious and requires system knowledge that they would rather not learn.

The specifics of Coda's optimistic replica control protocol for disconnected operation are given in later chapters of this document. However, it is appropriate to say here that, in actual usage of Coda, the disadvantages of optimistic replication have not proved overwhelming. Primarily, this is due to the fact that infrequent write-sharing in Unix environments makes incorrect partitioned executions unlikely to occur. Hence, the system is "mostly correct most of the time," and the frequency of manual repair is low. Chapter 8 gives empirical support for these claims.

Rationale Specific to Disconnected Operation. The rationale of the preceding subsection applies equally well to the cases of server replication and disconnected operation. Essentially, the argument is that the likelihood of partitioned, conflicting accesses is so low in typical file system usage that the availability cost of pessimistic replica control is not worth paying. On top of this, however, second-class replication has certain characteristics that make optimistic replica control absolutely essential. The most important of these are the following:

– longer-duration partitionings.
– the need to hoard.
– client autonomy assumptions.

The first characteristic basically reaffirms the generic availability argument, whereas the latter two go towards usability and administrative concerns. Each characteristic and its consequences is explained more fully below.

Longer-Duration Partitionings. Disconnected operation is likely to lead to longer-duration partitionings than server replication because of mobile clients. One of the attractions of a mobile computer is that it can be taken to a distant location and used for an extended period of time. One can imagine a mobile client being taken home for the weekend, or out of town on a business trip, or to the beach on a week-long vacation. A design goal of Coda is to support voluntary disconnections like these, lasting for periods of a few days to perhaps a few weeks.

Lengthy disconnections have both positive and negative implications for optimistic replica control. On the negative side, they mean that more partitioned, conflicting accesses will occur, with some fraction of those requiring manual resolution. On the positive side, the availability benefits of the optimistic approach become more valuable as disconnection duration increases. For example, it may be tolerable for an object to be inaccessible for a few tens of minutes, but completely unacceptable for it to be unavailable for a few days. Moreover, a few hours or tens of minutes may be below the typical threshold for noticing inaccessibility, whereas a day or a week is likely to be well above it.

The net effect of long partitionings comes down to whether sharing or the likelihood of assignment errors increases faster with disconnection duration. Chapter 8 presents evidence from an AFS environment that write-sharing increases very slowly. For example, the likelihood of sharing within one-week of a mutation was found to be only 62% more than within one-hour. The likelihood of assignment errors is more difficult to measure, but intuitively one would expect a much faster rate of increase than this. Under such conditions, long-duration partitionings favor optimistic over pessimistic replica control.

The Need to Hoard. Disconnected operation requires clients to *hoard* copies of individual objects that they expect to need during disconnections. This requirement is treated in depth in Chapter 5. It follows from the fact that clients have relatively small amounts of persistent store, and so cannot practically host the entire namespace or even significant portions of it. This is in contrast to server replication, where each replication site stores a substantial and logically related portion of the namespace (e.g., a set of volumes).

Hoarding has serious consequences for pessimistic replica control. To see why, consider the most appropriate pessimistic protocol for second-class replication, *token-passing.* This protocol is used in Echo and AFS-4, although only in support of connected operation. The basic idea is that a client must possess a read or write token for an object in order to perform the corresponding class of operation. Write tokens imply exclusive access and read tokens shared access, analogously to conventional locking schemes. A token request which conflicts with outstanding tokens cannot be granted until the outstanding tokens are revoked (and any dirty data written back). Tokens are granted and revoked by servers, which maintain a database of which clients have which tokens for which objects. Token-passing is therefore similar to callback, with the major distinction being that there are two types of "callback promises" rather than just one.[15]

---

[15] Token-passing can also be seen as a variant of classical weighted voting, in which "votes" are dynamically reassigned with each token granted or revoked. Classi-

To extend token-passing for disconnected operation, clients must hoard tokens along with the objects they represent. In general, a client will not know whether an object will be needed for read or for write access during some future disconnection. Since a write token implies read as well as write permission, there is incentive to hoard write tokens as that leaves one's options completely open. Unfortunately, a single write token excludes all other tokens, both read and write. Hence, if more than one client wishes to hoard an object, and at least one insists on write access, an unstable situation is created. Granting one client's token request requires revocation of at least one other site's token. The *token-contention problem* refers to the "ping-ponging" of tokens back and forth between clients attempting to hoard the same object.

The token contention problem may be manageable if only voluntary disconnections need be catered for. Clients could hoard objects without tokens during connected operation and then, just before disconnecting, grab tokens for all desired objects. However, this strategy does not work for involuntary disconnections since, by definition, they cannot be predicted. The position of Coda is that involuntary disconnections are and will continue to be significant in many environments. If wireless networking becomes widespread, then this will certainly be the case. Token contention remains, therefore, as a serious limitation of pessimistic replica control.

Optimistic replica control, in contrast, does not suffer from contention problems related to hoarding. The legality of an operation is checked after the fact, so permission need not be acquired beforehand. A client does need to keep fresh versions of objects hoarded, and will need to re-fetch them as other clients make updates. However, clients are not in competition with each other for the latest copy, so no instability results.

Client Autonomy Assumptions. A premise of the AFS/Coda model is that distributed file systems can grow gracefully only if clients have a large degree of autonomy. If clients cannot be turned off or relocated or rebooted at the whim of their owners then a system will not scale. In AFS and Coda, this freedom is ensured by strictly differentiating between clients and servers and isolating clients from each other as far as possible. Explicit dependencies exist only between clients and servers, not between individual clients. Disconnected operation is an attempt to enhance autonomy even further, by tempering the dependence of clients on servers.

Pessimistic control of second-class replicas defeats the relaxation of client-server dependence – and therefore client autonomy – because it introduces inter-client dependencies. To see how, reconsider the token-passing protocol. A connected client needing a token that conflicts with one held by a disconnected client must wait until the disconnected site reconnects. Therefore, to be a "socially responsible citizen," the disconnected site should strive to reconnect at the earliest opportunity. Moreover, a client should avoid discon-

---

cal weighted voting itself is not suitable for second-class replication, because it assumes relatively static replication sets.

nections in the first place, since each disconnection carries the risk of blocking fellow users.

Avoiding disconnections is, of course, in a client's own interest. It is the fact that it is in other client's interest as well that is the problem. This fact fundamentally alters the view from a client, changing its role from an autonomous personal computer to a critical player in the system. For example, turning off one's machine for the weekend or over a vacation is no longer an innocent, power-saving act, but one that potentially inhibits a colleague from accessing data.

This unwelcome result – the loss of autonomy – is avoidable with optimistic replica control. In any situation in which a pessimistic server would delay connected clients pending communication with an inaccessible client, an optimistic server can declare the latter site disconnected after a short period and resume connected mode processing. When the disconnected client reconnects, it can be forced to merge its disconnected transactions with the state at the server. The burden of recovering from inconsistent activity can be placed on the disconnected client, not the server or connected clients. Indeed, connected clients can be made entirely unaware of the whole proceedings, except perhaps for a brief pause when the server is initially timing out the disconnected site. For its part, the disconnected client has the flexibility to detach and reattach whenever it desires, without inconveniencing others to any measurable degree.

The cost of inter-client dependency could be reduced while retaining pessimistic control by associating fixed lifetimes with tokens. This would effectively turn them into *leases*, as introduced by Gray and Cheriton [30]. A connected client's dependence on a disconnected lease-holder would be limited to the term of the lease, rather than the duration of the disconnection. A lease-based approach has several problems, however, which inhibit its use. First, there are conflicting pressures on setting the term of leases, with no clear means of resolving them. Specifically, the holder of a lease would like its term to be as long as possible – to give itself the most flexibility in event of involuntary disconnection, while all other clients would like it to be as short as possible – to minimize their waiting time in event of the same. Second, when a lease expires at a disconnected client who has updated the object, the update is no longer valid and cannot be blindly propagated at reconnection. Some mechanism for recovering from this situation would have to be supplied. Third, leases do not solve the contention problem arising from the need to hoard.[16]

---

[16] Gray and Cheriton present leases as essentially timed callback promises, rather than timed read and write tokens as implied here. However, they do note the use of time-outs on typed access tokens as a natural extension of their work.

2.3.5 Replica Control Summary

Partitioned replica control is at the core of any high availability file or database system. This section has presented the rationale for Coda's replica control strategy. Four elements are paramount. First, a computation model which makes explicit the dependencies between data accesses is essential for achieving high availability. Coda employs the model of transactions to this end. Second, to maintain compatibility with existing software, the system infers transactional boundaries rather than altering the standard file interface. Third, the specification of Coda transactions is optimized for high availability. Only slight modification to the semantics of certain Unix operations is necessary to achieve this. Fourth, Coda uses algorithms for both server replication and disconnected operation that manage replicas optimistically. This allows a much larger range of the partitioned activity permitted by the computation model to be realized in practice. Table 2.4 recaps the four main elements of the Coda approach, summarizing the advantages and disadvantages of each.

The Coda model results in a classification of legal versus illegal partitioned file system activity that is intuitively acceptable to most users. Basically, partitioned file operations are allowed as long as they do not update the same file contents or attributes, and partitioned naming operations are allowed as long as they do not update the same directory entry. This is essentially the same availability as is offered by other optimistically replicated file systems based on the Unix model (e.g., Ficus [34, 33]). However, no one else has justified this availability with the type of careful semantic analysis given in this section. The value of this analysis is significant in at least three respects. First, it makes plain the assumptions that are required for partitioned operation to be correct, and thereby identifies the cases where unsatisfied assumptions may lead to problems. Second, it provides a guide for disambiguating subtle cases of correctness versus incorrectness. Finally, it provides a framework for extending the system to support explicit transactional operation. This extension could eliminate the two most serious drawbacks of the current approach: the possibility that unsatisfied assumptions about "true" computation boundaries may lead to undetected violations of correctness, and the need to manually recover from detected cases of incorrect execution.

Feature	Advantages	Disadvantages
Transactional Model	dependencies among operations are explicit; many read/write conflicts between partitioned, independent computations can be permitted; queries can be permitted in any partition.	transactions are foreign to the Unix interface and culture; multi-item queries are only weakly-consistent.
System-Inferred Transactions	maintains backward-compatibility with existing software base; provides convenient upgrade path to programmer-supplied transactions.	incorrect inferences can result in incorrect computations.
Availability-Optimized Transaction Specification	partitioned, mutating operations can be permitted on distinct directory entries and distinct attribute fields; protection changes by one user do not conflict with partitioned operations by other users.	time attribute fields are not accurately maintained (except for file `modify-time`).
Optimistic Enforcement of Correctness	can recognize all syntactically correct histories, including those involving partitioned read/write conflict; avoids early binding of operations to partitions; can (potentially) resolve incorrect executions automatically via system re-submission of transactions; is especially-well suited to disconnected operation (longer-duration partitionings, the need to hoard, client autonomy assumptions).	system is correct only at equilibria; manual repair is (currently) required to resolve incorrect executions.

Table 2.4. Summary of Coda Replica Control Features

3. Architecture

Chapter 1 identified disconnected operation as a general client-based approach to improving service availability. The idea is simple: disconnected clients employ local resources to emulate services normally obtained remotely. For complex services, an agent is needed to assist in the emulation.

Disconnected file service in Coda is based on the premise that this agent should be the cache manager. An architecture which overloads caching for disconnected operation has overwhelming advantage over one which employs independent subsystems. First, the integrated approach yields a constant semantics and seamless transitions between connected and disconnected modes. The segregated model, in contrast, exposes transitions to users and yields arbitrary data-sharing semantics. Second, segregation can result in duplication of data; in the worst case, utilization of local resources is reduced by 50%. Third, temporal locality effects mean that the cache subsystem has useful knowledge of what objects will be requested during the next disconnection. With a segregated architecture, this knowledge cannot be exploited to improve disconnected service.

Despite the advantages of integration, Coda is unique in employing it. The only other file system supporting general disconnected operation, FACE [4, 15], uses a segregated approach. Although the FACE designers noted the advantages of integration, they chose to forego them in the interest of implementation simplicity.

This chapter provides an overview of the Coda disconnected operation architecture. Subsequent chapters elaborate on the system design and the implementation that was produced.

3.1 The View from Venus

Intuitively, disconnected file service has three requirements. First, the client agent must have local copies of data that will be accessed during a disconnection at the time it begins. Second, the agent must satisfy disconnected file requests using its own copies, and remember the operations that it performs. Third, the agent must make those operations visible to servers sometime after disconnection ends.

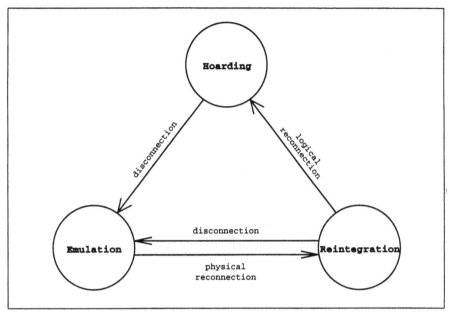

Fig. 3.1. Venus States and Transitions

This intuitive decomposition maps directly onto the set of states visited by the Coda cache manager. Prior to disconnection, Venus is in the *hoarding* state, satisfying connected mode file requests and attempting to keep its cache full of useful objects. Coherence of its copies with the servers' is maintained via the AFS-2 callback protocol. During disconnection, Venus is in the *emulation* state, servicing requests out of its cache and recording operations. Upon reconnection, it enters the *reintegration* state, in which disconnected operations are sent to servers for validation and incorporation into the shared file store. Following reintegration, Venus returns to hoarding and the cycle begins again. Figure 3.1 depicts the three Venus states and the transitions between them.

The two steady states at Venus are hoarding and emulation, which represent normal connected and disconnected operation, respectively. Reintegration is not a steady state, but rather an extended transition. Venus is physically connected during reintegration, but user computation is suspended until the process completes or physical connectivity is again lost. In the former case – which is by far the most common – reconnection occurs logically with the transition to hoarding. In the latter case, logical reconnection cannot occur, and Venus must transit back to emulation.

It is often convenient to think of Venus as monolithically being in one of the three states. However, this is not true in general, as Venus will normally have objects cached from several servers, each of which has an independent connectivity relationship with it. Venus may therefore be in one state with respect to some cached objects and in another state with respect to others. Internally, state is recorded at the granularity of volumes, since all objects in a volume have the same custodian. The cases where state is constant across all volumes are called *fully-connected* and *fully-disconnected*, where Venus is hoarding for each volume in the former case and emulating for each in the latter.

3.2 Decoupling from Server Replication

The Coda architecture allows server replication and disconnected operation to be seamlessly integrated in the same system. Server replication occurs at the granularity of a volume, with the set of servers hosting a volume known as the *volume storage group* (VSG). Each client independently maintains its own view of the system topology. At any point in time and for any volume, the VSG members that the client is currently communicating with is known as that volume's *accessible volume storage group* (AVSG). The client is in the hoarding state for the volume as long as its AVSG is non-empty. When the AVSG membership falls to zero, the client enters the emulating state and is operating disconnected. When connectivity is restored with any VSG member, reintegration is performed and the client subsequently returns to the hoarding state.

Although the integrated model of server replication and disconnected operation is elegant and simple to understand, the mechanics of combining the two facilities are non-trivial. Moreover, server replication by itself is a complex facility with many interesting performance and usability issues specific to it. For these reasons, the rest of this dissertation presents disconnected operation in isolation from server replication. This considerably simplifies certain aspects of the presentation, and allows us to stay focused on the issues pertinent to disconnected operation. Other Coda papers [86, 83, 49] contain details of server replication and its relationship to disconnected operation.

3.3 Masking Disconnection

Section 1.5.1 identified five types of client/server communication that must be masked in order to successfully support disconnected operation. The Coda mechanisms for masking each of these types are previewed in this section.

3.3.1 Cache Miss Avoidance

A connected cache miss can be serviced fairly quickly by just fetching the data from the appropriate server. But disconnected cache misses cannot be serviced in a reasonable period of time, and therefore impede user computation. Venus employs four techniques to minimize their occurrence. First, *hints* concerning future file references are sought and recorded, and hinted objects are pre-fetched into the cache. Second, hints are combined with usage observations to form even better predictions of future reference streams. Pre-fetch and replacement decisions are driven by this refined notion of working-set. Third, naming information is factored into cache management, so that cached objects are never rendered inaccessible due to misses during path expansion. Finally, whole-file caching is used to ensure that misses never occur on parts of objects.

3.3.2 Replica Control

Replica control traffic results from the need to make updates made by one client visible to others. A server which commits an update transaction breaks callback promises to other connected clients that have cache copies, causing those copies to be discarded. A disconnected client, however, cannot see the callback breaks generated by other clients' updates, nor can its own updates cause the immediate invalidation of other clients' copies. In either case, subsequent accesses by clients not in the updater's partition could lead to incorrect computations.

Coda addresses this general problem – partitioned access to replicated data – optimistically, as motivated in Chapter 2. Disconnected and connected clients are allowed to access objects in their own partitions unrestricted, without concern for invalidations that cannot be received from the other partition. When a disconnected client reconnects, its transactions are reintegrated only if they are 1SR with those committed at the server during the partitioning. If they are not, then Venus aborts the reintegration and preserves the effects of the disconnected transactions in a local *closure* file. A user can anytime thereafter examine the closure using a simple tool, and decide him or herself what type of recovery ought to be taken.

In order for the system to detect whether a reintegration is legal or not, Venus *logs* certain information about each disconnected update transaction it performs. This includes the transaction read and writeset and the versions of the data items that were accessed. Read-only transactions are not logged and reintegrated, as that is not needed to ensure 1SR. Unlike other optimistic protocols, this merge process – reintegration – requires logs from only one of the two merging sites. Servers do not need to log transactions committed by connected clients in order to participate in reintegration. This strategy is attractive in that it puts the burdens of logging and of recovering from inconsistency only on the sites that are actually benefitting from disconnected operation.

3.3.3 Update Buffering

Update buffering is needed to make disconnected updates globally visible upon reconnection. Buffering is naturally integrated with the logging mechanism required for replica control. In each log record Venus records the new values that the transaction wrote, as well as state required to verify transaction legality. Since local storage is a scarce resource, logging must be carefully optimized. Venus recognizes two classes of *cancelling* optimizations, which allow log and cache space that is no longer needed to be reclaimed. In addition, duplication of plain file data is avoided by keeping references to cache copies in store log records rather than actual values.

3.3.4 Persistence

Recoverability of disconnected state requires that both file contents and system meta-data be kept in non-volatile store. To address the mismatch between disk and main memory speeds, Venus uses both in-memory caching and write-behind of updated data. Two features of its approach are novel. First, a *variable-deadline* scheduling algorithm is used for meta-data writes, with deadlines determined by the mode of the update – connected or disconnected. Second, meta-data is accessed via a lightweight transactional subsystem which supports atomic update. This reduces the need for complex and time-consuming invariant-recovery at startup, since the subsystem is guaranteed to recover a consistent meta-data state.

3.3.5 Security

A connected client may contact a server for security purposes in two situations. First, it contacts an authentication server when it needs to verify that a user is who he or she claims to be. The details of this process are discussed later in Section 4.2.2. Second, it contacts an object's custodian when it does not have cached access rights for the user performing a transaction. Protection in Coda is enforced via an access matrix, with objects in one dimension and users in the other. Since there may be tens of thousands of users in the system, it is impractical for Venus to cache the rights of all users for any given object. It therefore caches only the rights of a small, fixed number of users for each.

The inability to authenticate disconnected users is accounted for as follows. Venus takes the word of the local kernel that a user is who they claim to be. Thus, it makes protection checks for a disconnected transaction using the cached access rights of the user associated with the system call(s). However, it refuses to attempt reintegration until the user has re-authenticated him or herself. Until that occurs, the corresponding volume remains in the emulating state, regardless of when physical connectivity with the file server is restored.

The inability to fetch missing access rights while disconnected is obviated in two ways. First, access rights obtained while connected are cached in persistent store for the most recent users of each object. This makes it highly likely that the requesting user's rights will be found on subsequent disconnected accesses of the object. Second, Venus always caches the rights of the "anonymous" principal, System:AnyUser, for every object. These rights serve as a floor for every real user, and hence can be used as a conservative approximation to missing real rights.

Finally, it is important to note that disconnected operation offers no new avenue of attack for a malicious individual. Servers validate disconnected operations during reintegration using the same protection and integrity checks that they make in the connected case. So although a disconnected client may be attacked and subverted without the system's knowledge, this is no different than in the absence of disconnected operation. Moreover, the system guarantees that in any subversion – connected or disconnected – damage will be confined to the portions of the namespace accessible to the subverted user. No system which admits insecure client machines can do any better than this.

3.4 Computation Correctness

Most replicated file systems have side-stepped the issue of partitioned computation correctness, and settled for behavior that was a reasonable – but typically unspecified – approximation to a non-replicated reference system. An important goal of Coda is to provide a well-defined and consistent semantics that applies regardless of whether a computation is performed under partitioned or non-partitioned conditions.

Recall from Chapter 2 that the model of computation in Coda is that of inferred transactions. The basic standard of correctness for transactions over replicated data is one-copy serializability. Optimistic replica control schemes satisfy this criterion through the combination of two sub-protocols. The first is a concurrency control protocol which ensures that intra-partition transaction processing is 1SR. The second is a merge protocol which makes the union of the transaction histories of two formerly separate partitions 1SR. As part of this process, some transactions in one or both of the partitioned histories may need to be undone. Global 1SR is attained when all partitionings have been merged. Therefore, to prove that disconnected operation in Coda is 1SR, it must be shown that each of the sub-protocols is correct.

3.4.1 Intra-Partition Transaction Processing

Disconnected operation admits two types of partitions: connected and disconnected. A connected partition consists of a server and the various clients that are in communication with it. A disconnected partition consists of only a single client, who is not in communication with the server. Correct transaction processing in a disconnected partition is straightforward since only one site is involved. The Coda cache manager at such a site ensures local serializability using a simple locking protocol.

In a connected partition, Coda transaction processing is governed by the AFS-2 caching protocol. This protocol uses a simple *version certification* mechanism to ensure that transactions are serializable within the partition. Performing a transaction with this protocol has three steps. First, Venus ensures that it has a cached copy – with callback promise – of every object in the transaction's read and writesets.[1] The descriptor for each copy also contains a *version-id*, which identifies the last committed transaction which wrote this copy of the object.[2] Second, Venus performs the data accesses and computational steps of the transaction on the cache copies. Third, the transaction is certified for correctness, and committed if the certification succeeds. In the case of an update transaction, certification is performed at the server and involves locking every object in the read and writesets and comparing the transaction begin version-id of each one with its current value. Certification succeeds only if every version-id is unchanged. Commitment entails recording the new data values, installing a new version-id for updated objects, and breaking callback promises to other clients. In the case of a read-only transaction, certification and commitment occur locally at Venus. Certification consists simply of a check that callback promises on the readset have not been broken since transaction begin, and commitment merely returns appropriate results to the invoker of the transaction. If certification fails for either an update or a read-only transaction then the transaction is aborted by Venus and retried from scratch.[3]

The correctness of this certification protocol is immediate from the fact that every history it admits would also have been admitted by a two-phase locking (2PL) scheduler.[4] To see this, imagine that Venus acquires read or write locks (as appropriate) at servers at transaction begin rather than verifying or acquiring callback promises. Assume further that locks are held until transaction commitment. Then certification of a transaction in the real Coda protocol succeeds precisely in those cases where there would be no lock contention under 2PL. Certification fails and transactions are retried in those cases where 2PL would have observed contention. The fact that read-only transactions are certified at Venus rather than the server is simply a positive side-effect of there being no real locks to release.

---

[1] The read and writesets of all Coda transactions are known at transaction begin time. Writeset is generalized here to include the increment and decrement sets as well.

[2] Version-ids have also been referred to as *storeids* in other Coda papers.

[3] Transactions which are coincident with a single system call are retried automatically by Venus. The only Coda transactions not of this sort are the readdata and writefile types. The terminating system calls of those transactions receive a special ABORT error code, and it is up to the application to retry the transaction if it so desires.

[4] The fact that a 2PL scheduler admits only serializable executions is well known. See, for example, Bernstein et al [6] for a proof of this.

3.4.2 Merging

The idea behind reintegration is to use the same basic certification mechanism
for merging as is used in normal, connected-partition transaction processing.
Venus therefore processes disconnected transactions in much the same way
as connected transactions. The main difference is that in the disconnected
case, version state is preserved in log records and certification is *deferred* until merge time. During reintegration, transactions are certified by the server
in the order in which they were committed at Venus. As long as transactions are certified successfully, the server tentatively updates its state as if
it were committing connected mode transactions (callback promises are broken, version-ids are updated, etc). If the entire log certifies successfully, then
the tentative updates are made final by committing the reintegration as a
whole. However, if any transaction fails certification, then the reintegration
is aborted and the server undoes all tentative updates. Venus forms a local
closure file in this case and discards the corresponding log records.

The fact that this reintegration procedure always results in a 1SR history
is easy to prove. There are two cases: reintegration succeeds and reintegration
fails. Let H_d be a disconnected transaction sub-history being reintegrated,
H_c be the corresponding connected-partition sub-history, and $\hat{H}_d$ and $\hat{H}_c$ be
serial equivalents of those sub-histories.[5] If reintegration succeeds, then the
committed global history, $H_c \cup H_d$, is view equivalent to the serial, one-copy
history $\hat{H}_c \cdot \hat{H}_d$. Thus it is in the set 1VSR (and, of course, 1SR as well).
View equivalence is guaranteed because version certification ensures that no
transaction in H_d reads any logical data item written by any transaction in
H_c. Every transaction therefore reads from the same writer in $H_c \cup H_d$ as it
does in $\hat{H}_c \cdot \hat{H}_d$, which in turn means that the reads-from relationships for
the entire histories must be identical. If reintegration fails, i.e., it is aborted,
then the committed global history is $H_c \cup \emptyset = H_c$, which is equivalent to $\hat{H}_c$
(by assumption) and therefore 1SR.

Asymmetry. Reintegration is unlike other optimistic merge algorithms because of its asymmetry. This property arises directly from the separation of
sites into clients and servers in the Coda model. Merge asymmetry is evident
in two key respects. First, the transactions in the connected sub-history are
un-abortable. That is, whenever the algorithm determines that partitioned
transactions are incompatible with each other (i.e., they prevent the global
history from being 1SR), the transaction(s) in the disconnected sub-history
are always chosen for abortion, never those in the connected sub-history. This
reflects itself in terminology which speaks of connected-partition transactions
as always being "correct," and disconnected-partition transactions as being
judged "correct" or "incorrect" at reintegration time.

---

[5] The assumption of correct intra-partition transaction processing ensures that
sub-histories $\hat{H}_c$ and $\hat{H}_d$ do exist.

The second element of merge asymmetry concerns the restoration of mutual consistency between replicas. After establishing that the global history is 1SR, reintegration makes the copies at only one of the sites consistent with the final state of the one-copy history. That is, only the server receives the new values written in the "other" partition. The reintegrating client does not directly receive the new values written by connected-partition transactions while it was disconnected. This is quite natural since, as a caching site, it may not even be interested in the objects updated at the server. So, instead, the client simply discards all callback promises upon disconnection and relies on the normal validation procedure to lazily refresh its cache copies after reconnection.

Problems with Version Certification. Although the version certification algorithm described above admits only correct partitioned histories, it admits far fewer correct histories than we would like. In particular, because version-ids are associated with entire Unix objects rather than with independently accessible data items, the algorithm is vulnerable to the false conflict problem described in Section 2.3.3. This means, for example, that connected- and disconnected-partition transactions which mutate different name bindings in the same directory would not be allowed. Version certification would falsely conclude that the disconnected transaction makes the global history incorrect and thereby abort the reintegration.

An obvious way to address this problem would be to maintain version-ids at the sub-object rather than the object level. This would be feasible with respect to the various attribute data items, since they number only a few per object. But it would not be at all practical to do this for directory contents or for access rights. Recall from Figure 2.8 that the former consists of 256^{256} logically independent elements and the latter consists of 2^{32}.

The approach that is used in Coda is to augment version certification with a second mechanism called *value* certification. The basic idea is to log old values for certain types of transactions in addition to version-ids, and to use the old values during certification to determine whether the data item in question actually changed or not at the server. If not, then the disconnected transaction is compatible with the connected history and reintegration can continue. With this approach it is possible to avoid false conflicts altogether. Chapter 7 discusses both types of certification in greater detail, and shows that the Coda hybrid certification algorithm is indeed correct.

Read-Only Transactions. The read-only transactions, readstatus and readdata, dominate the Coda transaction mix regardless of whether Venus is in connected or disconnected mode. Logging these transactions during disconnections and certifying them at reintegration would impose tremendous time and space overheads on the system.

Fortunately, there is no compelling reason to log and certify read-only transactions, and Venus simply ignores them for reintegration purposes. As explained in Section 2.3.1, the result of not regulating partitioned queries is that they may be only weakly consistent. It was argued there that this exception is justified in the light of the much greater availability it permits. From a technical standpoint, the admittance of weakly consistent queries means that the histories recognized by the Coda certification algorithm are contained within the augmented set 1VSR' rather than 1VSR itself.

It is important to note that, although serializability is little affected by Venus' lightweight treatment of queries, the *currency* of the data that such transactions read is not. It is legal – in serializability terms – for Venus to satisfy a disconnected query using *any* version of a specified data item, regardless of how "stale" it may be. This concern is addressed by the hoarding actions of Venus, which limit the staleness of any disconnected object to be the length of the disconnection plus a small constant (typically a few minutes). Chapter 5 discusses this and other aspects of hoarding in depth.

3.5 Detailed Design and Implementation

The details of the architecture and its implementation are presented in the next four chapters. The presentation is organized around the Venus state model, with a chapter devoted to each of the hoarding, emulation, and reintegration states. Issues which span more than one state, for example data persistence, are discussed with the state they most critically affect. Preceding the three state chapters is an "internals" chapter, which gives additional Coda background useful for the main discussion.

4. Coda Internals

This chapter provides a functional overview of Coda clients and servers. The focus is on the general system framework rather than issues that are specifically due to disconnected operation. The following three chapters consider those issues in great detail.

4.1 Client Organization

Client support for Coda is divided between a small, in-kernel *MiniCache* module and a much larger, user-level cache manager, Venus. This approach is consistent with the now-popular *micro-kernel* model of system organization, in which a very small system kernel is augmented with a suite of user-level processes providing traditional operating system services. Mach [1], Chorus [76], and Amoeba [59] are examples of systems that have popularized the micro-kernel approach.

From the Coda point of view, there are two key advantages of mostly user-level implementation. First, development, debugging, and maintenance are all much easier with user-level than with kernel code. For example, source-level debuggers can be used to debug the cache manager, and the machine does not have to be rebooted every time the cache manager suffers a fatal error. Second, portability is enhanced by moving as much functionality as possible from the kernel to user-level. Machine-specific issues tend to disappear at the user-level, as do configuration difficulties and undesirable interactions with other system software modules.

The main disadvantage of user-level implementation is lower performance. Performance degradation occurs primarily because more context-switching and more copying between address-spaces is required. The performance penalty of user-level services can be reduced in several ways. The primary technique employed in Coda is to locate small, select bits of functionality in the kernel beyond those which are absolutely necessary. This reduces both the number of kernel-Venus interactions and the amount of data that must be passed between the two. An alternative approach would be to take advantage of micro-kernel technology that allows efficient address-space sharing and various communication and scheduling optimizations. This approach has not yet been taken in Coda, but it may well be taken in the future.

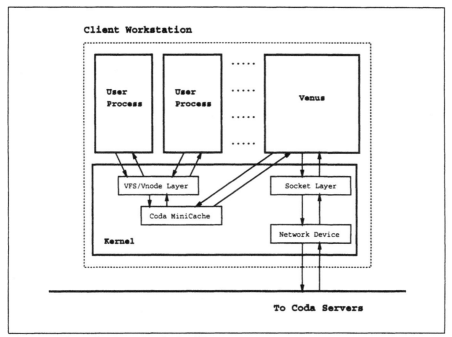

Fig. 4.1. Organization of a Coda Client

The Coda client software has been ported to two operating system environments. The initial and still most-widely used environment is the standard 4.3 BSD kernel. The second, more experimental environment is the Mach 3.0 [29] micro-kernel with a user-level BSD server. In the former case, the Coda MiniCache is a module in the kernel itself, while in the latter it is a module in the BSD server. In both cases Venus runs as a normal user-level process. The distinctions in the two environments are not particularly important for this thesis, and will not be considered further. The rest of the discussion assumes the standard 4.3 BSD environment, since it has been in use far longer. Figure 4.1 illustrates the relationship between Venus, the MiniCache, the rest of the kernel, and regular user processes in the standard 4.3 BSD environment.

4.1.1 Cache Manager

Venus runs as a privileged, user-level process on each client workstation. The AFS-2 equivalent Venus – i.e., the agent without server replication or disconnected operation support – has three main responsibilities:

- handling file system requests from local user processes.
- handling callback break messages from Coda servers.
- ensuring that its cache usage stays within pre-defined limits.

High availability support imposes additional responsibilities on Venus, which are touched on briefly in this section. Those responsibilities that are specific to disconnected operation are treated in detail in Chapters 5 through 7.

Process Structure. Venus is a complex and highly concurrent piece of software. It is structured as a collection of coroutines executing infinite server loops. These coroutines are known as *lightweight processes* (LWPs) because they share the Unix process' address space and are scheduled within its time slice by their own, non-preemptive scheduler. An LWP gives up control either by invoking a yield primitive or by waiting on a condition variable. In the latter case, another LWP must signal the condition in order for the waiting LWP to become runnable again.

About a dozen distinct types of LWPs are used in Venus. In some cases several instances of a type may be active at once. The purpose and behavior of each type is discussed briefly below. This information is summarized in Table 4.1.

Name	Number	Function
Worker Multiplexor	1	distribute local file system requests to worker LWPs.
Worker	variable (3)	process local file system requests; update cache and interact with servers as necessary.
Callback Handler	variable (3)	receive callback break messages from servers and flush invalid objects.
Cache Daemon	1	maintain cache usage within pre-set limits.
Probe Daemon	1	periodically probe servers to detect topology changes.
Resolver	variable (3)	supervise resolutions when unequal server replicas are detected.
Hoard Daemon	1	pre-fetch hoardable objects into the cache and keep the cache in priority equilibrium.
Reintegrator	variable (3)	supervise reintegrations when disconnections end.
IoMgr	1	multiplex I/O activity for all of the process' LWPs.
Socket Listener	1	multiplex all incoming RPC2 packets for the process.
SFTP Listener	1	multiplex all incoming SFTP packets for the process.

LWP types which may have a variable number of instances have a typical number listed in parenthesis.

Table 4.1. Summary of Venus LWPs

Worker Multiplexor. One LWP serves as a dispatcher for all file system requests made by user processes. These requests are forwarded to Venus by the kernel over a Unix character device, the *cfsdev*, which acts as a simple message passing channel. On receiving a request, the multiplexor first looks for an idle worker LWP to pass it on to. If all workers are busy, it creates and dispatches a new one, provided that a pre-set limit on the number of workers has not been reached. If the limit has been hit, the message is placed on a pending-request queue which workers check as they complete their current assignments.

Workers. Worker LWPs interpret the messages dispatched by the multiplexor and perform the corresponding file system transactions. If the client is disconnected with respect to the objects involved, then the operation is performed using only cached data. Otherwise, the worker performs the transaction as per the AFS-2 caching protocols. When the transaction has been completed, the worker constructs a reply message containing any OUT parameters and a return code and passes it back to the kernel through the cfsdev.

Workers, like all Venus LWPs, communicate with Coda servers via a user-level RPC package called RPC2 [80]. RPC2 employs the User Datagram and Internet Protocols (UDP/IP) [70, 71] for unreliable delivery of packets from one Unix process to another. It provides *at-most-once* execution semantics [63] on this base using a connection setup protocol and sequence numbering of packets. Making an RPC requires a connection which has been bound to a particular service instance, as specified by an <IP-ADDRESS, UDP-PORT, RPC2-SUBSYSTEM> triplet. A process indicates its willingness to become a service instance by calling a library routine which *exports* the particular subsystem.

An RPC is synchronous with respect to the thread of control which invokes it. The LWP is blocked while the server is performing the operation and communicating its results. Mechanism within RPC2 ensures that the entire process does not block, however. Having multiple worker LWPs is thus quite useful because it allows more concurrency in the processing of file system calls. Remote processing of one user request can be overlapped with local or remote processing of another.

Callback Handler. A set of LWPs service callback break RPCs that arrive from file servers. These are triggered by updates to locally cached objects that have been performed by other workstations. The fid of the object being "broken" is an argument of the call. The callback handler looks up and flushes the object from the cache so that the next reference will cause the current copy to be fetched. If the object happens to be involved in a transaction at the time of the break, then the flush is deferred until the transaction is finished.

Cache Daemon. A daemon runs at regular intervals to check that cache limits have not been exceeded. Limits are placed on the number of status descriptors, the number of data blocks, and the number of VLDB mappings that are cached. The daemon flushes descriptors, blocks, and mappings in inverse priority order to keep totals within *soft* limits. *Hard* limits, which are somewhat higher, are checked and enforced by workers every time they cache something new. The purpose of the daemon is to perform as much housekeeping as possible in the background, out of the path of user request handling.

Probe Daemon. A daemon wakes up periodically to send *probe* RPCs to sites in the client's "universe." A client's universe consists of those servers which are custodians for objects it has cached. The purpose of probing is to detect topology changes in a timely fashion. From the point of view of disconnected operation, a DOWN to UP transition means that reintegration can be attempted for corresponding volumes, and an UP to DOWN transition means that newly submitted transactions should be performed in disconnected rather than connected mode. The default values for the DOWN- and UP-server probe intervals are 4 and 10 minutes respectively.

Resolver. In the Coda implementation of server replication, partitioned transaction histories are merged *lazily* rather than aggressively. Merging is triggered as a side-effect of the normal caching protocols, whenever Venus finds that the version-ids associated with server replicas are unequal. The merge procedure for first-class replicas is known as *resolution*, and it is performed in coordinated fashion by the servers constituting a replication suite. The role of Venus in resolution is merely to invoke it when replica inequality is detected. Dedicated resolver LWPs are used to make these invocations and wait for them to complete.

Hoard Daemon, Reintegrator. The functions of the hoard daemon and reintegrator LWPs are to keep the cache in priority equilibrium and to supervise reintegrations, respectively. These LWPs are central to disconnected operation, and their behavior is discussed in detail in Chapters 5 and 7.

IoMgr. The LWP package optionally provides a thread called IoMgr which aggregates requests to wait for input and/or timeouts. The standard way of doing event-waiting in Unix is to invoke the select system call, specifying a set of I/O descriptors and a timeout value (if any). However, direct invocation of select by an LWP causes the entire process to block since LWPs are not scheduled by the Unix kernel. To avoid this problem, an LWP calls a library routine, IoMgr_Select, which combines its request with those of other pending selectors and puts it to sleep on a condition variable. When no application LWP is able to run, the IoMgr does a real select using the merged arguments. When the call returns the IoMgr interprets the results and signals those LWPs whose logical selects were satisfied.

Socket Listener. All RPC2 communication for a process is multiplexed over a single Unix datagram socket. The RPC2 library employs a dedicated LWP, the socket listener, to receive all incoming packets and decide how each should be handled. A reply to an outstanding request is passed on to the LWP which issued it. Old (i.e., duplicate) replies are quietly discarded. A new request is passed to an idle LWP if there is one; otherwise the socket listener sends a "busy" response to the requester, instructing it to wait and try again later.

Retried requests result in the socket listener sending a busy, sending a saved response, or ignoring the packet depending on whether it matches the current, the last completed, or an earlier request on the connection.

SFTP Listener. Coda makes use of a companion protocol to RPC2 for efficient bulk-transfer of data. SFTP (for Smart File Transfer Protocol) streams packets from either Venus or file server to the other end using a sliding window and selective retransmission. It has its own dedicated LWP, SFTP listener, which performs a function analogous to that of the socket listener. File transfer is performed as a *side-effect* of a fetch or store RPC using the generic side-effect interface provided by RPC2. RPC2 side-effects are initiated by a server after it has received a request and before it has sent its response. The enclosing RPC remains in progress until the side-effect is complete, at which point the server finishes the call.

Cache Representation. Venus caches three types of data in non-volatile storage:

- status descriptors for files, directories, and symbolic links. These structures encapsulate the vnodes described in Chapter 2.
- the actual data contents for each type of object.
- VLDB mappings.

Two different persistent storage mechanisms are used to support these caches.

Cached meta-data, meaning everything except the contents of plain files, is stored in *recoverable virtual memory* (RVM) segments which are mapped into Venus' address space. An RVM library [87, 56] provides routines for mapping and unmapping segments, and for efficient, atomic update of data. The use of RVM to manage cached meta-data is a feature that was added specifically to support disconnected operation. Before that, some meta-data was cached only in virtual memory and the rest was stored in local Unix files and explicitly buffered in memory. The switch to RVM was motivated primarily by the need for atomic update. A detailed discussion of this issue appears in Section 6.3.

Local Unix files are used as containers for the contents of cached plain files. A protected directory contains a fixed number of container files, each of which corresponds to a status descriptor in RVM. The number of descriptors/containers is fixed, and can only be changed with a complete re-initialization of Venus. The number of disk blocks in use varies over time, but is kept below a maximum value by the actions of the cache daemon. An object which is status-only cached will have this noted in its RVM descriptor, and the corresponding container file will be zero-length. The same is true of a container associated with a descriptor for a directory or symbolic link.

4.1.2 MiniCache

In-kernel support for Coda at clients consists of a small MiniCache module. The purpose of the MiniCache is twofold: to intercept user file system requests on Coda objects and redirect them to Venus, and to minimize the cost of redirection by handling certain simple and very common requests itself.

Coda achieves compatibility with other file systems by conforming to a standard file system intercept mechanism, Sun Microsystems' *Virtual File System* (VFS) interface [46]. This interface allows multiple Unix-like file systems to co-exist in the same namespace through a mount facility very similar to that of conventional Unix. A VFS mount operation establishes an entry in a local table, which is consulted during path translation to indirect from one virtual file system to another.

The VFS layer of the kernel is entered immediately on each file system call. It translates the file descriptor and pathname arguments of the call to *virtual inodes* (vnodes) representing the objects.[1] A vnode is a data structure containing some fields common to all VFS types and an optional pointer to data which is VFS-specific. One of the fields is an *operations vector*, which contains pointers to functions that can be invoked on the vnode. The operations themselves are specified by the VFS interface, but each file system type provides its own code to implement them. Following derivation of the vnodes, the VFS layer calls the appropriate routine from the operations vector, passing the vnodes and the remaining system call arguments as parameters.

A VFS-ized kernel requires each file system type to provide two operations vectors: one for vnode-level and one for VFS-level operations. Table 4.2 lists the operations constituting these two interfaces. Together, they correlate very closely with the BSD file system interface shown earlier in Table 2.1. The most significant difference is in pathname translation, where new VFS/Vnode calls (vfs_root, vn_lookup) abstract out functionality from the main UFS translation routine (namei). This relationship reflects the intent of the VFS design, which was to support the joining of namespaces in a clean, modular way.

Coda VFS Module. The MiniCache exports the operations vectors for VFSs and vnodes of type Coda. A MiniCache routine is entered by a kernel thread running in the context of the user process which invoked the UFS call. The straightforward implementation of each routine performs a cross address space procedure call to Venus. This entails packing the operation code and any IN parameters into a message block, sending the message to Venus through the cfsdev, waiting for the reply, and unpacking the return code and any OUT parameters.

Blind redirection of VFS calls is simple, but it gives poor performance because of excessive context switching and copying of data. Coda addresses this problem by adding functionality to the MiniCache which allows it to service many calls on its own. Of course, in the extreme, this strategy equates to moving Venus into the kernel, which is undesirable from several perspectives.

---

[1] The name clash on "vnode" from contractions of Vice-inode and virtual-inode is unfortunate. However, the use of virtual-inode is confined to this chapter only, and within this chapter the correct interpretation should be obvious from context.

vfs_mount	Mount the specified VFS on the directory vnode corresponding to the specified path.
vfs_unmount	Unmount the specified VFS.
vfs_root	Return the root vnode of the specified VFS.
vfs_statfs	Return file system information for the specified VFS.
vfs_sync	Write out all cached information for the specified VFS.
vfs_vget	Return the vnode corresponding to the specified fid in the specified VFS.
vn_open	Perform appropriate open protocol on the specified vnode.
vn_close	Perform appropriate close protocol on the specified vnode.
vn_rdwr	Read or write the specified file vnode.
vn_ioctl	Perform an ioctl on the specified vnode.
vn_getattr	Get attributes for the specified vnode.
vn_setattr	Set attributes for the specified vnode.
vn_access	Check access permissions for the specified vnode.
vn_lookup	Return vnode mapped to by the specified component name in the specified directory vnode.
vn_create	Create a new file with the specified component name in the specified directory vnode.
vn_remove	Remove a file with the specified component name in the specified directory vnode.
vn_link	Link the specified vnode to the target name in the target directory vnode.
vn_rename	Rename the vnode in the specified directory vnode to the target name in the target directory vnode.
vn_mkdir	Create a new directory with the specified component name in the specified directory vnode.
vn_rmdir	Remove a directory with the specified component name in the specified directory vnode.
vn_readdir	Read entries from the specified directory vnode.
vn_symlink	Create a symbolic link with the specified component name and contents in the specified directory vnode.
vn_readlink	Read the specified symbolic link vnode.
vn_fsync	Write out all cached information for the specified vnode.
vn_inactive	Indicate that the specified vnode is no longer referenced by the vnode layer.

This table describes the interface to the VFS and Vnode layers used in Coda. This version of the interface corresponds to the specification in Kleiman's original paper [46]. Several revisions have been made by Sun since that time (see Rosenthal [75]), but the differences are not important for purposes of this dissertation. The table excludes some operations in the original specification that addressed interactions between the file and virtual memory subsystems.

Table 4.2. VFS and Vnode Interfaces

The key is to identify functionality which is simple to implement but has high payoff in performance. Four such techniques are employed in Coda.

Read/write indirection. The reply from Venus to a vn_open message includes a handle for the UFS file containing the locally cached copy. This handle is used to establish a pointer from the Coda vnode to that of the cache file. Subsequent vn_rdwr, vn_readdir, and vn_fsync calls are satisfied by following the pointer and invoking the operation on the cache file's vnode. No interaction with Venus is required until the session-ending vn_close call is received, at which point the link between the two vnodes is destroyed.

Name translation caching. Each component in a pathname normally requires a vn_lookup call during name translation. The cost of crossing the kernel-Venus boundary for these operations can be a substantial fraction of the total time to handle a system call. The MiniCache greatly reduces lookup costs by remembering the results of successful vn_lookup calls in a small LRU cache. Subsequent lookups of the same keys are satisfied quickly, without talking to Venus.

Symbolic link caching. Pathname translation also requires symbolic links to be evaluated. In many environments the number of symbolic links is large, particularly at upper levels of the namespace. A vn_readlink call for each evaluation, as performed in the naïve implementation, imparts a significant amount of overhead. The MiniCache eliminates most of that overhead by caching link contents in the vnode the first time they are read.

Attribute caching. One of the most common vnode operations is vn_getattr, which corresponds to the UFS stat call. The attribute block returned by the call is fairly small (a few tens of bytes), and changes infrequently for most objects. Hence, it is an excellent candidate for caching. A copy of the attributes is stored in the vnode on the first vn_getattr call, and used in subsequent calls to bypass Venus.

These optimizations are implemented in only a few hundred lines of code – as compared with several tens of thousands in all of Venus. Yet their impact on performance is dramatic. Steere et al [94] reports measurements which show a 67% drop in performance on a standard benchmark from disabling just the last three of the optimizations. Moreover, the difference between Coda (with all optimizations) and AFS-3 (which uses an in-kernel cache manager) on the same benchmark is negligible.

A negative consequence of caching state in the MiniCache is that it needs to be kept coherent with that stored by Venus. A separate interface is needed for Venus to invalidate MiniCache state in response to certain events (for example, a callback break). Invalidations are passed as messages through the cfsdev in the opposite direction from VFS requests. The Venus-to-MiniCache interface is listed in Table 4.3.

cfs_invalidate	Flush all MiniCache data.
cfs_invalidate_user	Flush all MiniCache data pertaining to specified user.
cfs_invalidate_fid	Flush all MiniCache data for specified object.

Table 4.3. Venus-to-MiniCache Interface

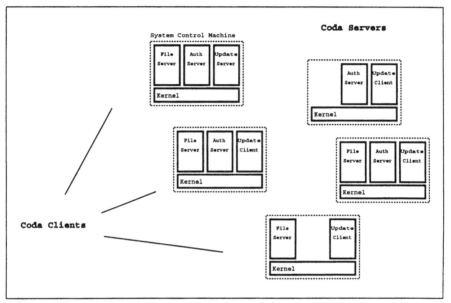

Fig. 4.2. Typical Organization of Coda Servers

4.2 Server Organization

Server machines run several different Coda processes. These include a *file server*, an *authentication server*, and an *update client*. One machine, the *system control machine* (SCM), runs the *update server* rather than a client. A machine need not run both a file and authentication server, although that is the usual arrangement. All of these processes run at the user-level. A small number of kernel modifications are also required to support efficient operation of the file server. A typical configuration of Coda servers is shown in Figure 4.2.

4.2.1 File Server

The file server runs as a privileged, user-level process. The AFS-2 equivalent file server has three main responsibilities:

- handling file system requests from Veni.
- maintaining callback state and notifying Veni when their cached copies become invalid.
- handling requests for administrative operations on volumes.

High availability requires servers to also participate in the replica merge procedures – resolution in the case of server replication and reintegration in the case of disconnected operation.

Process Structure. Like Venus, the file server is composed of several types of LWPs executing infinite server loops. The LWP types and their functions are discussed in brief below, and summarized in Table 4.4.

Name	Number	Function
Vice Worker	variable (5)	service RPC2 requests on the Vice subsystem.
Resolution Worker	variable (2)	service RPC2 requests on the Resolution subsystem.
Volutil Worker	variable (2)	service RPC2 requests on the Volutil subsystem.
Probe Daemon	1	periodically probe replication cohorts and clients that have callback promises.
IoMgr	1	multiplex I/O activity for all of the process' LWPs.
Socket Listener	1	multiplex all incoming RPC2 packets for the process.
SFTP Listener	1	multiplex all incoming SFTP packets for the process.

LWP types which may have a variable number of instances have a typical number listed in parenthesis.

Table 4.4. Summary of File Server LWPs

Vice Workers. A number of LWPs, typically around five, are created at startup to service RPC requests from Veni on the *Vice* subsystem. The interface to this subsystem is specified in Table 4.5. About half of the calls map directly onto operations in the VFS/Vnode interfaces. The others deal primarily with fetching objects, manipulating access-control lists, querying volume information, and managing RPC2 connections. The Vice interface also has calls for invoking resolution and reintegration.

Request handling for the common, VFS/Vnode equivalent calls consists of the following basic steps:

1. Look up and lock status descriptors using the fids specified in the request. Some operations first require directory name lookups to derive the fids.
2. Perform protection and integrity checks to verify legality of the request. This revalidates the checks made by Venus, and is necessary to guard against subverted clients.
3. Perform the semantic part of the call; for example, bulk-transfer of data or insertion of a new directory entry.
4. Set any OUT parameters and unlock the status descriptors.

Callback promises are also established and/or broken during request handling. Promises are recorded in a virtual memory data structure keyed by fid. A new promise is established at the conclusion of ViceGetAttr, ViceFetch and the object-creating operations – ViceCreate, ViceMakeDir, and ViceSymLink. Promises are broken by the Vice worker just before performing the semantic part of a mutating operation. Break RPCs are made on the *CallBack* subsystem, which is enumerated in Table 4.6.

Resolution Workers. A small number of LWPs are employed to service requests on the *Resolution* subsystem. These requests arrive from other file servers, which are acting as resolution coordinators. The resolution procedure is entered by a Venus invoking a ViceResolve RPC on a coordinator.

Volutil Workers. Several LWPs are dedicated to servicing incoming requests for the *Volutil* subsystem. The subsystem exports operations for creating, deleting, cloning, moving, and various other administrative functions on volumes. Requests arrive from utility programs run by system administrators. Authenticated and secure connections are used to protect volume integrity.

Probe Daemon. As in Venus, an LWP is dedicated to probing sites in the server's universe. The universe of a server consists of other servers with which it is a replication cohort, as well as clients which have outstanding callback promises from the server.

IoMgr, Socket Listener, SFTP Listener. These LWPs serve exactly the same functions in the file server as they do in Venus.

Persistent Storage Representation. The file server stores five types of data in non-volatile storage:

- status descriptors for files, directories, and symbolic links. These are the server-side representation of Vice-inodes (vnodes).
- the actual data contents for each type of object.
- volume descriptors.
- the volume location database (VLDB).
- the protection database (which specifies the domain of users and groups, and the membership of each group).

As with Venus, this data is mapped by type onto RVM segments and local Unix files.

Vnodes, directory and symbolic link contents, and volume descriptors are all kept in RVM. This data is mapped into the server's virtual memory space at startup, and read thereafter as normal memory. Writes also use normal memory operations, but must be bracketed by RVM library calls which specify the begin and end of atomic actions. Using RVM for this meta-data has two key advantages over the alternative of Unix files. First, atomic actions eliminate the need for complex and time-consuming application-specific recovery at startup. RVM's internal recovery mechanism suffices to restore all file server invariants. Second, the Coda protocols for server replication require

ViceFetch	Retrieve the status and data of the specified object.
ViceGetAttr	Retrieve the status of the specified object.
ViceGetAcl	Retrieve the access-control list of the specified directory.
ViceStore	Store the data of the specified file.
ViceSetAttr	Set the attributes of the specified object.
ViceSetAcl	Set the access-control list of the specified directory.
ViceRemove	Remove the specified directory entry.
ViceCreate	Create a new file with the specified name and parent.
ViceRename	Change the name of the specified object.
ViceSymLink	Make a symbolic link with the specified name, parent and contents.
ViceLink	Make a hard link to the specified file.
ViceMakeDir	Make a directory with the specified name and parent.
ViceRemoveDir	Remove the specified directory.
ViceGetRootVolume	Retrieve the name of the root volume.
ViceGetVolumeInfo	Retrieve location information for the specified volume.
ViceGetVolumeStatus	Retrieve status information for the specified volume.
ViceSetVolumeStatus	Set status information for the specified volume.
ViceConnectFS	Initiate dialogue with a server.
ViceDisconnectFS	Terminate dialogue with a server.
ViceProbe	Probe the server for purposes of topology management.
ViceAllocFid	Allocate a range of fids for the specified volume.
ViceResolve	Initiate conflict resolution for the specified object.
ViceReintegrate	Initiate reintegration for a volume.

Table 4.5. Vice Interface

CallBackBreak	Revoke the callback promise for the specified object.
CallBackProbe	Probe a Venus for purposes of topology management.
CallBackFetch	Fetch a file from Venus in the course of reintegration.

Table 4.6. CallBack Interface

durability of updates. Achieving this with RVM is much simpler and permits more concurrency than with Unix files.

The contents of Coda files are stored in local Unix files, much the same as they are at Venus. The major difference is that container files on the server are not named in any Unix directory. Instead, container inodes are allocated directly using a new icreate system call. The container file's inode number is recorded in the associated vnode, and thereafter it is accessed by number via other new system calls (iopen, etc). This optimization eliminates path expansion overhead which would duplicate work already performed by Venus. The kernel changes implementing the new system calls is localized in one source file, and consists of about 200 lines of code.

The volume location and protection databases are each mapped onto a plain Unix file. These databases are read-only from the point of view of the file server. Update occurs via atomic replacement of the whole database, as described later in Section 4.2.3.

4.2.2 Authentication Server

Authentication servers run on trusted Vice machines. They manage a database of passwords, and participate in a protocol for establishing secure RPC connections between Veni and file servers. The passwords belong to the users of the system, plus there is one password which collectively belongs to file server processes. The protocol is derived from the Needham and Schroeder private key authentication scheme, and is described fully in Satyanarayanan [81].

The RPC2 package permits mutually suspicious clients and servers to authenticate themselves to one another during its bind procedure. Authentication is based on a 3-phase handshake, in which each party must produce evidence that it knows a particular secret or *key*. Successful completion of the handshake not only assures each party that the other knows the secret, but distributes a session key that they can use to encrypt traffic on the newly established connection.

A naïve use of this mechanism would employ the user's password as the handshake key, and require the user to produce it every time Venus needed to set up a connection with a file server. An obvious improvement is to have the user type in his or her password once – e.g., to the login program – and store it in the clear at Venus. This approach is much more convenient, but it is also risky. An attack on Venus which captures the password exposes the user to unlimited future damage.

Coda and AFS mitigate this danger with a level of indirection provided by the authentication server. The procedure is as follows. When a user logs in to a workstation, his or her password is used to establish a secure, short-lived connection between the login program and an authentication server. The server constructs and returns a pair of *authentication tokens*, which are suitably structured and encrypted to serve as a new shared secret between

Venus and file servers. Login passes the tokens to Venus, then exits. Venus subsequently uses the tokens as the handshake key for establishing secure connections on behalf of the user.

The advantage that tokens have over passwords is that they are time-limited. So capturing a user's tokens still exposes him or her to damage, but only for the duration of the tokens' lifetime. Coda tokens typically expire 24 hours after they are issued. Upon token expiry, servers discard all connections for the corresponding user, and insist that fresh tokens be acquired to reestablish authenticated communication. A user who does not have valid tokens may still access Coda objects. However, the connections that Venus establishes will be unauthenticated, and the access rights applied by the server will be those of the "anonymous system user." Tokens may be reacquired without logging out and logging back in via the log program, which is functionally identical to login.

4.2.3 Update Client/Server

The *Update* subsystem maintains the system databases used by file and authentication servers. The SCM acts as the master for the volume location, authentication, and protection databases. Modifications are allowed only on the copy at the SCM; copies at other sites are read-only slaves. The single instance of the update server runs at the SCM. All other server machines run update clients which periodically check whether their database copies are current. When a new master version is detected, the client fetches it over and atomically installs it in place of its current copy. Secure RPC is used between update clients and servers to protect the integrity of the databases.

This update mechanism is acceptable for the system databases because they are slowly-changing and the occasional use of stale data is not fatal. For example, after a user changes his or her password there is a short period during which either the old or new password may authenticate successfully, depending on which authentication server is approached. Similarly, a new volume will become visible to Veni at different times depending on the file server they direct their VLDB lookups to.

5. Hoarding

The hoarding state is so named because a key responsibility of Venus in this state is to hoard useful data in anticipation of disconnection. However, this is not its only responsibility. Rather, Venus must manage its cache in a manner that balances the needs of connected and disconnected operation. For instance, a user may have indicated that a certain set of files is critical but may currently be using other files. To provide good performance, Venus must cache the latter files. But to be prepared for disconnection, it must also cache the former set of files.

Hoarding really refers, then, to the process of cache management in the face of both connected and disconnected operation. A "hoard" is the same as a cache, except that the resource is managed under a broader set of guidelines. This chapter motivates the design of the hoarding subsystem in Coda, and gives a detailed description of its implementation.

5.1 Idealized Cache Management

The hoarding task can be likened to managing a portfolio of investments. A client's "investments" at any given time are the set of objects it has in its cache. The "return" on an investment is the reduction in latency it provides during execution of the future reference stream. A connected mode hit yields a "dividend" proportional to the cost of fetching data from a server – a few milliseconds to a few seconds, depending on the size of the object. A disconnected hit yields a higher dividend, representing the value of being able to access the object immediately versus not being able to access it at all.

A portfolio manager buys and sells investments in order to maximize the value of the income stream from the portfolio. A cache manager behaves analogously, fetching and replacing objects to maximize the value of cache hits. Both managers face constraints in their activities: the portfolio manager is limited by the current assets of the portfolio holder, the cache manager by the amount of cache space allocated to it. The cache manager is also inhibited from making certain investments at certain times; in particular, it cannot fetch an object when it is disconnected from the object's custodian.

In the theory of finance, income streams are evaluated in terms of their *utility*. Each investor x has a utility function, U_x, which ranks streams according to their intrinsic value to that individual. In very simplified terms, the job of the portfolio manager is to determine the income streams of all possible investments and, subject to available assets, select that combination which maximizes U_x.

An analogous, idealized specification of hoarding can be derived. Assume given a cache size limit, a stream of future references, and a future disconnection schedule. These parameters define a set of *feasible executions*. An execution is a listing of the reference stream, with each reference classified as a *connected-hit*, *connected-miss*, *disconnected-hit*, or *disconnected-miss*. Feasibility means that the obvious constraints are obeyed in the execution: cache size limit is never exceeded, an object must be cached at time $t-1$ in order to be hit at time t, and an object cannot be fetched when its custodian is disconnected from the client. Assume further a utility function for the workstation user which ranks executions for any reference stream. The cache manager's task is then simply to identify the feasible execution with the highest utility, and perform pre-fetches and replacements consistent with that execution.

5.2 Practical Cache Management

The utility model provides a useful theoretical foundation for hoarding. It forms a basis for choosing rationally in the allocation of scarce resources. However, it does not translate directly into a practical implementation. Its use is complicated by the following:

- future references are not perfectly predictable. Predictability declines the further into the future one looks. Moreover, disconnected references are heavily influenced by earlier disconnected misses.
- involuntary disconnections are not predictable. Uncertainty may be associated with voluntary disconnections as well; for example, the time at which the disconnection will end may be only approximately known.
- user utility functions are not easily characterized. Enumerating and explicitly ranking executions is infeasible, since their number grows exponentially (i.e., each reference may hit or miss in the cache, so for a reference stream of length n there are 2^n distinct executions). Furthermore, ranking even a small sampling of alternatives would be too tedious for users.
- remote update activity also affects cache management. Data that is being hoarded for future use should be re-fetched sometime after another site mutates it.

A practical design for cache management based on utilities must address the uncertainty reflected in the items in this list.

Coda performs hoarding in the spirit of utility maximization, but with mechanisms that are pragmatic rather than perfectionist in construction.

The design recognizes that perfect information is never possible in practice, and that higher quality information must normally be paid for – with computational resources, with user attention, or with both. The intent is to balance information gathering and processing costs against the quality of utility approximation they provide.

The crux of the Coda design is to keep a "useful" set of objects cached at all times, where useful means *likely to lead to high utility valuations, given expectations of future reference streams and connectivity state*. New information which indicates that a more useful set of objects than current cache contents might exist causes the cache to be re-evaluated. The following design features are central to the approach:

– use of explicit reference information.
– combining implicit and explicit information.
– use of naming information.
– whole-object caching.

Each of these features is motivated in a separate subsection below. A description of the detailed design and implementation follows in Section 5.3.

5.2.1 Use of Explicit Reference Information

Explicit reference information is information which cannot be derived by the cache manager through observation of normal file system activity. Typically, it is supplied by a workstation user, though it may instead be provided by a third party such as a system administrator or an application program.

Implicit information, in contrast, can be collected by the cache manager without outside assistance. In this respect it is superior to explicit information, since there is never any obligation on the part of the user. Having the user supply reference information reduces the transparency of the system and may be a significant source of irritation.

Cache management in Coda incorporates explicit reference information despite this potential pitfall. To understand why this design choice was made, consider the alternative of using only implicit information. Such an approach relies on the fact that recent reference activity is an excellent predictor of near-future references in typical filing environments. This fact is well-known and has been exploited successfully in distributed file systems for many years. In a typical implementation the cache manager simply notes references as it processes requests, and makes replacement decisions based on how recently or how often objects have been used.

Reference-based algorithms work well in the context of connected operation, but they have at least two serious limitations when one considers the need to support disconnected operation as well. First, the correlation of recent and future references declines the further out onto the "horizon" one looks. Beyond some point, say a few hours, the correlation may be quite weak. This means that if a disconnection were to occur, the frequency of cache misses would increase with time, and perhaps reach an intolerable level in a very short period. Hence, supporting disconnections of longer duration – several hours to several weeks – would be dubious.

The second limitation of reference-based algorithms is that they give no information about the importance of particular references. This is not a problem for connected-only management, since the utility lost on a cache miss is roughly constant for all objects. Disconnected misses, in contrast, vary widely in the pain they cause the user. For example, a miss on the exec of one's editor is likely to be far more serious than one on the open of an accounting file. With only implicit, reference-based information, the cache manager would have a difficult time ensuring that more important objects are hoarded in preference to lesser ones.

Using explicit reference information avoids both the problems of short predictive horizons and homogeneous miss penalties. Explicit information is supplied in Coda by passing pathnames of "interesting" objects to Venus. A value may be associated with a name to indicate the degree of interest. Names and values serve as *hints* to Venus that the corresponding objects should be cached if at all possible. Hints may be supplied directly by workstation users or indirectly by one of several means.

The Coda design is careful to minimize the burden on users of gathering and supplying information. The view taken is that user assistance for hoarding is acceptable provided that:

– it is optional.
– the mechanisms are easy to use.
– the payoff is high.

Section 5.3.1 describes in detail the mechanisms which satisfy these criteria.

5.2.2 Combining Implicit and Explicit Information

The preceding subsection argued that implicit information cannot adequately support disconnected operation. Explicit information is needed to enable operation during lengthy disconnections, and to make sure that critical objects are hoarded with commensurate effort. On the other hand, it's also true that reference information is important for good connected mode performance, and that it can contribute to availability for shorter-term disconnections.

The Coda strategy, therefore, is to combine implicit and explicit information to try to realize the benefits of both. The means of combination is a *prioritizing function*, which computes a priority for each cache object based on raw implicit and explicit measures of goodness. An *horizon* parameter weights the two measures, and is adjustable to suit the preferences of the workstation user. A short horizon weights the implicit measure more heavily, favoring recently referenced objects that are likely to be referenced again in the near-term. A long horizon does the opposite, favoring explicitly named objects that will/would be useful in event of later disconnection.

Priorities are the basis of all cache management decisions in Venus. The goal is to continuously maximize the total priority of objects that will fit in a cache of given size. Objects may enter the cache in one of two ways: on demand, via a normal file system operation, or by pre-fetch. Pre-fetching occurs when the cache has free space or when the priority of an explicitly named, uncached object exceeds that of a cached object. The object chosen for replacement in any cache full situation is the one with the lowest current priority.

The intent of the Coda scheme is to make priority maximization as good a proxy for utility maximization as possible. An object's priority represents both the likelihood that it will be used, and the value of hitting on it if it is indeed used. This is precisely the information that would factor into an implementation of the idealized hoarding model outlined in Section 5.1. Of course, priorities are a simplification of the notion of utility. For example, they assume that objects are independent of one another, and therefore do not capture *conditional* utility relationships that clearly exist.[1] However, simplifications are needed to realize a practical implementation, and the priority model has proved to be a good compromise.

5.2.3 Use of Naming Information

The Unix namespace is organized hierarchically, as a directed acyclic graph rooted at a single node. In Coda there are three types of naming objects: directories, symbolic links, and volume mount points. Naming objects can be accessed directly, for example in the listing of a directory. But from the viewpoint of hoarding, their more important role is in pathname expansion. Expansion is the translation of high-level into low-level names which identify the actual arguments of system calls. As an example, handling the system call

```
open(/coda/usr/jjk/src/venus/venus.c)
```

involves reading at least 6 directories in order to derive the fid for venus.c. If translation encounters symbolic links or mount points then they – and perhaps additional directories – must be read as well.

The significance of path expansion for hoarding is that a cached object is inaccessible if any naming component is uncached during disconnection. Having such an object cached is thus counter-productive, since it occupies space that might otherwise be devoted to a nameable object. Note that this is not an issue for connected-only cache management, since a missing naming object can always be fetched.

---

[1] Consider a window manager application that requires a particular font. A disconnected hit on the application binary obviously has different utility depending on whether the font file is hit or not, but this cannot be directly expressed with simple priorities.

In utility terms, this phenomenon signifies conditional utility relationships between naming objects and the files they identify. That is, the utility contribution of having a file cached during disconnection will be 0 if any pathname component is missing, and some positive value if all components are cached.[2]

An intelligent implementation of hoarding can account for naming effects by managing the cache hierarchically. The priority of leaf nodes must be reflected back up the graph, so that internal nodes are never replaced before their cached children. In effect, the priority of an internal node should be equal to that of its highest priority descendant. The means for achieving this in Coda are described in Section 5.3.2.

5.2.4 Whole-Object Caching

Whole-object caching was a key element of the AFS-2 design, as described in Chapter 2. The arguments for the approach are simplicity and efficiency; those against it are primarily higher latency and the inability to access very large files. The two disadvantages motivated the switch to a large-block caching scheme in AFS-3, and led to consideration of a similar change for Coda.

Supporting disconnected operation, however, is much cleaner and more effective if whole-objects are cached rather than incomplete portions of them. There are several reasons for this. First, although it is quite feasible to maintain reference information at the granularity of blocks, it is unrealistic to gather hints at that level. It is difficult enough for users to identify useful objects, let alone specific ranges of them. Second, caching blocks of objects independently ignores very strong conditional utility relationships. For example, a disconnected miss on one block of a large executable could render all of its blocks useless. Similarly, a source file with a few blocks missing could not be compiled, possibly negating the value of those blocks that were cached.

A third argument in favor of whole-object caching is even more pragmatic. Although not an endorsement of such programming practice, it's undeniably true that many programs are more resilient to open failures than they are to read or write failures. Hence, a missing block which reveals itself during a disconnected read is much more likely to crash a program than is a completely missing file. In the best case, the programmer will have anticipated unsuccessful opens, and provided fallback capability to allow the program to continue. As a realistic example, consider a window manager application which tries a list of substitute font files when an open on the first choice file

---

[2] Objects may be accessed via paths *relative* to a process' current directory, as well as *absolute* paths which start at the root node of the system. Hence, a disconnected object may be accessible – and therefore have positive utility – even though some component in its absolute path is missing. However, this does not affect the basic result that an object's utility is conditional on the ability to name it.

fails for any reason. Even in less benign cases, where the program fails anyway, the failure is likely to be much more graceful as a result of missing on open than on read or write (dirty buffers flushed, helpful error message, etc).

It's conceivable that one might choose a block over a whole-object caching design in spite of the aforementioned factors. A few special provisions, such as hoarding hinted objects in their entirety and using a large block size, would mitigate the disadvantages of the block approach. This could expand the domain of the system – albeit mostly in connected mode – to include applications such as large CAD/CAM systems which are currently not well supported. However, if disconnected support is a primary goal, then whole-object caching as used in Coda is the better choice.

5.3 Detailed Design and Implementation

The central pieces of information managed by Venus are known internally as *file system objects* (fsobjs). An fsobj contains all of the meta-data for a file, directory, or symbolic link. It is the Venus-side implementation of the Vice-inode structure introduced earlier, and is analogous to an inode in traditional Unix file systems. As mentioned in Chapter 4, fsobjs are stored on disk and mapped into Venus' address space using the RVM package.

The format of an fsobj is illustrated in Figure 5.1. The primary means of access is via a hash table which is keyed by fid. Fsobjs consist of several distinct sub-descriptors, the most important of which for hoarding are the *status, data, priority* and *hierarchy* blocks. The status block consists of standard Unix attributes plus version state, a callback promise flag, and access control rights for local users. The data block is a pointer which identifies one of the following, depending on the type of object: a container file, a directory page descriptor, or symbolic link contents. If the object's data is uncached, the pointer is null.

The priority and hierarchy blocks contain the key information used in hoarding. Fsobjs are linked into a priority queue in the order determined by current priority values embedded in the priority blocks. A replacement is made by taking the lowest priority entry off the queue and re-initializing it. If the replaced object had data cached then it too is freed on replacement. New objects which enter the cache have their priorities computed and are inserted in the appropriate place in the queue.

The rest of this chapter focuses on fsobj priorities. It explains how individual priorities are derived, and the global actions of Venus in maximizing total fsobj priority.

5.3.1 Hoard Database

One component of an fsobj's priority is the value ascribed to it by way of an explicit *hint*. Hints are received by Venus over a special interface, and

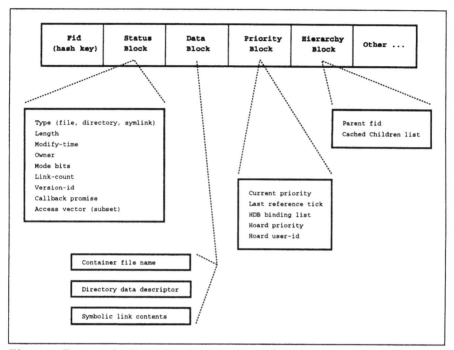

Fig. 5.1. Format of a Venus File System Object (fsobj)

maintained in a database known as the *hoard database* (HDB). The HDB is stored in RVM, and has a maximum size that is fixed at Venus genesis (1000-10000 entries covers the typical range).

Format and Interface. Each HDB entry (hdbe) has the format shown in Figure 5.2. Entries are keyed by the combination of the volume-id and pathname suffix fields. A hash table based on this key is maintained so that the lookup operation is efficient. "Pathname suffix" refers to the part of an absolute path which lies within the volume actually containing the object. The other fields of an hdbe are the user-id of the hint supplier, the hoard priority associated with the hint, flags indicating whether the entry is to be *meta-expanded*, and a pointer to a *name-context*. The hoard priority field allows some hints to be more influential than others. Its role in the overall object priority computation is described in Section 5.3.2. The purposes of the name-context and the meta-expansion flags are explained later in this section.

The interface to the HDB is via a simple message-passing facility built on the ioctl system call. A program wishing to access the HDB builds a structure containing the command and its arguments, opens a special control file in the Coda namespace, issues the ioctl on the control file descriptor with the structure as its argument, and finally closes the descriptor. The command makes its way through the MiniCache and across the kernel/Venus

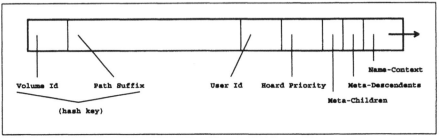

Fig. 5.2. Format of a Hoard Database Entry

Command	Function
add *filename* [*priority*] [c	c+	d	d+]	Add *filename* to the database with optionally specified *priority* and *meta-expansion attributes* (c and d indicate children and descendant expansion respectively, with + indicating the dynamic rather than the static variant).
clear [*uid*]	Clear all database entries or those for specified *uid*.
delete *filename*	Delete database entry with specified *filename*.
list *filename* [*uid*]	List all database entries or those for specified *uid* to specified output *filename*.
walk	Perform an immediate hoard walk.

Table 5.1. Hoard Program Command Set

interface as a vno_ioctl request. Venus validates the request, performs it, and returns a result.

The HDB command set includes the following: add an entry, delete an entry, clear all entries, list all entries, and "walk" the database. HDB walking is the process of reconciling hdbes and fsobjs, and is discussed in detail in Section 5.3.3.

The interface is fully exposed and commands may be issued by any program, although at present only one program actually does so. That is a simple, front-end program called hoard. The hoard command set is identical to that of the HDB interface, except in the arguments of a few commands. The hoard command set is summarized in Table 5.1.

HDB Entry Expansion. Users and application programs refer to objects via high-level, human-readable pathnames. At some point, a pathname needs to be expanded, component by component, to derive the low-level name of the object. In normal file system processing, expansion is done "on-demand," as an early step in the handling of a call.

However, expanding a pathname submitted as a hint is not so straightforward. The most convenient strategy from the system point of view is to expand the hinted pathname immediately – i.e., at the time of the HDB add command. With such an approach the HDB entry could simply contain a fid rather than a path, and Venus' processing effort would be limited to one expansion per entry.

Unfortunately, immediate or *static* expansion is usually the wrong approach from the user's point of view. Consider the following simple example. The pathname

/coda/usr/jjk/.login

is submitted as a hint, and Venus expands it to the fid 7f000184.8C. The file is then edited, and the editor renames fid 7f000184.8C to .login.BAK. The new contents it writes to a fresh fid, 7f000184.98, under the name .login. Now, the hinted object – with its elevated priority – is one which the user cares little about, and the one which he or she does consider important is being managed with unamplified priority.

The alternative to static expansion is to expand names *dynamically*, re-evaluating them in response to events which may change the expansion. This is the approach adopted in Coda. It solves the problem typified by the .login example above, as well as others, like the hinting of a name which does not bind to an object immediately but does so later when a new object is created. The disadvantage to dynamic expansion is that it is more complex to implement efficiently than is the static approach. However, the behaviors which thwart static expansion are so common that a usable system cannot be based upon it.

Dynamic expansion requires state to be maintained in order to make it efficient. The purpose of the state is to minimize the computational effort that must be expended in re-performing expansions. To this end, Venus pre-compiles expansions into instances of a data structure known as a *name-context* (namectxt). A namectxt consists principally of the <volume-id, path-suffix> pair being expanded and an ordered list of *name-bindings*. Name bindings, or just "bindings," are small blocks of store that associate pathname components with the fsobjs they currently map to. The effect of a binding is to transfer the priority of its hdbe to its fsobj. Figure 5.3 illustrates the linkage between hdbes, namectxts, bindings, and fsobjs with an example.

Linking together hdbes and fsobjs permits the effect of events affecting one of them to be reflected back on a minimal subset of the other. For example, a callback break on an fsobj causes only those hdbes which are linked to it to be re-evaluated, not the entire set of entries. Similarly, deleting an hdbe results in priority re-computation of only those fsobjs it was linked to, not all fsobjs. The full set of events which cause hdbe re-expansion or fsobj priority re-computation are listed in Section 5.3.3, along with discussion of the activity they entail.

The expansion strategy described above and implemented in Coda is not completely dynamic. Rather, the approach is a hybrid, in which the pathname prefix is bound to a volume at HDB add time and only the suffix is

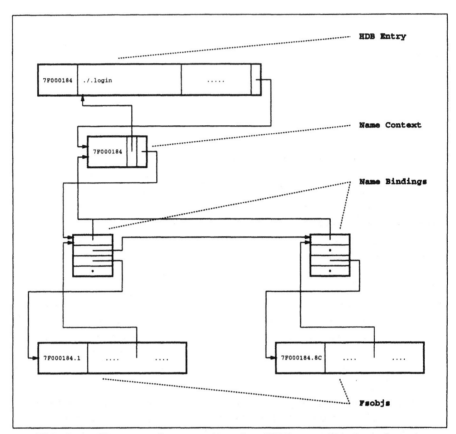

This figure illustrates the expansion of an HDB entry keyed on the pair
<7f000184, ./.login>. The fsobj on the left, with fid 7f000184.1, corresponds
to the root directory of the volume. The fsobj on the right, with fid
7f000184.8C, corresponds to the file currently named .login in that directory.

Fig. 5.3. Sample HDB Entry Expansion

expanded dynamically. The motivation for choosing this approach over a fully
dynamic one is twofold. First, considerable space savings can be achieved by
the encoding of prefixes into volume-ids. The former are often tens of bytes
long, whereas the latter is only a 4-byte quantity. Second, volume-level re-
organization of the namespace – which may be troublesome to the hybrid
approach – is rare. Hence, hybrid expansion realizes most of the benefits of
the fully dynamic scheme with little of the disadvantages of the static.

Meta-Expansion. To simplify the specification of hints, Coda supports
meta-expansion of HDB entries. Meta-expansion is an additional level of
mapping, which is applied in conjunction with the expansion described in
the preceding section. It maps a single high-level name into multiple high-
level names. Each new, high-level name is then expanded into a sequence of

low-level names – i.e., fids – just as if the path had been specified directly in an HDB entry. Two flavors of meta-expansion are supported in Coda: *descendant* and *children*. The former maps a pathname into the set of names representing all descendants of the bound directory. The latter maps a name into the set representing only immediate children.

The meta-expansion options in Coda take advantage of *naming locality* in file access patterns. Co-location in the same directory or sub-tree is typically strong evidence that objects are semantically related, and therefore that when one is accessed others will be accessed as well. Hence, a hint for a particular object is likely to be correlated with hints for other objects in the same directory or sub-tree. Meta-expansion recognizes and exploits this fact to reduce the effort of gathering and submitting hints. For example, instead of submitting a dozen names, one for each of the objects in a directory, a user need only submit a single name, that of the directory itself. In effect, meta-expansion leverages off of the effort already expended by users, applications writers and system administrators in organizing the namespace.

Meta-expansion is implemented by growing trees of namectxts off of HDB entries. A meta-expanded namectxt employs two fields which are unused in the non-meta case: a parent pointer which identifies the namectxt it was expanded from, and a list of children pointers which identify the namectxts it expands to. The pathname field of a meta-expanded namectxt is the same as its parent's, except that it has one additional component added onto the end. The structure formed by this process mirrors that of the directory hierarchy rooted at the meta-designated HDB entry. Figure 5.4 depicts a sample instance of descendant meta-expansion. Once a namectxt has been meta-expanded, the task of binding it to fsobjs is then identical to the non-meta case.

Like normal hdbe expansion, meta-expansion conceivably can be performed either statically or dynamically. That is, a pathname could be expanded into children or descendant paths once, at the time of HDB add, or it could be expanded continuously, in response to local or remote naming activity. Coda has mechanisms which support both of these meta-expansion styles.

Dynamic meta-expansion is supported directly by Venus. As with normal hdbe expansion, the dynamic variant is both the more useful and the more complex one to implement. Dynamic meta-expansion is more useful because it adapts to naming activity automatically, without further intervention from the user. Objects which become nameable in meta-designated directories automatically "become hinted," and those which lose their nameability automatically lose their hinted status. Implementation complexity results from the fact that the system must determine when an entry should be meta-expanded, and to what extent. The latter problem becomes obvious if one considers a request to descendant meta-expand /coda (i.e., the file system root). The interpretation of such a request is to dynamically track

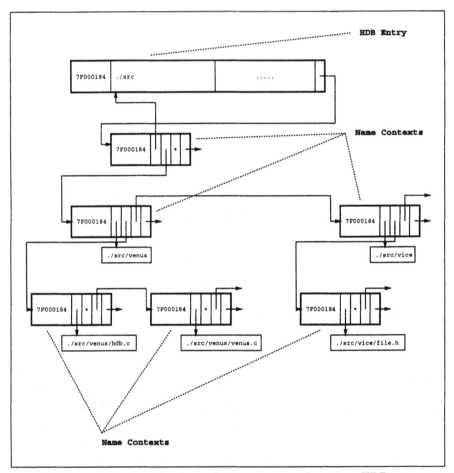

This figure illustrates the descendant meta-expansion of an HDB entry
keyed on the pair < 7f000184, ./src>. Fsobjs and the bindings which associate
them with name contexts are omitted for clarity.

Fig. 5.4. Sample Meta-Expansion

and hoard the entire shared filestore! Section 5.3.3 describes when dynamic
meta-expansion is performed, and how it copes with expansions that may
exceed local resources.

Although static evaluation is useless for normal hdbe expansion, it is
sometimes useful for meta-expansion. Static meta-expansion effectively takes
a "snapshot" of a directory or sub-tree, and issues a uniform hint for the
snapshot. This may be preferable to dynamic evaluation if the user anticipates
that "uninteresting" files may be added to a directory or sub-tree sometime
in the future. An example might be a system font directory which currently
contains only a small number of "useful" font files, but may have extraneous
fonts added to it later.

Static meta-expansion is not directly supported by Venus, but it can be easily provided by any client of the HDB interface. Standard Unix library routines and utility programs provide for enumerating directories and performing tree walks. The names they generate for a given root can then be submitted individually as non-meta-designated hints. This simple technique is used by the hoard program to implement static meta-expansion. Referring back to Table 5.1, static evaluation is specified by using the c or d modifier in an add command (for children or descendant expansion respectively), and dynamic evaluation is specified by using c+ or d+. Since Venus only knows about dynamic meta-expansion, unqualified use of the term "meta-expansion" should be interpreted hereafter as referring to that style.

Hoard Profiles. The cost of generating caching hints can be significant. Hint generation may involve scanning directories, gratuitously executing programs, even examining source code. It takes time and attention away from more directly productive tasks. Hence, there is considerable incentive to re-use hints; doing so amortizes cost over many sessions instead of it being borne by just one.

Coda has a simple, yet effective, mechanism for re-using hints. It makes use of the hoard program's ability to read commands from a file rather than the user's terminal. The procedure is simply to store related add commands in files, and pass the filenames to the hoard program instead of executing the commands directly. A file containing such a list of add commands is known as a *hoard profile*.

Profiles are an informal encapsulation mechanism. Typically, they reflect a grouping of objects based on a task; for example, the set of executable and support files needed to run a text editor. In some cases, such as a mail reading application, program and data files may be easily grouped into a single profile. In other cases, where the mapping of programs to data is not one-to-one, it may be more convenient to separate program and data components into their own profiles.

Profiles can amortize the cost of hint generation in two ways. First, if a user engages in the same tasks over time, then the effort he or she spends up front in constructing profiles can be spread over many of his or her own task executions. Second, if different users engage in a task, or variants of a task, then one person's efforts can benefit many others. An important example of this is an application maintainer constructing a profile of his or her application and making it publicly available. A user can then "hoard" that application simply by submitting its profile to the hoard program on his or her machine. Similar leverage can be gained by having system administrators construct and export profiles for utility programs and other system objects. As a final example, users cooperating on a project, say development of a piece of software, may share a project profile. This not only minimizes the initial profile construction cost, but allows each member to continue to see a common view of things as the project evolves.

```
# Home directory                          # X11 files (from X maintainer)
a /coda/usr/jjk 1000:c+                    a /usr/X11/bin/X
a /coda/usr/jjk/.MESSAGES/mail 1000:c+     a /usr/X11/bin/Xvga
a /coda/usr/jjk/bin 100:c+                 a /usr/X11/bin/mwm
a /coda/usr/jjk/lib 100:d+                 a /usr/X11/bin/startx
                                           a /usr/X11/bin/xclock
                                           a /usr/X11/bin/xinit
# Thesis                                   a /usr/X11/bin/xload
a /coda/usr/jjk/thesis/FIGS 20:d+          a /usr/X11/bin/xrdb
a /coda/usr/jjk/thesis/bib 100:d+          a /usr/X11/bin/xset
a /coda/usr/jjk/thesis/dissertation 1000:d+  a /usr/X11/bin/xterm
a /coda/usr/jjk/thesis/notes 100:d+        a /usr/X11/include/X11/bitmaps c+
a /coda/usr/jjk/thesis/proposal 10:d+      a /usr/X11/lib/app-defaults d+
                                           a /usr/X11/lib/fonts/misc c+
                                           a /usr/X11/lib/rgb.dir
# Venus sources (shared among developers)  a /usr/X11/lib/rgb.pag
a /coda/project/coda/alpha/src/venus 100:c+  a /usr/X11/lib/rgb.txt
a /coda/project/coda/alpha/include 50:d+   a /usr/X11/lib/system.mwmrc
a /coda/project/coda/alpha/lib 20:c+       a /usr/ucb/uncompress
                                           a /usr/lib/cpp
```

These are real hoard profiles used by the author. Each profile is interpreted
independently by the hoard program. The ''a'' at the beginning of a line
indicates an add-entry command. Note that pathnames beginning with
/usr are actually symbolic links into /coda.

Table 5.2. Sample Hoard Profiles

The normal pattern of hint generation for a novice Coda user is the following. Step one is to identify existing profiles that would be useful. This
typically includes public profiles for window managers, text editors and other
common applications. It might also include profiles covering project-related
data. Step two is to organize one's personal data into a series of private profiles. Step three is ongoing, and involves using the profiles and adapting them
to changing user behavior. This may entail trying different combinations of
profiles, modifying profiles, or constructing entirely new profiles to represent
new applications or activities. Table 5.2 displays several real profiles used by
the author in his day-to-day use of the system. They illustrate the use of the
three common types of profiles: public, project and personal.

The effectiveness of hoard profiles results from two usage phenomena.
First, the set of activities a typical user engages in is moderately-sized and
slowly-changing. Hence, the number of profiles he or she must be concerned
with at any time is generally small. Second, the set of objects used in most
tasks is usually either quite static, or can be tracked successfully using simple meta-expansion. The amount of profile revision and fine-tuning typically
needed is therefore also small. Taken together, the two phenomena mean that
a few, well-constructed profiles can capture long-term working-sets reasonably well, and without substantial maintenance effort.

Reference Spying. Use of the system has shown that "well-constructed"
profiles can indeed capture long-term working-sets. However, there remains
the problem of constructing "well" profiles in the first place.

In some cases the task is straightforward. For example, the data files containing a student's homework assignments may all be stored underneath the directory hw in his or her home directory. A profile with a single, meta-designated add command might be all that is needed in this case. Similarly, the complete TEX text-formatting package might be specified by a profile containing the line ''add /usr/misc/.tex d+''.

There are at least two reasons, however, why profile construction is not always so simple. One is that profiles which are too broadly specified are counter-productive. An overly inclusive specification will cause many un-needed objects to be cached, perhaps excluding other objects which will later be referenced. This danger is particularly acute with descendant meta-expansion, where a single hint can expand into a subtree containing tens or hundreds of megabytes of data. It is often wiser to select subsets of a tree than to meta-expand the root, even though each finer step in working-set specification requires correspondingly more effort.

A second impediment to profile construction is that many file reference are non-obvious to users. A classic example is a window manager application that uses a variety of fonts. The font files often have obscure names which even sophisticated users do not know. Similarly, an executable or a script may – unknown to the user – invoke other executables or scripts in the course of its execution. Under these circumstances, simply knowing the names of top-level executables and data subtrees may not be enough to capture a task's required files.

Coda addresses these problems by allowing users to observe file references. The spy program connects to a Venus, receives the full pathnames of files as they are opened, and writes the names to its standard output stream. A user can capture the names of objects required for a high-level task with the following simple procedure:

– start a background execution of the spy program, and redirect its output to a file.
– perform the high-level task.
– terminate the spy process.

Now the file generated by spy can be edited into a hoard profile, to be used to hoard for future executions of the task.[3]

Editing of spy-generated files is needed primarily to make use of meta-expansion. There are currently no smarts built into the system for making "meta-inferences" from plain reference streams. Editing is also needed

---

[3] The file saved will actually contain references for all active tasks, not just the one of interest to the user. Better strategies, which record references only from selected processes or process trees, could be implemented without too much trouble. However, on a primary-user workstation the spy interference from concurrent activities is normally small, so cross-task interference has not been a serious problem in practice.

if the user wishes to specify non-default priorities for some entries. If meta-expansion and non-default priorities are not needed for a particular task, then profile generation can be completely automated. The user need only replace the startup of the spy process in the first step above with the following Unix pipeline:

```
spy | sort -u | awk '{print "add " $1}' > $hoardfile &
```

Access Control. Access to the HDB is largely restricted to the user logged-in at the console of the machine. This follows from the environmental assumptions that most Coda clients are primary-user workstations, and that possession of the console equates with primacy. Other users are viewed as "guests" of the primary-user. As guests, it would be unreasonable for them to be able to control the long-term caching behavior of the machine.

The primary-user is allowed to perform any HDB command, including the deletion of entries that were added by other users. Among other things, this allows a user logging-in to a public or group workstation to start off with a clean state. Secondary users are allowed only limited access to the command set. In particular, they are not allowed to add new entries to the database, nor are they allowed to list or delete entries belonging to other users. Their only options are to delete or list their own entries (which must have been added at some point when they were primary). An exception is made for the Unix *super-user*, who is treated the same as the primary. Attempting to restrict super-user access would be futile, since the kernel gives him or her full access to the bare machine.

5.3.2 Object Priorities, Resource Allocation, and Naming Effects

Prioritizing Function. The function which computes an object's *current priority*, p, is a linear combination of two components:

$$p(f) = \alpha \cdot h(f) + (1 - \alpha) \cdot r(f)$$

$h(f)$ and $r(f)$ are functions computing the object's *hoard* and *reference* priority respectively. α is the *horizon* parameter introduced in Section 5.2.2. The higher its value the more heavily weighted is the hoard priority, and thus the further out on the "reference horizon" is the cache oriented. The horizon parameter is set to .75 by default, although it may be overridden at Venus startup.

Hoard Priority. The function h computes an object's hoard priority as the maximum of the priorities of the set of hdbes that are currently bound to it. This set is accessible via a list rooted in the fsobj. The current hoard priority is stored in the fsobj for efficiency reasons, and is recomputed whenever the set of bound hdbes changes. An fsobj with no bound hdbes has hoard priority 0. The maximum priority that can be associated with an hdbe – and thus the maximum hoard priority that an fsobj can take – is given by the constant $\mathcal{H}$ (1000 in the current implementation).

Reference Priority. Computation of the reference priority component is more complicated. The straightforward approach is to map the *least recently used* (LRU) ordering onto the integers; i.e., the least recently used fsobj gets reference priority 1, the next gets 2, and so on. Unfortunately, the reference priorities generated by this approach are not very useful for combining with hoard priorities. This is because LRU is inherently an ordinal measure, whereas cardinality is needed to combine multiple decision criteria into one. LRU effectively filters out all reference information except the ordering of each object's latest reference. With this filtering, it discards information that could establish cardinal relationships between objects. The problem is clearly illustrated by noting that LRU order always yields the same reference priority for the first- and second-most recently used objects, regardless of whether the first has been referenced just once or a thousand times consecutively.

Coda avoids the foregoing type of problem by using more than just relative order in computing reference priorities. The function r computes an object's reference priority based on the total number of references that have occurred since it was last referenced. r may be thought of as computing object *temperatures* – the more recently an object has been referenced the "hotter" its temperature and therefore the higher its reference priority. The approach differs from LRU in that an object's temperature declines when any other object is referenced, whereas its LRU order changes only when a (formerly) less recent object is referenced.

The actual reference priority function used is the following:

$$r(f) = max(\mathcal{R} - \frac{Ticks - t_f}{\beta}, 1)$$

$\mathcal{R}$ is a constant which represents the maximum reference priority that can be assigned to an fsobj. Typically, it is set to be the same as the maximum hoard priority. *Ticks* is a global "tick counter" which is incremented on every reference made at this Venus. t_f is the value of *Ticks* at the time f was last referenced. The per-object tick counters are stored in the fsobjs themselves, and they persist across Venus restarts. β is known as the *cooling* parameter. The higher its value, the slower inactive objects will move to lower temperature ranges. By default β is 16, meaning that objects whose latest reference is among the globally most recent 16 get reference priority $\mathcal{R}$, those whose latest reference is among the next 16 get $\mathcal{R} - 1$, and so on. A floor of 1 is enforced so that every cached object which has been referenced – no matter how far back in the past – will see some positive reflection in its reference priority.

Resource Allocation. Priorities are used in the allocation decisions for two key Venus resources, fsobjs and container file blocks. Every request for one of these resources is accompanied by a *request priority*. A request succeeds if enough free resources exist to satisfy it directly, or if a sufficient amount can be gathered by freeing allocated resources whose priority is lower than the request priority. An allocated fsobj's priority is its current priority, p; an allocated container file's priority is the current priority of the fsobj which owns it.

Request priorities depend on the source of the request. In the case of a request made on behalf of a user file system operation, the request priority is a large constant. This constant, $\mathcal{U}$, is likely to be higher than that of most allocated resources, and therefore the request is almost certain to succeed.[4] In the case of a request made during a pre-fetch operation, the request priority is a function of the particular hint driving the pre-fetch. The construction and use of priorities in this case is discussed in detail in Section 5.3.3.[5]

Accounting for Naming. Section 5.2.3 observed that disconnected operation induces hierarchical management of the cache. The basic reason for this is that disconnected misses during path expansion cannot be serviced. Thus, having a file cached does not by itself make the object accessible. If the file cannot also be named using only locally cached directories and symbolic links, then it cannot be accessed disconnected and might as well not be cached.

Hierarchical cache management reduces to two operational requirements:

– naming objects should be fetched and cached the first time they are used in expanding a path.
– naming objects should not be replaced as long as any of their descendants are still cached.

The first requirement is met automatically, as a side-effect of normal path expansion. The second necessitates linking objects together such that ancestor/descendant relationships are explicit. This is done in Coda by keeping a list of cached children in each directory fsobj, along with a back pointer from each fsobj to its parent. These fields constitute the fsobj *hierarchy block* depicted earlier in Figure 5.1. The linkage fields are updated immediately upon the caching of a new object or replacement of an old one.

With fsobjs linked hierarchically, bottom-up replacement can be ensured in at least two different ways. One approach is to augment the prioritizing function so that it computes a directory's priority simultaneously with its descendants. Specifically, an interior node's priority is taken to be the maximum of its own $p(f)$ value and those of all its cached descendants. The problem

---

[4] The exact value of $\mathcal{U}$ is $\alpha \cdot \mathcal{H}/2 + (1 - \alpha) \cdot \mathcal{R}$.

[5] A third resource ought to be allocated using request priorities, but currently is not. That is the RVM space which is used to hold directory and symbolic link contents. In the current implementation, no priority is associated with a request to allocate such space, and Venus simply aborts if the request cannot be satisfied out of the free list. The total amount of RVM space is fixed at Venus genesis, and is set large enough that exhaustion is very unlikely to occur. Nonetheless, the situation has arisen, and the request priority solution should be implemented in a future version of Venus.

with this approach is that substantial effort may be required to propagate priorities upward each time the priority of an outer node changes.

A much more efficient approach, and the one taken by Venus, is to simply regard any node with children cached as not replaceable. Such nodes are not linked into the fsobj priority queue, and hence cannot be replaced before their descendants. Of course, it is necessary to recognize when replacement of a child causes an interior node to become exposed, and when the caching of a child causes the inverse to occur. In the former case the directory fsobj must be entered into the priority queue, in the latter it must be taken off. The net effect of this scheme is the same as one in which all nodes are replaceable, but interior nodes are assigned infinite priority.

5.3.3 Cache Equilibrium

Earlier in this chapter, the idealized goal of cache management in Coda was stated to be utility maximization. Since true utility maximization is infeasible, an approximation based on object priorities was derived. Implementation of the priority maximizing approach reduces to satisfying the following conditions, which are known collectively as the *priority invariant*:

- no uncached object has higher priority than any cached object, and
- the cache is full or no uncached object has non-zero priority, and
- the version of every cached object is the same as that at its custodian.

When the priority invariant holds at a workstation, its cache is said to be in *equilibrium*.

Priorities of cached objects are computed as described in the last section. Uncached objects may have non-zero priority as a result of unexpanded namectxts. An unexpanded namectxt, having priority h, indicates the possibility of uncached objects with priority

$$\alpha \cdot h + (1 - \alpha) \cdot 0 \implies \boxed{\alpha \cdot h}$$

Let $\hat{h}$ be the priority of the highest-priority unexpanded namectxt, and denote $\hat{p} = \alpha \cdot \hat{h}$ the *pending priority*. Then the first two conditions of the invariant imply that either there are no unexpanded namectxts, or that the lowest priority cached fsobj has priority at least as great as $\hat{p}$.

It is not hard to see how *static* cache equilibrium could be achieved. That is, given initial cache and HDB states and an absence of remote system activity, how one would pre-fetch and replace objects in order to satisfy the priority invariant. But achieving equilibrium *dynamically* – in the presence of file activity occurring both locally and elsewhere in the system – is another matter. The mechanisms to do this are more complex, particularly given the need to perform the task efficiently.

Cache equilibrium may be perturbed by four classes of events:

- *local file system events* – non-mutating references to objects, extension or truncation of files, and creation or deletion of objects.
- *remote file system updates* – mutations of files and directories.
- *local HDB events* – additions and deletions of HDB entries.
- *local authentication events* – acquisition of new authentication tokens, or expiration of existing ones.

A scheme for maintaining equilibrium dynamically must account for these disequilibrating events. The rest of this chapter explains how this is done efficiently in Coda.

Periodic versus Continuous Equilibrium. The most obvious approach to maintaining equilibrium is to restore it immediately each time it is perturbed. This ensures that the priority invariant is satisfied *continuously*. Continuous satisfaction, in turn, means that the expected utility of the cache is always at a maximum.

Unfortunately, it is not practical for Venus to maintain equilibrium continuously. The major reason is that many disequilibrating events cannot be accounted for in real-time. This is particularly true for events which may precipitate remote communication; for example, remote file updates which induce the fetching of large amounts of data. A literal implementation of continuous equilibrium would suspend user file system activity while the priority invariant was being restored. Such behavior is obviously at odds with the interactive orientation of workstation computing.

The impossibility of continuous equilibrium is best illustrated by considering specific, massively disequilibrating events. Examples of such events, along with the requirements implied by continuous equilibrium, include the following:

- *remote rename of a directory* – when the new parent of a renamed object is a directory designated for descendant meta-expansion, the entire subtree headed by the object must be fetched. Continuous equilibrium implies that this fetch should occur instantaneously, despite the fact that the number of objects and the amount of data involved may be huge. The same scenario may also be entered through the local addition of an HDB entry specifying descendant meta-expansion.
- *reestablishing connectivity with a server* – since servers cannot break callback promises while partitioned, Venus must revalidate the currency of cached objects when connectivity with their custodians is restored. Continuous equilibrium demands that revalidation be done immediately, despite the fact that hundreds of objects may be involved. Moreover, when validations fail, other equilibrating actions such as hdbe re-expansion and data re-fetch may be needed as well. These too need be performed instantly in order to provide continuous equilibrium.
- *locally referencing an object* – this potentially alters the temperature of every cached fsobj – not just the one being referenced – as each unreferenced

object becomes one tick "cooler." There is always the chance that this cooling could cause the priority of an fsobj to fall below $\hat{p}$, indicating that that fsobj should be purged and an uncached object pre-fetched to replace it. Hence, continuous equilibrium demands cache-wide temperature computation after each reference, so that objects can be pre-fetched as soon as they enter the optimal cache set.[6]
 - *locally deleting or truncating a large file* – this frees up cache space, which can be reallocated to the highest priority uncached objects. Continuous equilibrium implies that those objects should be fetched immediately, before any other events occur.

Note that these examples are not contrived or obscure. Indeed, the most common file system event – simply referencing an object – is included among them.

Because continuous cache equilibrium is clearly impractical, Coda uses a *periodic* approach instead. With this type of scheme, the effects of disequilibrating events are allowed to accumulate, and action to restore equilibrium is taken only at specific, regularly-spaced points in time. At such points the priority invariant is guaranteed to hold, but within their intervals nothing is promised. Between equilibria there may be lower-priority objects cached instead of more valuable uncached ones, there may be vacant cache space despite the existence of unexpanded hdbes, and there may be versions of objects cached that are stale with respect to those at servers.

The key issue for a periodic approach is how frequently to perform equilibration. There are incentives to make the period both as short and as long as possible. A short period gives a better approximation to continuous equilibrium, and thus reduces the risk of disconnecting with sub-optimal cache contents. On the other hand, a long period is more efficient, since an equilibrating action can often account for a series of disequilibrating events. For example, if the same file is updated remotely 10 times in one minute, it is much more efficient to re-fetch the file once, rather than multiple times as might occur with a very short equilibration period. Similarly, cache-wide recomputation of reference priorities costs the same whether one or one thousand new references have occurred, so extending the period can significantly reduce that expense.

The choice of the equilibration period is thus fundamentally one which trades off optimality versus efficiency. However, the extent of the trade-off can be reduced by keeping state which focuses equilibrating effort. The idea is to have disequilibrating events identify specific equilibrating tasks that need to be done, so that the next equilibration need only concern itself with those tasks. Venus makes extensive use of such state, so that a given level

---

[6] Note that cache-wide dependence of references is not a property specific to the temperature-based algorithm, but is inherent in any reference-oriented scheme that normalizes priorities. For example, the obvious LRU and LOU (least-often used) algorithms suffer from the same limitation.

of optimality – that is, the same period – can be provided with less system computation.

The next subsection gives an overview of the equilibration process in Coda. Details of the process and other issues relating to equilibrium in general are presented in the subsections that follow.

Equilibration: Overview. Equilibration occurs in Coda through a process known as a *hoard walk*. Hoard walks are performed periodically by a background Venus LWP known as the *hoard daemon*. The walk period is 10 minutes by default, although it may be set to any value at Venus startup. A hoard walk may also be initiated on-demand, via an HDB command exported by the hoard program. The most common time to demand a hoard walk is just before a voluntary disconnection. This ensures that the cache is as current and balanced as possible at the moment of detachment.

A hoard walk consists of three distinct phases: *reference priority recomputation*, *status walking*, and *data walking*. Roughly speaking, the first phase equilibrates the cache with respect to implicit reference information, and the second and third phases equilibrate it with respect to explicit information. The division of the latter task into two phases reflects the organization of Venus' cache into separate status and data portions.

The three hoard walk phases are executed sequentially, in the order given below. Pseudo-code for each phase is presented at the end of this chapter.

Reference priority recomputation. The first phase accounts for temperature changes due to local object references. It iterates over the fsobjs, recomputing the reference priority of each one. For those whose reference priorities have changed since the last hoard walk, the procedure also recomputes their current priorities and updates their positions in the fsobj priority queue.

Status walking. The second phase puts the cache in status equilibrium. It ensures that the "equilibrium set" of fsobjs is cached and that each one's status is the same as that at its server, but it does not guarantee that data is cached along with the status. It verifies the bindings of hinted pathnames specified in the HDB, including pathnames hinted indirectly via meta-expansion. Naming activity since the last hoard walk may have made previous bindings invalid, or it may have enabled the establishment of new bindings.

The status walk begins by checking the validity of each cached fsobj. Any object that is stale has its old status and data purged and fresh status installed. Fsobj and data are de-allocated in the case of any object that was remotely deleted.

The heart of the status walk comes next, which is iterating over the set of namectxts in decreasing priority order. For each namectxt, the path is expanded just as if it were specified in a user system call such as an open. Expansion has the effect of caching both fsobj and data for each successfully looked-up, non-terminal component. The terminal component – if it is successfully looked-up – has only its fsobj cached at this point. Namectxt bindings are established, confirmed, or discarded as appropriate in the process.

An expansion may need to allocate one or more fsobjs in the course of its work. The request priority used in such cases is that which the object would have once it were cached, i.e., the product of α and the namectxt priority. Such allocations may have the effect of evicting lower-priority objects from the cache. An allocation will fail if the status-cache is full and every fsobj has higher priority than the candidate. If this occurs, then the iteration terminates prematurely. Otherwise, it continues until every namectxt has been expanded. In either case, the priority invariant will have been re-established with respect to object status.

Data walking. The third phase puts the cache in data equilibrium. It transforms a cache which has the optimal set of fsobjs into one which also has the optimal set of fsobjs-with-data. The effect of the data walk is to refresh stale data and to make use of newly vacant container space.

The data walk iterates over the fsobjs in decreasing priority order. For *hoardable* objects – those with non-zero hoard priority – it fetches data if it is not present. Missing data is not fetched for non-hoardable objects, however. The assumption is that if a non-hinted object does not have data cached as a result of the way it has been used (e.g., it was only the target of a stat call), then there is no cause for pre-fetching it.

In order to fetch data for a file, container file blocks must first be allocated. The request priority used in such cases is the priority of the already cached, but data-less fsobj. Analogously to fsobj allocation, this may lead to the purging of blocks associated with lower-priority objects. If such an allocation should fail, then the iteration terminates at that point. Otherwise, it continues until every fsobj has been examined. At either conclusion the cache will be in data as well as status equilibrium.

Using State to Reduce Equilibration Effort. The work involved in hoard walking – particularly in the status and data walks – can be substantial. A naïve implementation would expend a great deal of effort expanding pathnames and checking object currency with servers unnecessarily. Venus minimizes local computation and server communication by exploiting two kinds of state.

Namectxt validity. The first type of state is used to reduce the number of namectxts that must be expanded or re-evaluated during a status walk. Each namectxt incorporates its own state variable, which places the namectxt in one of three classes: *valid, indigent,* or *suspect.*

A valid namectxt is one which is fully- or partially-expanded, and whose bindings are all valid. That is, the

```
<parent-fid, child-component, child-fid>
```

triplets represented by the namectxt bindings correspond to the directory contents existing at the server. In addition, for a partially-expanded name-ctxt, the factor inhibiting binding of its first unbound component is one of the following:

- *missing mapping* – the component does not exist in the last bound directory.
- *missing server* – the component does exist in the last bound directory, but status for the mapped-to object cannot be fetched because its custodian is inaccessible.
- *missing privileges* – status for the mapped-to object cannot be fetched because the user associated with the namectxt does not have lookup permission in the parent directory.

An indigent namectxt is similar to a partially-expanded, valid namectxt. The difference is the factor inhibiting binding. In the indigent case, what is missing is not a mapping, a server, or privileges, but the priority to allocate an fsobj. That is, further expansion of the namectxt requires caching a new object and the status-cache is full, but the namectxt is too "poor" to displace the lowest-priority fsobj.

A suspect namectxt is one which is fully- or partially-expanded, but at least one of whose bindings is suspect. A binding – and thence its namectxt – becomes suspect due to one of the disequilibrating events discussed in the next subsection. A namectxt may also be suspect because it has never been evaluated; that is, it was created sometime after the last status walk.

The tri-furcation of namectxts allows status walks to be conducted with much less effort than if namectxts were unclassified. Valid namectxts do not need to be re-evaluated during a walk, since it is guaranteed that their bindings would not change. In the normal case most namectxts will be in the valid state, so this is a substantial savings. Suspect and indigent namectxts do need to be re-evaluated, however, and in decreasing priority order. The order requirement avoids situations where objects are fetched in re-evaluating one namectxt, only to be replaced in the subsequent re-evaluation of a slightly higher priority one. A priority queue of all suspect and indigent namectxts is maintained to support the order requirement. Following re-evaluation, a namectxt transits to either the valid or the indigent state. If the re-evaluation terminated with an ENOSPC return code – indicating that an fsobj could not be allocated at the namectxt's priority – then the namectxt becomes or remains indigent. Otherwise, it becomes valid. Figure 5.5 illustrates the state machine governing namectxt behavior.

The purpose of distinguishing indigent from suspect namectxts is to optimize the re-evaluation loop. Once a re-evaluation terminates for lack of space, it is pointless to re-evaluate subsequent indigent namectxts because their bindings could not possibly change. This is true because their existing bindings are valid (by definition), and additional bindings could not be established because a "richer" element has already failed to allocate a necessary

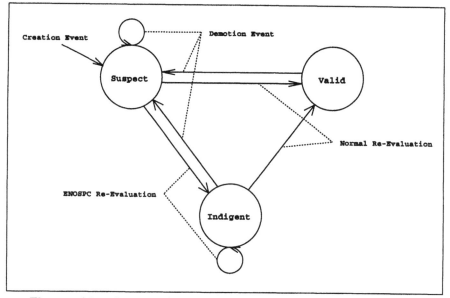

The transitions labeled "Demotion Event" and "Creation Event" are discussed in the disequilibrating events section, 5.3.3. Transitions corresponding to the purge of a namectxt logically emanate from each pictured state, but they and the target "dead" state are not shown for the purpose of clarity.

Fig. 5.5. Name-Context States and Transitions

resource. Hence, the iteration enters *clean-up* mode once a space failure occurs, in which it skips over subsequent indigent entries and re-evaluates only suspect ones. Cleaning is necessary to recover the state occupied by "dead" bindings, and to mark suspect entries indigent before the next status walk.

Fsobj validity. The second type of state is used to reduce server communication during status and data walks. It is simply the use of callback promises to protect the currency of cached information. The alternative to a callback scheme is "validate-on-use," as typified by Sprite or NFS.

With validate-on-use, the currency of every fsobj would need to be checked at least once at a server during a hoard walk. In contrast, with callback it is necessary to contact a server only in cases where an object's currency is suspect. Under normal conditions, most objects will not be suspect and thus their currency can be verified simply by examining local state. Only in relatively few cases is expensive server communication needed for currency checking.

Callback-based cache coherence is not something new to Coda, but rather is a feature inherited from AFS-2. This fact – and the superiority of callback over validate-on-use – was noted in Chapter 2. The purpose of re-visiting the comparison here is to point out that hoarding makes the superiority of callback even more pronounced. The Sprite designers showed that at small-scale and for connected-only operation, the simplicity of validate-on-use could outweigh the efficiency advantage of callback [64]. However, in a system supporting disconnected operation it's clear that validate-on-use would be disastrous even at small-scale. Such a system would entail the gratuitous open of every cached file at every client on every hoard walk. The overhead of this approach, particularly the load imposed on servers, would be intolerable.

Disequilibrating Events. The distinction between continuous and periodic cache equilibrium is analogous to that between interrupt-driven and polling I/O. Continuous equilibrium corresponds to equilibrating entirely within an interrupt service routine (ISR). Periodic equilibrium, in its naïve form, corresponds to ignoring interrupts and restoring equilibrium from scratch at each poll.

The preceding subsections have argued that a purely interrupt-driven approach to cache equilibrium is infeasible, and that a naïve polling approach is inefficient. An intermediate approach is to note the occurrence of a disequilibrating event in its ISR, and to use such notations to direct equilibrating activity at periodic polls. This is the approach employed most heavily in Coda. However, there are a few events for which the extreme approaches are used; that is, the event is accounted for entirely in its ISR, or it is accounted for – at least partially – by undirected polling.

The following discussion returns to the classification of disequilibrating events in the introduction to Subsection 5.3.3, and explains what happens in each ISR. The discussion is summarized in Table 5.3.

Local file system events. This class of events breaks down into three sub-classes. The first includes non-mutating references to files and directories, which most commonly correspond to open or stat system calls. The only ISR activity in this case is to update the global and per-fsobj tick-counters, which will be read during the next cache-wide reference priority recomputation. Note that equilibration cannot be directed in this instance, i.e., the set of fsobjs needing recomputation cannot be refined, since object temperatures are dependent on each others' references.

The second sub-class, local directory mutations, does entail actions for directing equilibration. In this case, the ISR finds the namectxts associated with the object or objects being mutated and forces each one to the suspect state. Such a transition – from any state to the suspect state – is known as a *demotion*, and ensures that the namectxt will be re-evaluated during the next status walk. Locating the relevant namectxts is fast since each fsobj contains a list of the namectxts that are bound to it. In addition to demoting namectxts, the ISR updates the fsobjs and local data contents to reflect the mutation being performed. This includes allocating new fsobjs when a name insertion is accompanied by object creation (e.g., in a mkdir operation), and de-allocating fsobjs and data blocks when a name removal is accompanied by object deletion.

Event	Status- and Data-Cache Action	Name-Context Action
Local non-mutating operation	update global tick-counter and that of referenced fsobj	∅
Local directory mutation	update fsobjs and data contents as necessary, including allocation/de-allocation of fsobjs and data blocks	demote namectxts associated with fsobjs
Local file mutation	allocate/de-allocate data blocks as necessary	∅
Remote directory mutation	demote mutated fsobjs	demote namectxts associated with fsobjs
Remote file mutation	purge mutated fsobj and data blocks	demote namectxts associated with fsobj
Server re-connection	demote fsobjs hosted by re-connecting server	demote namectxts associated with fsobjs
HDB add-entry operation	∅	create new namectxt (in suspect state)
HDB delete-entry operation	re-prioritize fsobjs formerly bound to namectxt	purge namectxt
Auth token acquisition	∅	demote namectxts associated with user
Auth token expiration	∅	demote namectxts associated with user

Table 5.3. Summary of Disequilibrating Events and ISR Actions

The third sub-class, local file mutations, is like the first in that its ISR does nothing special to direct equilibration. Venus merely performs the mutation on its cached data, allocating new container blocks in the case of file extension, and de-allocating blocks in the case of file truncation. The vacant cache space created in the latter case will be re-allocated during the next data walk if there are any hoardable, data-less objects at that time. Note that since plain file mutations do not affect the naming hierarchy, there is no need to demote namectxts as there is in the case of directory mutations.

Remote file system updates. This class also breaks down into three subclasses. The first represents remote directory mutations which are signalled by callback breaks. As in the local case, all associated namectxts are de-moted in the ISR to ensure their re-evaluation on the next status walk. The distinction between the local and remote cases is significant, however, in the handling of fsobjs and data contents. In the local case, mutations are per-formed on cached objects as well as being written through to servers, so local and remote copies remain identical and callback promises remain valid. But in the remote update case, local cache copies become stale with respect to the server copies, as indicated by the break message. The most obvious response to a callback break is to purge the fsobj and data contents (if they exist), since more recent information is available at servers.

However, the purge approach is risky in a system supporting disconnected operation, and it is highly pessimistic in the case of directory objects. The risk stems from the fact that critical data could be rendered inaccessible if a disconnection were to occur before the next hoard walk. Purging is pessimistic for directories because the local data is likely to be only "slightly stale" after a callback break. That is, most of the mappings contained in the local directory copy will still be valid; the callback break normally signifies only that one new mapping has been entered or one existing mapping has been removed. Hence, the chance of "getting into trouble" by retaining a stale directory is small, whereas the potential payoff of keeping it is large. For this reason, Venus only demotes a directory fsobj on callback break – i.e., it simply discards the callback promise. If the client stays connected, then the directory will be re-fetched at the next hoard walk or user reference to it, whichever comes sooner. But if a disconnection should occur first, a stale copy will be available until the client can reconnect.

The second sub-class of remote update events represents file mutations which are signalled by callback breaks. In contrast to the directory case, a callback break on a plain file causes Venus to purge the cached fsobj and data contents (if they exist). The reasons for treating files more severely than direc-tories are twofold. First, the consequences of disconnecting suddenly without a critical file are generally less than those for a directory, since a missing direc-tory may leave a whole sub-tree of critical files inaccessible. Second, files are updated by completely overwriting their contents, unlike directories which are updated by incremental changes to particular entries. Hence, a stale di-rectory is likely to be much more similar to its fresh counterpart than is a stale file. Moreover, the directory-entry independence assumptions of Coda mean that many disconnected updates to stale directories can be reintegrated transparently, whereas a disconnected update to a stale file is guaranteed to force manual repair. A consequence of purging file fsobjs on callback break is that Venus must also demote associated namectxts since, although the nam-ing hierarchy has not changed, the final namectxt component is no longer bound.

The third sub-class concerns remote updates that are discovered indi-rectly, via re-connection with a server, rather than those signalled directly by callback break. Re-connection means that every cached object hosted by the server could now be stale. That is, each object could have been updated at the now re-conversant server during the partitioning. Callback breaks notifying the client of those updates obviously could not have been delivered because of the communication failure. As a result, Venus must check the validity of each such object before using it again. This is arranged by simply demoting the fsobjs belonging to the affected volumes. Along with the demotion of directory fsobjs, associated namectxts are demoted as well. This ensures that expansions which are no longer valid will be examined and updated during the next status walk.

The effect of the server re-connection ISR is similar to performing a callback break for each affected object, but it is not identical. The difference is that file fsobjs and data are only demoted on server re-connection rather than being purged. This reflects the certainty of staleness in the two cases: with a real callback break an object is known to be stale, but on re-connection there is only the possibility of staleness. Furthermore, the likelihood of staleness for any given file is quite small. Hence, purging would almost always be unnecessary, and would result in considerably more re-fetch activity.

Local HDB events. Disequilibrating HDB events are of two types: adding new hdbes and deleting existing ones. The ISR for adding an hdbe creates a new namectxt and attaches it to the hdbe, but does not immediately expand it. Instead, the namectxt is initialized in the suspect state, guaranteeing that it will be expanded on the next status walk. This delayed expansion is useful when sourcing a large hoard profile or a series of profiles which specify multiple priority levels. In such situations eager expansion would often result in extra work; for example, fetching many objects into a nearly full cache, only to have them replaced during successive expansions of slightly higher priority namectxts. The danger of "thrashing" like this is particularly high when meta-expansion is involved.

The ISR for deleting an hdbe does much more in the way of equilibration than does the one for adding. It first purges the namectxt corresponding to the hdbe, then purges the hdbe itself. Purging a namectxt entails detaching each binding from the fsobj it was bound to, then de-allocating the bindings and the namectxt itself. Detaching a binding requires that the hoard priority of the formerly-attached fsobj be re-evaluated. If the detaching binding was the only one bound to the fsobj, then the new hoard priority is 0. Otherwise, the fsobj's list of (still) bound namectxts is traversed to find the one with the next highest priority. That value then becomes the new hoard priority. If the fsobj's hoard priority changes as a result of the detachment, then its current priority and its place in the global priority queue are recomputed as well. This activity completely accounts for the effect of the hdbe deletion, unless the decline of an fsobj's hoard priority causes its current priority to fall below $\hat{p}$. In that case, the next hoard walk is needed to fully account for the event.

Local authentication events. Authentication token events are the final class of disequilibrating event. Acquiring or losing tokens perturbs cache equilibrium because the identity of the user effectively changes. Recall that servers check permissions for requests by token-less users with respect to the "anonymous" principal, which is known as System:AnyUser. Acquiring tokens therefore changes one's identity from System:AnyUser to a real principal, and losing tokens (through their expiry) effects the opposite transition.

A change in identity will be accounted for automatically in future on-demand accesses, as Venus will use the new identity in checking access rights. However, automatic adjustment does not hold for hinted pathnames that have been expanded in earlier hoard walks. Certain expansions may now be incomplete or illegal, and – without some stimulus – might not be re-evaluated in the normal course of events. Specifically, there may be partially-expanded namectxts that could now be expanded further because the new principal has lookup permission in a directory that the old principal didn't. Conversely, bindings in other namectxts may now be illegal because the old principal had sufficient expansion privileges and the new one does not.

To make sure that imbalances caused by identity changes are eventually corrected, the token acquisition and expiry ISRs demote all namectxts associated with the given user. Each such namectxt will be re-evaluated during the next status walk. In the case of amplified rights, new objects may be fetched or already cached fsobjs may have their priority increased. In the case of reduced rights, fsobjs may have their priority decreased as a result of detaching bindings that are no longer legal.[7]

Meta-Expansion. Meta-expansion is a powerful conceptual tool, but its implementation requires care. The danger of a careless implementation is that it may take many more than the minimal number of expansions and fetches to reach equilibrium. Redundant activity of that type not only consumes workstation cycles that could be used for user computation, but also imposes higher load on servers.

Recall that, in the abstract, meta-expansion refers to a class of rules for mapping single pathnames into sets of pathnames. The two rules or meta-expansion variants supported in Coda are called children and descendant. The children variant derives the members of a pathname set by concatenating the input path with the entries of the directory bound to its last component. The descendant variant consists of applying the children variant recursively to each path for which the last component binds to a directory or symbolic link.

---

[7] Acquiring tokens cannot reduce a user's privileges because a real principal's rights are guaranteed to be a superset of those of System:AnyUser for any object. Hence, in the acquire ISR it is really only necessary to demote those namectxts whose full expansion has been inhibited by missing permission. This optimization has not been implemented, and token events are sufficiently rare that its benefit would be slight.

The implementation of meta-expansion in Coda is directed by the following set of observations and induced requirements:

- the derivation of a pathname set itself requires cache resources; i.e., it requires fsobjs and data space for the directories and symbolic links it traverses. Hence, meta-expansion must operate within the existing priority framework for cache resource allocation.
- derived pathname sets evolve over time, as names are added to and removed from directories. The system must be able to account for such changes by re-performing meta-expansion. But, to make efficient use of computational resources, this process should occur no more often than is necessary.
- it is trivial to specify a pathname derivation whose satisfaction would require more cache resources than the total available at a typical workstation. Hence, the system must be able to perform partial derivations, and to extend them incrementally as space permits.

The framework supporting these requirements consists of *derived namectxts*, with one derived namectxt corresponding to each derived pathname. Derived namectxts are organized into trees, with each one rooted at the (non-derived) namectxt belonging to a meta-designated hdbe. This organization was introduced earlier in Section 5.3.1, and illustrated in an example in Figure 5.4.

Representing derived pathnames as their own namectxts simplifies the integration of meta-expansion and the cache equilibrating mechanisms. A derived namectxt is treated the same as a non-derived namectxt in most respects: it competes for resources based on its priority, it is bound to fsobjs in the course of namectxt evaluation, and it is updated in response to disequilibrating events such as callback breaks and server re-connections.

The issues which differentiate derived and non-derived namectxts are creation and deletion. A non-derived namectxt is created and deleted by explicit HDB operations, but for a derived namectxt these events are implicit. To explain how creation and deletion occur in the derived case, it is helpful to have some more precise terminology. Namectxts may be classified into five disjoint sets: *non-meta* (NM), *meta-root-children*, (MRC), *meta-root-descendant* (MRD), *meta-branch-children* (MBC), and *meta-branch-descendant* (MBD). MRC and MRD are namectxts associated with children and descendant meta-designated hdbes, respectively. These types, together with NM, correspond to the earlier notion of non-derived namectxt. The other two types, MBC and MBD, represent derived namectxts. The term *meta-expanded* is used as a synonym for derived, and *meta-expandable* denotes the types that may have namectxts derived from them (MRC, MRD, and MBD).

Creation. The time to consider meta-expanding is when a directory that is the terminal component of a meta-expandable namectxt path has been cached for the first time, or when a new version of its contents have been fetched. These situations correspond precisely to the transition of a fully-bound, meta-expandable namectxt to the valid state during a status walk.

Hence, following each such transition Venus invokes the meta-expansion procedure on the newly valid namectxt.

The task of the meta-expansion algorithm is to make the existing set of child namectxts agree with the new directory contents. If the namectxt has never before been meta-expanded, then the child set will be empty. Otherwise, it will correspond to an earlier incarnation of the directory. The new incarnation may be the same as the old, or it may differ substantially. The four steps of the algorithm are:

1. create an empty list for the children of the new incarnation.
2. enumerate the new directory contents. For each directory entry, scan the namectxt's current children list:
   - if a namectxt is found which matches the directory entry, move that namectxt from the current to the new children list. A match occurs when the directory component is equal to the tail element of the namectxt path.
   - otherwise, create a new namectxt corresponding to the directory entry, and add it to the new children list.
3. any namectxt left on the current children list corresponds to an entry which existed in the old directory incarnation but not the new. Recursively delete each such namectxt.
4. delete the now-empty current children list, and make the new children list the current.

Meta-expanded namectxts created in step 2 of the algorithm are initialized in suspect state and immediately placed on the namectxt priority queue, just like new, non-derived namectxts. The priorities of these namectxts are inherited from their parents. Therefore, they will enter the queue, be expanded, and be meta-expanded (if appropriate) before all other namectxts previously enqueued but of lower-priority. This behavior is essential for achieving equilibrium in the minimum number of steps. If newly meta-expanded entries did not enter the queue and participate in the status walk immediately, then either equilibrium would not be achieved or it would require multiple iterations over the queue.

The meta-expansion algorithm given above derives pathname sets one level at a time. A single level is all that is required in the case of the children meta-expansion variant, so namectxts of type MBC are not themselves meta-expandable. But for descendant meta-expansion, any number of levels may be required to reach the leaf nodes of a subtree. Hence, MBD namectxts are subject to meta-expansion just like either of the root types. The level-by-level approach makes it possible to partially perform meta-expansions that would not fit in available cache space.

Deletion. The converse of meta-expansion is meta-contraction. A tree of meta-expanded namectxts obviously must be contracted if the hdbe associated with the root namectxt is deleted. Such an act means that the user no longer wishes to hoard the directory's children or descendants.

But suppose a meta-expanded namectxt becomes unbound, say because the object attached to its final component is deleted. No explicit order to delete the hint has been given, but in most cases Venus scavenges it (and any descendants) anyway. The motivation for doing so is space efficiency. Keeping the partial namectxts around would not affect correctness in any way, but over time it could be a serious drain on Venus' memory pool.

Eagerly contracting partial, meta-expanded namectxts is safe in the majority of cases. This follows from two facts. First, deleting the namectxt cannot affect the priority of any fsobj, because each fsobj it is bound to must also be bound to at least one ancestor. Second, with the exception noted below, the normal meta-expansion process will re-derive the namectxt at any future point at which it could again be fully bound.

Eager contraction can occur at two different points. One is during step 3 of the meta-expansion procedure, where unmatched children are scavenged following the directory enumeration. The other point it can occur is following re-evaluation of the meta-expanded namectxt itself. When re-evaluation yields a partial expansion inhibited because of missing mapping, server, or privileges, then it is appropriate to contract the namectxt and its descendants. Re-appearance of the missing element is guaranteed to demote the parent namectxt, resulting in its re-evaluation and subsequent meta-expansion.

The exceptional case, in which eager contraction must be tempered, is when a re-evaluation is only partially satisfied due to allocation failure. In that situation, the event which would re-enable full expansion of the namectxt – de-allocation of resources – will not signal its parent. The hoard walk algorithm presumes that vacated space will be re-claimed through the polling of indigent entries, not the signalling of those entries or their ancestors. Hence, when ENOSPC is returned from the re-evaluation of a meta-expanded namectxt, the namectxt must stick around instead of being scavenged. But there is no reason to retain descendants of such a namectxt – they can be re-derived if/when that becomes feasible. Thus contraction still occurs in this case, but it must skip over the "leading-edge" of indigent entries.

Batch Validation. The use of callback greatly reduces the need for Venus to communicate with servers in validating cache entries. However, there is one situation in which remote validation cost still can be substantial. That situation is a status walk following restored communication with one or more servers. Recall that restoring communication invalidates callback promises for objects hosted by the re-connecting server. Each such object needs to be validated at the start of the next status walk (if not before). In cases where all servers reconnect at once, such as at client restart or the conclusion of a voluntary disconnection, this may mean remotely validating thousands of objects at a time.

In early versions of Coda, validations were performed one at a time, and status walks following full-reconnects could spend several minutes in vali-

```
const int  R = 1000;        /* maximum reference priority */
const float  α = .75;       /* horizon parameter */
const float  β = 16.0;      /* cooling parameter */
int Ticks;                  /* global tick counter */
PriorityQueue FPQ;          /* priority queue of replaceable fsobjs */

void ReferencePriorityRecomputation () {
    for (each fsobj f) {
        int new_rpri = max (R - (Ticks - f.tick_counter) / β, 1);
        if (f.rpri != new_rpri) {
            if (f.replaceable) FPQ.remove (f);
            f.rpri = new_rpri;
            f.pri = α * f.hpri + (1 - α) * f.rpri;
            if (f.replaceable) FPQ.insert (f);
        }
    }
}
```

Fig. 5.6. Reference Priority Recomputation

dation. To alleviate this problem, a batch validation facility was added.[8] It allows up to 50 validation requests for the same volume to be piggybacked on a normal validation RPC. The savings realizable from batching are substantial, because communications costs are a very large portion of the validation process. For example, in the most intensive validation cases, batching has been found to reduce latency by roughly one order of magnitude.

Hoard Walking in Pseudo-Code. The preceding sections have motivated and described the hoard walk procedure in increasing detail. The chapter concludes with a summary of the procedure in pseudo-code. Figures 5.6, 5.7, and 5.10 contain the code for the three hoard walk phases. Figure 5.8 covers the namectxt re-evaluation subroutine, and Figure 5.9 covers meta-expansion. Each code fragment is written in C++, and is identical to the current production code except for the omission of minor details.

---

[8] This facility was implemented by Lily Mummert.

```
PriorityQueue NPQ;        /* priority queue of suspect and indigent namectxts */

void StatusWalk () {
    /* Ensure that status is valid for every cached object. For an object */
    /* discovered to be stale, old status and data (if any) are discarded, */
    /* and fresh status is installed. Validation requires server communication */
    /* only in cases where no callback promise is outstanding. */
    for (each fsobj f)
        (void) f.GetStatus (f.huid);

    /* Re-evaluate suspect and indigent namectxts. Iteration must be in */
    /* decreasing priority order. If status-cache becomes full, enter */
    /* "clean-up" mode, in which indigent entries are skipped. */
    bool cleaning = FALSE;
    for (each namectxt n ∈ NPQ) {
        if (cleaning && n.state == INDIGENT)
            continue;

        int result = n.CheckExpansion ();
        if (result == ENOSPC)
            cleaning = TRUE;
    }
}
```

Fig. 5.7. Status Walk

```
#define META_EXPANDED (n)    ((n).type ∈ {MBT, MBNT})
#define META_EXPANDABLE (n)  ((n).type ∈ {MRC, MRD, MBNT})

int namectxt::CheckExpansion () {
    /* expand() is a global routine which performs path expansion */
    /* path, priority, and bindings are data members of class namectxt */
    /* priority will be used in any fsobj allocation; */
    /* bindings list will be updated as a side-effect */
    int result = expand (path, priority, bindings);

    /* perform meta-expansion if namectxt expansion succeeded */
    /* and it is a property of this namectxt */
    if (result == 0 && META_EXPANDABLE (this))
        result = MetaExpand ();

    /* take appropriate transition to next state */
    NameCtxtState next_state;
    switch (result) {
        case 0:                             /* success */
            next_state = VALID;
            break;

        case ENOENT:                        /* unbound component */
        case ETIMEDOUT:                     /* server inaccessible */
        case EACCES:                        /* no lookup permission */
            next_state = VALID;
            break;

        case ENOSPC:                        /* fsobj could not be allocated */
            next_state = INDIGENT;
            break;

        default:
            assert (FALSE);
    }
    transit (next_state);

    /* meta-contract on any failure; */
    /* if the namectxt is indigent, only contract its descendants */
    if (result != 0 && META_EXPANDED (this))
        if (state == INDIGENT) KillChildren ();
        else Suicide ();

    return (result);
}
```

Fig. 5.8. CheckExpansion Routine Invoked During Status Walk

```
int namectxt::MetaExpand () {
    binding *b = bindings.last ();
    fsobj *f = b->bindee;

    /* meta-expansion applies only to directories */
    if (f->type ! = DIRECTORY)
        return (0);

    /* only status is guaranteed to be cached at this point; data is needed too! */
    int result = f->GetData ();
    if (result ! = 0)
        return (result);

    /* basic task is to make existing set of child namectxts agree with new */
    /* directory contents: */
    /*    1. create empty "new_children" list */
    /*    2. move still valid namectxts from current children list to new */
    /*    3. create new namectxts for direntries not found in current list, */
    /*       and add them to new */
    /*    4. delete remaining entries in current list */
    /*       (they have no corresponding current direntry) */
    /*    5. delete (now empty) current list, and rename new to current */
    list *new_children = new list;
    for (each direntry de ∈ f->dirdata) {
        bool found = FALSE;
        for (each namectxt *child ∈ *children) {
            if (de.component == tail (child->path)) {
                move (child, children, new_children);
                found = TRUE;
                break;
            }
        }
        if (!found) {
            /* constructor initializes child's priority and type from the parent's */
            namectxt *n = new namectxt (this, de.component);
            new_children->append (n);
        }
    }
    for (each namectxt child ∈ *children)
        child->suicide ();
    delete children;
    children = new_children;

    return (0);
}
```

Fig. 5.9. MetaExpand Routine Invoked During Status Walk

```
PriorityQueue FPQ;                    /* priority queue of replaceable fsobjs */
#define HOARDABLE (f)  ((f).hpri > 0)

void DataWalk () {
    /* Iterate over replaceable fsobjs in decreasing priority order, guaranteeing */
    /* that data is cached for "hoardable" objects. Non-replaceable fsobjs do */
    /* NOT need to be checked, since the preceding status walk ensured that */
    /* they either already have data cached or aren't hoardable. */
    for (each fsobj f ∈ FPQ) {
        if (!HOARDABLE (f))
            continue;

        /* Finish early if an fsobj is too "poor" to allocate needed data blocks. */
        int result = f.GetData (f.pri, f.huid);
        if (result == ENOSPC) break;
    }
}
```

Fig. 5.10. Data Walk

6. Server Emulation

The server emulation state represents the behavior of Venus when it is disconnected. The name is actually a bit misleading, since the primary task of even ordinary cache managers is emulating server activity. What distinguishes a disconnected-capable cache manager from an ordinary one is the extent of its emulation capabilities. As identified in Section 1.5.1, an ordinary cache manager is limited by the need to communicate with servers in many situations. When one of those situations arises during a disconnection, file service is impeded.

The Coda cache manager eases this limitation through two basic techniques: *avoiding* the need to communicate while disconnected, and *deferring* unavoidable communication until disconnection ends. These techniques allow Venus to effectively *mask physical disconnection* in many cases. In the ideal situation, users and applications are not even aware that disconnection has occurred.

This chapter describes the mechanisms used by Venus to mask physical disconnection while it is in progress. It begins with a brief overview of the basics of disconnected file system processing, then proceeds to describe the key masking mechanisms in detail.

6.1 Disconnected Processing

The activity at a fully- or partially-disconnected Venus is of two types:

− user transaction processing.
− hoard walking.

6.1.1 User Transaction Processing

Venus processes a user transaction in disconnected mode if it is in the emulating state for the corresponding volume. By construction, each Coda transaction can access objects in a single volume only, so the mode of a transaction is always clearly defined.

The processing of a transaction in disconnected mode is as similar to the connected case as possible. Recall from Chapter 3 that processing a transaction in connected mode has three basic steps:

1. Venus ensures that it has a cache copy, with callback promise, of every object in the transaction's read and writeset. If an object is not cached, Venus fetches the latest copy from the server. A callback promise is established as a side-effect of the fetch. If an object is cached but without a callback promise, then Venus makes a validate RPC to verify that its copy is still current and to obtain a callback promise. If its copy turns out not to be current, then the old copy is discarded and a fresh one fetched.
2. Venus performs the data accesses and integrity checks of the transaction on the cache copies only.
3. Venus certifies that the transaction executed without interference, and commits or retries the transaction as appropriate. In the case of an update transaction, certification and commitment occur at the server, and updated values are made globally visible as part of commitment. In the case of a read-only transaction, certification and commitment occur locally, without server communication.

In disconnected mode, server communication is impossible by definition, so steps 1 and 3 of the algorithm require modification. If a needed object is missing from the cache at transaction begin, then there is obviously nothing that can be done to avoid that, and Venus returns an error to the transaction-initiating system call. If all objects are cached, however, then Venus can mask other server communication that would have been required in connected mode. The key operational changes to support this are the following:

– at transaction begin, Venus does not have callback promises for any of the objects involved in the transaction. Callback promises must be discarded for cache objects as soon as their volume enters the emulating state, since invalidation messages obviously cannot be received from a partitioned server. However, Venus ignores the fact that callback promises are missing, and proceeds to step 2 of the connected-mode processing algorithm as long as it has some copy of each required object.
– at transaction end, Venus *locally commits* the transaction in lieu of the normal certification and global commitment procedure. Local commitment entails logging enough information in persistent store so that the transaction can eventually be certified and – if certification succeeds – globally committed. Local commitment also involves installing fresh version-ids for the copies of objects that were updated.

Transaction logging enables certification and global commitment to be deferred until reconnection with the server occurs. The logging process is discussed in detail in Section 6.2. Chapter 7 describes what happens when the period of deferment is over.

6.1.2 Hoard Walking

Despite their name, hoard walks are performed regardless of whether Venus is fully-connected, fully-disconnected, or connected for some volumes and disconnected for others. The rationale in the fully-disconnected case is that much of the equilibrating work of a hoard walk can be performed using just local information. For example, fsobj temperatures can still be computed, local HDB operations can still be internalized, and local naming operations can still affect HDB entry expansion. Continuing to perform hoard walks ensures that priorities reflect the best available information, and that replacement decisions continue to be made in a utility-maximizing fashion. The fact that some information is unavailable simply means that the utility approximation is more approximate than it would be otherwise.

The rationale in the mixed scenarios is similar to the fully-disconnected case. Again, it is worthwhile to take advantage of local equilibrating information to the fullest extent possible. However, with only partial disconnection, it is also possible to internalize remote events that affect volumes which are still connected. For example, if a callback break is received for a cached file, then it is sensible for Venus to purge its copy just as it would in the fully-connected case. Similarly, pre-fetching of objects hosted by still connected servers ought to continue as long as their priorities warrant it. This occurs automatically when hoard walking is performed irrespective of connectivity state.

The mechanics of hoard walking with full or partial disconnection are nearly identical to the fully-connected case. There are only two significant differences. First, during the status walk it is not possible to validate the currency of objects which are disconnected. The iterator recognizes disconnected objects immediately and simply skips over them. Subsequent HDB entry and meta-expansion is performed under the assumption that disconnected cache copies are indeed valid. Real validation will occur on the first hoard walk following reconnection to the partitioned server(s). Second, during the data walk it is not possible to pre-fetch the contents of disconnected, hoardable objects. Again, the iterator simply skips over such objects, and attempts to pre-fetch only from still connected servers. Partitioned pre-fetch candidates will be accounted for later, at the first non-partitioned hoard walk.

The remainder of this chapter ignores hoard walking, and focuses on issues associated with disconnected transaction processing. However, it should be borne in mind that hoard walking is an ongoing background activity, which occurs regardless of the foreground state of each volume.

6.2 Transaction Logging

Logging disconnected transactions at Venus serves two purposes. First, it makes it possible to distinguish correct from incorrect disconnected computations. Second, it allows the updates of correct disconnected computations to be made globally visible.

The challenges of logging are in making it efficient. There are two types of costs that must be minimized: the extra latency imposed on disconnected operations, and the local storage that is consumed by log records. The latency cost can be reduced by using asynchronous disk writes, so that mechanical delays are not borne directly by user requests. However, this approach introduces problems of data persistence and of recovering to a consistent state following a crash. Section 6.3 discusses persistence and recovery issues in depth. The other type of cost, local storage consumption, is reduced through a combination of techniques. One important factor is not having to log read-only transactions, which is possible because of the acceptance of weak-consistency for queries in the Coda model. Two other space optimizations are discussed in this section, following an overview of log organization and the record format.

6.2.1 Log Organization and Record Format

Venus maintains a separate log in persistent storage for each volume for which it has any cached objects. A record is constructed and appended to the appropriate log at the time an update transaction locally commits. The format of a log record closely matches the specification of the transaction type it corresponds to. Figure 6.1 depicts the format of a link transaction log record as an example. It shows that a record has two parts: a set of type-independent fields, and a set of type-specific ones. The former set consists of pointers to the preceding and succeeding records of the log, a list of the fsobjs associated with the record, time and author fields denoting when and for whom the transaction was performed, an operation code identifying the transaction type, and a globally unique transaction identifier.

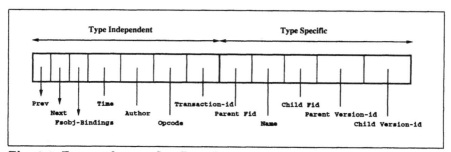

Fig. 6.1. Format of a link Log Record

The type-specific fields of a record contain the information needed to certify the transaction and to make its effects globally visible. The certification procedure needs to know the transaction read, write, increment, and decrement sets, as well as the start-of-transaction version-ids of the corresponding objects. The former are derivable from the record opcode and other fields such as fids and name components. The latter are included explicitly in the record. Making the transaction's effects globally visible requires the *new values* of the data items in its write set and the amounts that each counter is

incremented or decremented. These values are also derivable from the record
opcode or are represented explicitly as type-specific fields of the record.

Table 6.1 lists the various log record types and the type-specific fields
of each one. The record types map almost exactly onto the set of update
transaction types identified earlier in Tables 2.2 and 2.3. The only difference
is that there is no record type corresponding to the setrights transaction
type. This reflects the fact that setrights transactions cannot be performed
at disconnected clients. The cause of this restriction is that clients do not
have copies of the users and groups databases; hence, they cannot convert
rights specifications to and from access-control lists.

chown	*fid, new_owner, version_id*
chmod	*fid, new_mode, version_id*
utimes	*fid, new_modifytime, version_id*
store	*fid, new_length, new_contents, version_id*
link	*parent_fid, name, child_fid, parent_version_id, child_version_id*
unlink	*parent_fid, name, child_fid, parent_version_id, child_version_id*
rename	*from_parent_fid, from_name, to_parent_fid, to_name, child_fid, from_parent_version_id, to_parent_version_id, child_version_id*
mkfile	*parent_fid, name, child_fid, mode, parent_version_id*
mkdir	*parent_fid, name, child_fid, mode, parent_version_id*
mksymlink	*parent_fid, name, child_fid, mode, contents, parent_version_id*
rmfile	*parent_fid, name, child_fid, parent_version_id, child_version_id*
rmdir	*parent_fid, name, child_fid, parent_version_id, child_version_id*
rmsymlink	*parent_fid, name, child_fid, parent_version_id, child_version_id*

Table 6.1. Log Record Types and their Type-Specific Fields

6.2.2 Cancellation Optimizations

File system activity often involves a great deal of *cancelling* behavior. The
case of a file that is repeatedly stored is a prime example: the last store
serves to cancel the effects of all earlier ones. Another common example
is the creation and later deletion of an object, interspersed perhaps with
other updates to it. The delete effectively cancels the create, as well as the
intervening operations.

Venus exploits cancelling behavior to significantly reduce the cost of logging. The basic idea is to recognize cancelable subsequences of transactions
and use them to transform the log into a shorter – but equivalent – representation. The benefits of shorter logs are twofold. First, they mean that less
space needs to be dedicated for logging at Venus. Or, stated differently, more

disconnected activity can be buffered without exhausting a fixed allocation. Second, shorter logs mean that less data needs to be communicated during reintegration and less work needs to be done by servers in processing it. Reintegration latency is reduced as a result, as well as the load imposed on servers and the network.

Venus recognizes and takes advantage of two distinct types of cancelable subsequences. These are termed *overwritten* and *identity* subsequences, and they are defined precisely in Subsections 6.2.2 and 6.2.2. Subsection 6.2.2 enumerates the specific instances of these classes that are recognized and cancelled by Venus, and explains how this is done efficiently. These three subsections are preceded by a discussion of what it means for a cancellation optimization to be correct.

Correctness Criteria. An intuitive requirement of disconnected transaction log transformations is that they preserve "correctness." But what, exactly, does this mean? The most obvious interpretation is that the result of reintegrating an optimized log should always be identical to that of reintegrating its unoptimized counterpart. We can formalize this notion with the definition below. Note that disconnected log and sub-history refer to the same thing, and are used interchangeably hereafter.

Definition 6.2.1. *A cancellation optimization is reintegration transparent if for every subsequence of transactions Σ that it cancels from a disconnected transaction sub-history H_d and for every connected-partition transaction sub-history H_c, the following are true:*

1. *$H_d - \Sigma$ reintegrates successfully with H_c if and only if H_d reintegrates successfully with H_c.*
2. *the server state following reintegration of $H_d - \Sigma$ with H_c is the same as that following reintegration of H_d with H_c.*

The first condition says that reintegrate-ability is preserved by the optimization. The second says that each optimized reintegration produces the same final state as its unoptimized counterpart.

Although reintegration transparency is a simple and useful correctness criterion, it is too limiting in many important situations. The history in Figure 6.2 illustrates the problem. The disconnected transaction log of that history is not reintegrateable, and yet the global history is 1SR and an optimized version of the log can in fact be reintegrated. The unoptimized log is not reintegrateable because disconnected transactions T1 and T2 cannot be certified after the execution of connected transaction T3. However, the null log – which results from optimizing out transactions T1 and T2 – clearly is reintegrateable, and it yields a post-reintegration state identical to a serial, one-copy execution of the transactions (specifically, T1 · T2 · T3).

The preceding example raises the interesting point that optimization can actually increase the set of legal histories that are recognized. This stems from the fact that certification recognizes only a fairly small subset of the 1SR

Disconnected Partition	Connected Partition
T1: mkfile[d, "foo", f, u]	T3: mksymlink[d, "foo", s, u]
T2: rmfile[d, "foo", f, u]	

Fig. 6.2. A 1SR History whose Log is Reintegrateable only after Optimization

histories. In particular, only those histories that have one-copy equivalents in which all disconnected transactions follow all connected transactions are certifiable. Optimization can effectively enlarge the set of certifiable histories by eliminating non-certifiable subsequences from disconnected sub-histories. If, in every case, reintegrating the remaining sub-history generates a final state equivalent to a one-copy execution of the entire set of transactions, then the optimization clearly preserves "correctness." We can formalize this second notion of log transformation correctness with the following definition.

Definition 6.2.2. *A cancellation optimization is 1SR-preserving if for every subsequence of transactions Σ that it cancels from a disconnected transaction sub-history H_d and for every connected-partition transaction sub-history H_c, the following are true:*

1. *$H_d - \Sigma$ reintegrates successfully with H_c if H_d reintegrates successfully with H_c.*
2. *if $H_d - \Sigma$ and H_d both reintegrate successfully with H_c, then the resulting server state is the same in each case.*
3. *if $H_d - \Sigma$ reintegrates successfully with H_c but H_d does not, then:*
   (a) the original, global history $H_c \cup H_d$ is 1SR.
   (b) the server state following reintegration of $H_d - \Sigma$ with H_c is the same as that following some serial, one-copy execution of the transactions in $H_c \cup H_d$.

Thus, 1SR-preservation is identical to reintegration transparency, except that the optimization is allowed to reintegrate additional histories which can be proved 1SR by other means.

In the following, both reintegration transparency and 1SR preservation will be used as correctness criteria. It should be clear that reintegration transparency is a stricter criterion, with every reintegration transparent class of optimization also satisfying 1SR-preservation. The reason for retaining reintegration transparency is that it is easier to prove than 1SR-preservation when both are true.

Overwrite Cancellation. The basic idea behind the *overwrite* class of optimization is that a transaction which reads all of the data items read and writes all of the data items written by a set of earlier transactions makes that earlier set redundant. Hence, the overwritten set can be removed from the log and not be reintegrated without affecting correctness. A more formal definition of this class of optimization and a proof that it indeed preserves correctness is given below.[1]

Definition 6.2.3. *A subsequence Σ_o of a disconnected transaction sub-history is an **overwritten** subsequence if there is an **overwriter** transaction $T \notin \Sigma_o$ in the same sub-history such that:*

1. $\forall T_k \in \Sigma_o \;\; T_k < T.$
2. $\forall T_k \in \Sigma_o \;\; \text{READSET}(T) \supseteq \text{READSET}(T_k) \;\wedge$
   $\text{WRITESET}(T) \supseteq (\text{WRITESET}(T_k) \cup \text{INCSET}(T_k) \cup \text{DECSET}(T_k)).$

The first condition says that every overwritten transaction must precede the overwriter. The second says that the overwriter's read set must encompass that of every overwritten transaction, and that its write set must encompass the write, increment, and decrement sets of the same.

Theorem 6.2.1. *Cancelling overwritten subsequences from a disconnected transaction sub-history is reintegration transparent.*

Proof   We need to show that both conditions of definition 6.2.1 are true for connected and disconnected sub-histories H_c and H_d and overwritten subsequence Σ_o.

Condition (1):   (if) Reintegration of a disconnected sub-history succeeds if every transaction is version certifiable. Since version certification of a transaction is independent of other disconnected transactions, every subsequence of a reintegrateable history is also reintegrateable, including $H_d - \Sigma_o$. (only if) Assume not. Then every transaction in $H_d - \Sigma_o$ is certifiable and at least one transaction in Σ_o is not. For each uncertifiable transaction there must be at least one transaction in H_c that writes into its readset. Denote an uncertifiable transaction in Σ_o by T_j and a transaction in H_c that writes into T_j's readset by T_k. From definition 6.2.3, T_k must also write into the readset of T, the overwriter of Σ_o. This means that T is also uncertifiable and hence must be in Σ_o. But, again from definition 6.2.3, T is not in Σ_o. A contradiction.

Condition (2):   From condition (1) we know that reintegration of H_d with H_c and $H_d - \Sigma_o$ with H_c either both fail or both succeed. If both fail, then the post-reintegration server state reflects just the final writes of H_c in either case. If both succeed, then the post-reintegration server state reflects the final writes of H_c and the final writes of either $H_d - \Sigma_o$ or H_d. From definition 6.2.3, we know that there are no transactions in Σ_o which perform final writes for H_d, since T follows all transactions of

---

[1] It is not necessary to understand the details of this proof and the one in the next subsection in order to appreciate the nature of the cancellation optimizations. The non-mathematical reader may wish to concentrate on the definitions and theorem statements and merely skim the proofs.

Σ_o and writes every data item that they write (or increment or decrement). Hence, post-reintegration server state must be the same when both reintegrations succeed as well.

Identity Cancellation. The basic idea behind the *identity* class of optimization is that a set of transactions whose final write values are identical to its initial read values is redundant. Hence, the identity set can be removed from the log and not be reintegrated without affecting correctness. Again, a more formal definition of this class of optimization and a proof that it indeed preserves correctness is given below.

Definition 6.2.4. *A subsequence Σ_i of a disconnected transaction sub-history H_d is an* **identity** *subsequence if:*

1. $\forall T_k \in \Sigma_i$ $(\forall d \in (\text{WRITESET}(T_k) \cup \text{INCSET}(T_k) \cup \text{DECSET}(T_k))$
   $\text{INITIALVALUE}(d, \Sigma_i) = \text{FINALVALUE}(d, \Sigma_i))$.
2. $\forall T_k \in \Sigma_i$ $(\forall T_j \in H_d$
   $((\text{WRITESET}(T_j) \cup \text{INCSET}(T_j) \cup \text{DECSET}(T_j)) \cap \text{READSET}(T_k) \neq \emptyset \vee$
   $\text{READSET}(T_j) \cap (\text{WRITESET}(T_k) \cup \text{INCSET}(T_k) \cup \text{DECSET}(T_k)) \neq \emptyset) \wedge$
   $T_j < T_k \Longrightarrow T_j \in \Sigma_i)$.

The first condition says that the last value written by the subsequence for every data item must be the same as that which the subsequence initially read. (Note that the last value "written" may be by way of an increment or decrement rather than a write.) The second condition says that all transactions which both conflict with and precede some member of the subsequence must be in the subsequence themselves.

Theorem 6.2.2. *Cancelling identity subsequences from a disconnected transaction sub-history is 1SR-preserving.*

Proof   We need to show that all three conditions of definition 6.2.2 are true for connected and disconnected histories H_c and H_d and identity subsequence Σ_i.

Condition (1):   Reintegration of $H_d - \Sigma_i$ succeeds if reintegration of H_d does because every transaction of $H_d - \Sigma_i$ is guaranteed to be version certifiable.

Condition (2):   Following successful reintegration, the server state reflects the final writes of H_c and the final writes of either H_d or $H_d - \Sigma_i$. From condition (1) of definition 6.2.4, it's clear that the value written by any final write in Σ_i must be the same as that which prevailed at the start of the partitioning. Hence, applying or omitting such writes must result in the same final server state.

Condition (3):   Let $\hat{H}_c$ and $\hat{H}_d$ be equivalent serial, one-copy sub-histories for H_c and H_d, and let $\hat{\Sigma}_i$ be the projection of Σ_i in $\hat{H}_d$.[2] Then we will show that:

(a) $\hat{\Sigma}_i \cdot \hat{H}_c \cdot (\hat{H}_d - \hat{\Sigma}_i)$ is a serial one-copy history which is equivalent to partitioned multi-copy history $H_c \cup H_d$.

(b) the server state following reintegration of $H_d - \Sigma_i$ with H_c is the same as that generated by the one-copy history identified in (a).

Claim (a) can be proved by showing that every transaction in each of the three subsequences reads the same values in the two histories.

Σ_i transactions: From condition (2) of definition 6.2.4, we know that a Σ_i transaction in the multi-copy history reads only pre-partitioning values and values written by preceding Σ_i transactions. This is clearly true in the one-copy history as well.

H_c transactions: An H_c transaction in the multi-copy history reads only pre-partitioning values and values written by preceding H_c transactions. In the one-copy history, an H_c transaction may instead read a value written by a Σ_i transaction. But because Σ_i is an identity subsequence, such a value must be the same as at the start of the partitioning (and thus the same as the transaction read in the multi-copy history). The fact that the value was written by different transactions in the two histories is of no consequence.

$H_d - \Sigma_i$ transactions: An $H_d - \Sigma_i$ transaction in the multi-copy history reads only pre-partitioning values and values written by preceding H_d transactions. In the one-copy history, an $H_d - \Sigma_i$ transaction reads from exactly the same transactions as in the multi-copy history. This must be true by the following two facts: (1) no one-copy history $H_d - \Sigma_i$ transaction reads from any H_c transaction, since otherwise the reintegration of $H_d - \Sigma_i$ and H_c would not have succeeded (an assumption), and (2) no one-copy history $H_d - \Sigma_i$ transaction reads from any Σ_i transaction that followed it in the multi-copy history, since such an $H_d - \Sigma_i$ transaction would have to have been in Σ_i itself (by condition 2 of definition 6.2.4).

Claim (b) follows from the fact that Σ_i contains no transactions which perform final writes for H_d, except those that re-write pre-partitioning values. Hence, the server state resulting from serial, one-copy execution $\hat{\Sigma}_i \cdot \hat{H}_c \cdot (\hat{H}_d - \hat{\Sigma}_i)$ must be the same as from serial, one-copy execution $\hat{H}_c \cdot (\hat{H}_d - \hat{\Sigma}_i)$. But reintegration of $H_d - \Sigma_i$ with H_c also produces that state (from the definition of reintegration in Chapter 3), and so the claim of equivalence is valid.

Implementation in Venus. The overwrite and identity cancellation optimizations can be utilized in any certification-based replica control context.

---

[2] Recall from Chapter 3 that H_c and H_d are guaranteed to be 1SR within their partitions. Therefore, $\hat{H}_c$ and $\hat{H}_d$ must exist.

There is no theoretical dependence on the particular transaction specification of Coda. However, recognizing cancelable subsequences in a system where transactions can access arbitrary sets of data items is a computationally hard problem. It entails set inclusion tests that are combinatorial in the number of transactions and data items accessed. In addition, to recognize identity subsequences the system must log old data item values and test them against new ones for equivalence. In the general case this is likely to be unprofitable, since data item sizes may be quite large and/or the likelihood of matching may be very small.

With the Coda specification, however, the recognition problem is tractable. A Coda transaction does not access an arbitrary set of data items, but rather a set that is pre-determined by its type. The type acts essentially as a *template*, with the transaction arguments instantiating the template to identify precisely the data items that are accessed. Transaction templates are used by Venus to define classes of subsequences that are *candidates* for overwrite or identity cancellation. The recognition problem then reduces to looking for candidate subsequences and performing additional checks to see if a candidate is a legitimate target for cancellation. This reduction is significant for at least two reasons. First, the number of candidate subsequence types is small, because the number of transaction types and the average number of data items accessed by most transactions are also small. Second, the set of candidate subsequences need not identify all possible cancellation opportunities. Effort can instead be focused on finding only those sequences which are most likely to occur and which offer the most benefit if found.

The remainder of this subsection enumerates the overwritten and identity subsequences recognized by Venus, and describes the recognition process in greater detail.

Overwritten Subsequences. Table 6.2 lists the set of overwritten subsequences recognized by Venus. Each entry in the table is a candidate subsequence, augmented with enough template information to determine when it is legitimate. The templates are those originally defined in Table 2.3. The interpretation of argument names is that whenever a name appears more than once in a subsequence the values must be the same everywhere in order for cancellation to be legitimate. A χ means that the argument value is irrelevant for matching purposes. The other syntax used in the specifications is that of regular expressions: "|" represents selection, "+" represents positive closure, and so on. So, for example, the first entry means that any non-empty subsequence of store and utimes transactions involving the same file and user is an overwritten subsequence if there is a later store by the same user.

It is easy to verify that the subsequences of Table 6.2 satisfy definition 6.2.3. Condition (1), which requires overwritten transactions to precede the overwriter in the history, is immediate from the construction of the table. Condition (2), which requires that the overwriter's read and write sets

Overwritten Subsequence	Overwriter
1. $(\text{store}[f,\,u] \mid \text{utimes}[f,\,u])^+$	$\text{store}[f,\,u]$
2. $\text{chown}[f,\,u]^+$	$\text{chown}[f,\,u]$
3. $\text{chmod}[f,\,u]^+$	$\text{chmod}[f,\,u]$
4. $\text{utimes}[f,\,u]^+$	$\text{utimes}[f,\,u]$
5. $(\text{store}[f,\,u] \mid \text{chown}[f,\,u] \mid \text{chmod}[f,\,u] \mid \text{utimes}[f,\,u])^+$	$\text{rmfile}[\chi,\,\chi,\,f,\,u]$
6. $(\text{chown}[s,\,u] \mid \text{chmod}[s,\,u] \mid \text{utimes}[s,\,u])^+$	$\text{rmsymlink}[\chi,\,\chi,\,s,\,u]$
7. $(\text{chown}[d,\,u] \mid \text{chmod}[d,\,u] \mid \text{utimes}[d,\,u])^+$	$\text{rmdir}[\chi,\,\chi\,d,\,u]$

Table 6.2. Overwritten Subsequences Recognized by Venus

encompass those of the overwritten transactions, can be verified by simple inspection of Table 2.3.

Identity Subsequences. The identity subsequences recognized by Venus are listed in Table 6.3. Each type consists of an initiator transaction, zero or more intermediaries, and a terminator. All three types are variants of the same phenomenon, which is that object-creating and object-deleting transactions are essentially inverses of each other. An object-creating transaction takes an object from "the void," and an object-deleting transaction returns it there. If we view the state of objects in the void as having the uninitialized value $\perp$ for every field, then a creation/deletion pair is clearly an identity transformation with respect to the object. It is also clear that intermediate transactions which read and/or modify only fields of the object itself – for example, store or chown – do not violate the identity property.

Object-creation and deletion transactions also involve updates to the parent directory of the object. In the simplest case, an object does not change its name or take on additional names after creation. The creation and deletion transactions are then inverses with respect to the parent directory as well: the former writes a fid into a formerly $\perp$-valued array element and increments the length attribute by the appropriate amount, and the latter writes $\perp$ back into the array element and decrements length by the earlier count.[3]

In more complex cases, intermediate transactions rename the object or give and take away additional names via link and unlink operations. It is not hard to see, however, that the net effect of intermediate naming activity is nil. This follows from the fact that Unix semantics prevent an object from being deleted until it has only one name left. Thus, by the time the object-deleting transaction is performed, the effect of every link and rename but one must have been inverted by an unlink or rename. The remaining uninverted

---

[3] If the object being created/deleted is a directory, then the parent's linkcount attribute is also incremented/decremented by 1.

| | Identity Subsequence | |
Initiator	Intermediaries	Terminator
1. mkfile$[\chi, \chi, f, \chi]$	(store$[f, \chi]$ | chown$[f, \chi]$ | chmod$[f, \chi]$ | utimes$[f, \chi]$ | link$[\chi, \chi, f, \chi]$ | unlink$[\chi, \chi, f, u]$ | rename$[\chi, \chi, \chi, \chi, f, \chi])^*$	rmfile$[\chi, \chi, f, \chi]$
2. mksymlink$[\chi, \chi, s, \chi]$	(chown$[s, \chi]$ | chmod$[s, \chi]$ | utimes$[s, \chi]$ | rename$[\chi, \chi, \chi, \chi, s, \chi])^*$	rmsymlink$[\chi, \chi, s, \chi]$
3. mkdir$[\chi, \chi, d, \chi]$	(chown$[d, \chi]$ | chmod$[d, \chi]$ | utimes$[d, \chi]$ | rename$[\chi, \chi, \chi, \chi, d, \chi])^*$	rmdir$[\chi, \chi, d, \chi]$

Table 6.3. Identity Subsequences Recognized by Venus

transaction is then taken care of by the object-deleting transaction itself. This property can also be verified from inspection of Table 2.3.

From the preceding discussion, it's clear that subsequences matching the templates of Table 6.3 satisfy condition (1) of definition 6.2.4. That is, the final values written by the subsequence are the same as those that prevailed at its beginning. A key point is that this fact is deducible from only the transaction type and argument information. It is not necessary to compare old and new values of data items to establish the identity property. Equivalence is implicit from the fact that certain transactions are known to take data items to and from the uninitialized state. This is of tremendous practical importance, because the space and time overheads of doing old versus new value testing make it too expensive for general use.

Although the templates satisfy condition (1) of the definition, they do not all guarantee that condition (2) holds as well. Condition (2) requires that all transactions which both conflict with and precede any member of the identity subsequence be in the subsequence themselves. It is easy to verify using Table 2.3 that templates 1 and 2 do indeed satisfy this condition, because all of the ways that files and symbolic links can be accessed are accounted for in their respective template specifications. Template 3, however, does not guarantee condition (2) because the directory created by a mkdir may be involved in transactions not covered by the template specification. In particular, elements of its contents array are mutated by mkobject, rmobject, link, unlink, and rename transactions in which it serves a parent role.

The exceptional cases involving template 3 can be divided into two subclasses, each of which has an implication for the algorithm that implements

the cancellations. The first sub-class involves *nested* identity subsequences,
as exemplified by the following:

```
T1: mkdir[d1, n1, d2, u]
T2: mkfile[d2, n2, f, u]
T3: rmfile[d2, n2, f, u]
T4: rmdir[d1, n1, d2, u]
```

In this example the mkdir/rmdir pair is not a legitimate identity subsequence
– even though it matches template 3 – because the mkfile and rmfile are not
in the subsequence yet they precede and conflict with a transaction that is.
Note, however, that the mkfile/rmfile pair is itself an identity subsequence,
and if it is cancelled then the enclosing mkdir/rmdir pair becomes legitimate.
Generalizing from this example, it should be clear that many illegitimate template 3 matches can be made legitimate simply by recognizing and cancelling
subsequences in an "inwards-out" fashion.

The other sub-class of exceptions concerning template 3 covers cases which
involve more than simple nesting. In these cases, the directory that has been
created and deleted at some point contained the name of some other, non-
deleted object. The transactions which inserted and removed the name precede and conflict with the enclosing rmdir transaction, yet they are not part
of the subsequence. Hence they "inhibit" the legitimacy of the mkdir/rmdir
pair (and any associated intermediaries). Two examples involving such *inhibiting conditions* are the following:

```
T1: mkdir[d1, n1, d2, u]          T1: mkdir[d1, n1, d2, u]
T2: mkfile[d2, n2, f, u]          T2: rename[d4, n4, d2, n2, f, u]
T3: rename[d2, n2, d3, n3, f, u]  T3: rename[d2, n2, d3, n3, f, u]
T4: rmdir[d1, n1, d2, u]          T4: rmdir[d1, n1, d2, u]
```

The common feature of these examples is that they involve a rename of some
object out of the created directory before that directory is deleted. In fact,
from examination of Table 2.3, it is possible to show that all exceptional
cases concerning template 3 involve only simple nesting or they have this
property. Consequently, truly illegitimate matches can be identified – and incorrect cancellation avoided – simply by having the algorithm check for this
"rename source" property.

On-line Algorithm. In order to get the most benefit from cancelling optimizations, an *on-line* approach must be taken. This means that Venus must
recognize and take cancellation opportunities greedily, as they are enabled.
This ensures that both goals of cancellation are met: minimizing the extent of log growth, and minimizing the data communicated and server work
performed during reintegration. The alternative approach, *off-line* or batch
cancellation at the start of reintegration, is attractive because it requires less
overall work to be done to recognize cancelable subsequences. However, it
addresses only the second of the two goals and therefore must be ruled out.

On-line recognition and cancellation is performed by Venus at the time a
transaction locally commits. The algorithm works by making 0, 1, or 2 scans

of the appropriate volume log, depending on the type of the transaction being committed. Let T be the transaction being committed, let *overwriter* be a predicate indicating whether the type of a transaction is one that can overwrite a subsequence, and let *identity_terminator* be a predicate indicating whether the type of a transaction is one that can terminate an identity subsequence. Then the steps of the algorithm are:

1. if *overwriter*(T), then scan through the log and use the template specifications of Table 6.2 to identify transactions that T overwrites. Remove each overwritten transaction from the log as it is encountered.

2. if *identity_terminator*(T), then scan through the log, determining whether an identity subsequence with T as terminator exists, and if so whether any inhibiting condition holds. If an uninhibited identity subsequence exists, again scan through the log, this time removing transactions in the subsequence as they are encountered.[4]

3. spool a log record for T, unless *identity_terminator*(T) and an identity subsequence prefix was successfully cancelled in step 2.

Indexing for Efficiency. The major expense in performing the cancelling optimizations is the scanning and matching required to recognize legitimate cancelable subsequences. One feature which reduces this expense is the segmentation of the log by volume. This means that fewer records need to be examined during most scans than if a single, Venus-wide log were kept. However, file system activity tends to be very localized, so it is still possible for volume logs to become quite large. Logs containing hundreds of records are not uncommon, and record counts much greater than one thousand have been observed.

To make the cost of scanning reasonable even with very large logs, Venus indexes volume logs by fid. The indices are organized as lists of log records rooted at each fsobj. Indexing by fid is useful because an overwriter transaction has the same fid in common with every transaction it overwrites, as does an identity-terminating transaction with the other transactions in its subsequence. Thus, every cancelable subsequence can be found by scanning just the records associated with particular fids rather than scanning the log as a whole. The reduction achieved by indexing is often significant. Typically, at most a handful of log records will reference the fid of a plain file or symbolic link, and not more than a few dozen will reference that of a directory. Hence, the cost of performing cancellations is generally unnoticeable, even when logs have grown to their largest allowable size.

Practical Effects. The cancellation optimizations have significant practical effect on disconnected operation. The key contributors to storage conservation are the following:

---

[4] Note that if a transaction is both a potential overwriter and identity-terminator, the first scan of the identity-checking step can be folded into the scan of the overwrite-checking step. Hence, the total number of scans in any case is no more than 2.

- overwrite cancellation 1 ensures that at most one store record per file and user is logged at a time.
- overwrite cancellation 5 ensures that any store record associated with a file does not persist beyond object deletion.
- the identity cancellations ensure that records resulting from naming structure expansion and contraction do not persist.

Empirical results concerning the effectiveness of the cancellation optimizations are presented in Chapter 8.

6.2.3 Store-Record Optimization

The logging procedure described so far places copies of all new values written by a transaction in its log record. The new values are needed, of course, to make the updates of the transaction globally visible at reintegration. In the case of most record types, new values account for only a few tens of bytes of storage. The total amount of space required to log most transaction types is about .25 kilobytes per transaction. The exceptional case is a store transaction, which requires a few tens of bytes plus whatever is the size of the new_contents of the file. In practice, the size of a stored file averages about 12 kilobytes, so the amount of space needed to log a store averages about 50 times that of other transaction types. Since stores typically account for 5-20% of all update transactions, they are – without further modification – the dominant consumers of log space.[5]

Fortunately, there is a simple way to drastically reduce the space required by store records. It is based on the fact that the cache container file contains exactly the bits that are needed for the new_contents field of a store record. So, rather than reproduce those bits in the store record, Venus merely logs a pointer to the container file in their stead. This *by-reference* log optimization makes the size of a store record comparable to that of other record types, and has a tremendous impact on the total amount of disk storage required at a client.

The feasibility of this optimization is dependent upon two conditions. First, it must be the case that at most one store record per file is in the log at any time. Otherwise, the referent of a non-final store would be invalid. This condition is enforced by on-line implementation of overwrite optimization 1, and by ensuring that only one user can store a given file disconnected (at a given client). (This latter restriction is enforced by allowing only one user to perform any disconnected update transactions on a given volume. Section 7.2.1 discusses this feature in more detail.) Second, it must also be the case that the container file referenced by a store is not replaced by Venus until after reintegration. Replacement would, of course, make the referent of

---

[5] Using .25k as the average size of a non-store record, 12k as the average size of a store record, and 12.5 as the percentage of stores in the update transaction mix, the percentage of log space consumed by store records is 87%.

the store invalid. Venus enforces this condition by setting a *dirty* flag in the fsobj owning the container file, and by keeping dirty fsobjs off of the priority queue. Replacement is re-enabled for a dirty fsobj when it becomes "clean" through reintegration.

The store record optimization also introduces two special cases that Venus must account for. First, there is the case in which reconnection occurs while an overwriting session is in progress. That is, a file which has been previously stored during the disconnection is again open for update. Reintegration cannot proceed immediately, because the referent of the logged store record is invalid. The solution is to pause the reintegration while the log record is cancelled "early." Reintegration can then continue, and be followed eventually by termination of the overwriting session. The second special case is similar to the first, and arises when the client crashes while an overwriting session is in progress. Upon restart, it may be the case that the referent of the logged store record is invalid. In that event, Venus quietly cancels the damaged log record and purges the corresponding container file. This is similar to the behavior of the fsck program [58], which recovers the state of a standard 4.3BSD file system following a crash.

6.3 Data Persistence

A disconnected user must be able to restart his or her machine after a shutdown and continue where he or she left off. In case of a crash, the amount of data lost should be no greater than if the same failure occurred during connected operation. To provide these guarantees, Venus must keep its cache and related data structures in non-volatile storage. With today's technology this means that clients must be equipped with hard-disk drives, since other forms of non-volatile storage are too expensive to employ in the quantity required.

Supporting decent persistence guarantees at Venus is complicated by two factors. First, because of crashes, the most recent updates to cached data may have been only partially performed, and thus non-volatile store may be in an inconsistent state at startup. The system must be able to detect such situations and *recover* a consistent state by undoing or completing partially-performed operations. Second, since a disk is being used as the non-volatile storage medium, there is tremendous relative latency associated with making updates persistent. Hence, for performance reasons it is essential that disk writes be performed asynchronously as often as possible, and that optimizations such as delaying and merging writes to the same block and scheduling disk accesses to minimize head movement be taken as well. But these behaviors are obviously at odds with the persistence objective, since they make the window between an operation's "completion" and its writes reaching non-volatile store much wider. Even more important, the disk optimizations make the recovery task much harder because writes may reach the disk in a different order than that in which they were issued. So, following a crash, it may be the case that not only are some operations partially performed, but that earlier writes on which a "committed" operation depends have not made it to disk. Without due care, this means that many operations – including some performed in the distant past – may need to be undone in order to reach a consistent post-crash state.

Providing both good performance and reasonable persistence at Venus turned out to be more difficult than expected. Simply using the AFS-2 and pre-disconnected operation Coda organization of non-volatile storage proved unacceptable, because a reasonable degree of persistence could not be guaranteed. The strategy that was developed took some of the pre-existing mechanism and added to it a new component that does guarantee acceptable persistence, but does not exact too high a penalty in performance. The mechanism that was retained is the use of local Unix files as containers for plain Coda file data. The feature that was added is the use of the RVM package to manage all of Venus' meta-data. These issues are discussed in more detail below.

6.3.1 Leveraging Off of the Local Unix File System

AFS-2 and pre-disconnected operation Coda both used the local Unix file system exclusively for the client's non-volatile storage requirements. This had significant practical benefit since the implementors did not have to write their own physical file system. The 4.3BSD fast file system [57] was already tuned to the usage patterns of the AFS/Coda environment, and yielded a reasonable balance between performance and persistence.

Utilization of the local UFS in the earlier systems had two parts, the first of which remained practical for disconnected operation, the second of which did not.

Container Files. The strategy of using local UFS files as containers for plain Coda files continues to work well with disconnected operation. Performance for reading and writing is good because the in-kernel UFS buffer cache reduces disk traffic substantially. Repeated reads of the same file typically hit in the buffer cache, and multiple writes of the same blocks are often combined into one. Writes are performed asynchronously and a certain amount of readahead is performed, so latency is often hidden from user programs. Disk accesses are reordered in the buffer cache so as to minimize head movement. Moreover, the VFS interface and the MiniCache enhancements described in Chapter 4 make the necessary indirection between Coda and UFS files clean and inexpensive.

Plain file persistence is also acceptable with the container file approach. There are two basic reasons for this. First, dirty blocks are flushed to disk at regular intervals – typically every 30 seconds – so there is a bound on the time it takes an updated block to reach non-volatile store. Second, by long tradition, Unix users and application writers are conditioned not to expect inter-

or even intra-file atomicity guarantees over their plain file updates. Post-crash anomalies such as "later" blocks appearing in a file but not "earlier" ones are tolerated as a cost of good normal case performance. Users accept the fact that their file updates have a "vulnerable period," during which data may be lost if a crash occurs. The condition which buys their acceptance is that the vulnerable period is bounded – the user knows that data last written more than t seconds ago is not at risk to a crash.[6]

Limitation: Meta-Data Recoverability. Both AFS-2 and pre-disconnected operation Coda used UFS files to store system meta-data, in addition to using them as containers for plain files. Meta-data in those systems consisted primarily of two types: the contents of cached directories and symbolic links, and descriptors for cached file system objects (i.e., fsobjs). Cached directories and symbolic links were mapped onto UFS container files, in the same manner as plain Coda files.[7] Fsobjs were stored on disk as a fixed-size array in a single UFS file. Flags in each descriptor indicated whether the descriptor itself and the corresponding container file were allocated or free. Portions of directories, symbolic links, and the fsobj array were explicitly buffered in Venus' memory, and written to disk – via the buffer cache – sometime after update.

The recovery strategy used in the earlier systems relied on the fact that virtually all information stored by a client was also stored at one or more servers. The only exceptions were files currently being updated at the client. It was therefore safe to purge any "suspicious" or "unstable" disk data during client recovery, since a consistent, up-to-date version of any object could be fetched from a server on demand. All the recovery algorithm needed to ensure was that every descriptor and container file pair were mutually and internally consistent. It did this by deriving a *stable-update* time, T_{stable}, and purging every descriptor or container file whose last-modified time was greater than or equal to T_{stable}. T_{stable} was conservatively computed as $T_{df} - \omega_1 - \omega_2$, where T_{df} was the last-modified time of the descriptor file, ω_1 was the period at which the sync daemon scheduled dirty kernel buffers for disk write, and ω_2 represented a bound on the time for all scheduled buffers to make it to disk.

Disconnected operation violates a premise of the "purge-unstable" recovery approach, which is that a server is always available and able to refresh a client's cache with the latest copy of an object. In the case of plain file data this is not a fatal problem, since – as noted above – only the most recently updated data is at risk. In the case of meta-data, however, the problem is much

---

[6] An assumption made throughout is that media failures may not occur. Obviously, if they may then data written anytime since disconnection is at risk. If media failures are a truly serious concern, then mirroring can be employed at the disk driver level, transparently to Venus.

[7] Note that Coda directories were mapped onto UFS files, not UFS directories. Mapping onto UFS directories is not useful because Coda and UFS directories have different internal structure. A similar argument applies to symbolic links.

more serious because the state at risk to a crash cannot be similarly bounded. There are at least two reasons for this. First, recall that an object must be nameable via cached directories in order to be used disconnected. Purging an unstable directory during disconnected recovery, then, would make an entire subtree inaccessible for the duration of the disconnection. If the directory in question were, say, the primary user's home directory, then the result would be catastrophic. Second, the ability to reintegrate disconnected updates depends upon a new form of meta-data, the per-volume transaction logs. Suppose that each log was mapped onto its own local UFS file in the obvious way. Then if a log were updated just before a crash, it would be purged at recovery, causing the entire set of disconnected updates for that volume to be lost. Clearly, that would be an unacceptable result.

It is possible to devise different persistence and recovery mechanisms that are more "disconnected-friendly" and which still rely on UFS files to store Coda meta-data. Indeed, a number of such mechanisms were explored and rejected before a non-UFS solution was adopted. In exploring the UFS-based options, it became clear that to provide a reasonable bound on the amount of data that could be lost or made inaccessible by a crash, some combination of the following techniques would be required:

- frequent and carefully placed fsync operations, which force all dirty buffers for a given file to disk.
- moving some Venus code into the kernel, so that inter-operation dependencies could be recognized and accounted for in the buffer cache.
- careful sizing and layout of persistent data structures to avoid "split-buffer" problems.
- special-purpose recovery code to undo partially-performed operations or deduce and re-perform missing ones.

The first three of these are *forward* techniques, which prevent potentially dangerous orderings from arising in the buffer cache. The last is a *backward* technique, which minimizes the amount of state that must be rolled-back to reach a consistent point. All four techniques have significant costs in performance, complexity or both. Most distressing is the difficulty of verifying correctness. The ad-hoc nature of these techniques means that every conceivable combination of operation order, buffer-cache optimization, and failure must be considered in order to be sure that a (non-trivial) legal state is always recovered. Moreover, each new type of meta-data or each new invariant that is introduced as the system evolves forces the verification process to be restarted from scratch.

6.3.2 Using RVM for Meta-Data

Venus avoids the problems associated with storing meta-data in plain UFS files by entrusting its meta-data to a local transaction facility instead. RVM [87, 56] is a library which may be linked into a Unix application to provide transactional access to one or more *recoverable segments* stored on disk. The application maps recoverable segments into its address space anytime after startup, and thereafter accesses the data using normal memory operations bracketed by begin- and end-transaction statements.

The major benefit to Venus of using RVM is that crash recovery is handled transparently by the library. Venus need only ensure that its meta-data is updated within transactions and that each transaction – executed in isolation and without failure – transforms the meta-data from one consistent state to another. It is RVM's responsibility, then, to ensure that a consistent state is recovered following any crash. Moreover, RVM guarantees that transaction roll-back during recovery is limited to transactions that were in progress at the time of the crash, plus, optionally, the set of transactions that committed within a specified period prior to the crash. So it is possible to make the sort of time-bounded persistence guarantee that users desire and which is difficult to provide with the UFS-based approach.

It is important to understand that the "application" utilizing RVM is Venus, not the set of arbitrary user programs. Processes other than Venus are, in fact, totally unaware of RVM's existence. Similarly, the "RVM transactions" performed by Venus are distinct from the "user transactions" that user programs make. In actuality, every updating user transaction does eventually lead to at least one RVM transaction, but some lead to more than one RVM transaction and some housekeeping RVM transactions do not correspond to any user transaction at all.

The remainder of this subsection discusses RVM and its use in Venus in greater detail.

The RVM Package. The RVM package was designed as a lightweight substrate for building persistent storage subsystems.[8] It bears some philosophical and surface-level resemblance to the Camelot distributed transaction facility [22], but it is intended to be lighter weight, more portable, and less monolithic. The RVM library provides two of the three properties required of transaction-processing systems, failure atomicity and persistence. It does not enforce the third transaction property, serializability. If the application requires serializability, then it must ensure it itself by synchronizing its accesses to shared data and to the RVM library routines. Similarly, RVM provides no direct support for nested or distributed transactions. If those facilities are needed then they must be provided by additional software layered on top of the base RVM library. The initial motivation for and application of RVM was in managing meta-data at Coda servers. Its use in Venus came later, as the persistence and recoverability needs of disconnected operation became apparent.

RVM exports the abstraction of *recoverable virtual memory* to its host application. The intent is to make recoverable storage appear as much like

---

[8] RVM was designed and built primarily by Hank Mashburn, with input from members of the Coda and Venari groups at CMU.

regular memory as possible. An application interacts with RVM in three basic ways. First, it associates and disassociates *regions* of recoverable segments with portions of its virtual address space. The library routines rvm_map and rvm_unmap are used for this purpose. Typically, an application maps in all of its regions at startup and does not unmap any until it terminates, although it may dynamically map and unmap regions if it so desires. Second, the application performs transactions over mapped-in data using the rvm_begin_transaction and rvm_end_transaction library routines. Rvm_abort_transaction is also available for explicit abort of active transactions. Accesses to mapped-in data are performed using normal memory read and write operations. Updated locations are written to disk when the transaction commits (or, optionally, sometime later). The application must tell RVM what address ranges a transaction has modified using the rvm_set_range routine, since the package has no way of deducing that information.[9]

The third way that an application may interact with RVM is to explicitly schedule disk writes. The package will perform all necessary writes transparently in default usage, but, for performance reasons, an application may wish to exercise its own control over disk activity. The two kinds of writing performed by RVM are called *flushing* and *truncating*. A transaction is flushed by appending *change records* containing the range specifications and new values it wrote to the RVM log on disk (hereafter referred to as just "the log"). Following the string of change records, a *commit record* is also written to the log, indicating that the transaction is complete. In default usage, a transaction is flushed synchronously with the rvm_end_transaction invocation. However, if the *no-flush* option is specified to rvm_end_transaction, then the package will instead buffer the transaction's change and commit records in memory. The application can later flush all buffered transactions to the log using the rvm_flush routine. Truncation is the process of applying the change records of the log to the recoverable segments. When it completes, the segments have been brought up to date and the old log records are effectively discarded. Truncation occurs by default when a flush causes the log to exceed a pre-determined size and also when the first rvm_map call is made by the application. The application may schedule a truncation at any other time by invoking the rvm_truncate routine.

The use of RVM's disk-write scheduling options is crucial to achieving good performance in Venus. Subsections 6.3.2 and 6.3.2 discuss this issue in further detail. Table 6.4 lists the exported RVM library routines, and summarizes the purpose of each.

Venus' Recoverable Segment. Venus maintains its meta-data in a single RVM segment. The segment consists of two regions, one large and one small. The large region – region 1 – contains a heap, from which recoverable store

---

[9] Explicit set-range calls could be avoided if RVM were tied more closely to either the compiler or the virtual memory system. Such arrangements were rejected for the base implementation in the interest of keeping it simple and portable.

RVM Interface Routine	Description
rvm_initialize	initializes state internal to the package.
rvm_terminate	cleans up state before terminating a session with the package.
rvm_map	maps a recoverable segment region into the address space of the application.
rvm_unmap	unmaps a previously mapped region.
rvm_begin_transaction	initiates a transaction.
rvm_set_range	defines a modification range pertinent to an active transaction.
rvm_abort_transaction	aborts an active transaction.
rvm_end_transaction	commits an active transaction.
rvm_flush	forces buffered log records for committed transactions to the RVM log on disk.
rvm_truncate	applies change records in the RVM log to the recoverable segment(s), then discards those records.

These are the main exported routines of the RVM library. A few additional routines are exported for setting options, collecting statistics, and so on. Consult the RVM manual for further details.

Table 6.4. RVM Library Interface Routines and Descriptions

can be dynamically allocated. The small region – region 0 – contains the roots of the heap plus a few other global variables. Both regions are mapped into Venus' address space at startup and are not unmapped until Venus terminates. Figure 6.3 illustrates the organization of Venus' address space, including the two recoverable regions.

The data in the heap logically represents three databases: a database of cached file-system objects – the FSDB, a database of cached volume information – the VDB, and a database of hoard entries – the HDB. Each database has as its core a set of descriptors and a hash table for efficient access. The descriptors in the case of the FSDB are fsobjs – the status blocks representing cached files, directories and symbolic links. The FSDB also contains the data parts of cached directories and symbolic links. For the VDB and HDB, the descriptors are volume and hoard entries respectively (volents and hdbes). Transaction log records are associated with logs in individual volents, and are thus also considered part of the VDB.

The size of the recoverable heap is fixed at Venus genesis and cannot be changed without a complete re-initialization. By default, Venus computes the heap size as a function of the container file usage limit, although this may be overridden if desired. The default computation typically results in a heap size about 20% that of the container file usage limit. In order to make sure that the heap is apportioned fairly among the various users of it, quotas are set

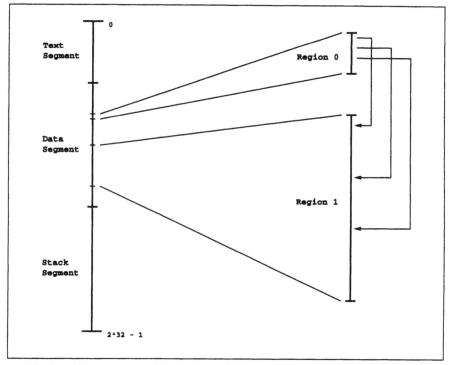

Region 0 is the recoverable root descriptor, and region 1 is the recoverable heap.

Fig. 6.3. Organization of Venus' Address Space

and enforced for most classes of heap data. If an object needs to be allocated and its class' quota is full, then the allocator must either free an allocated instance of that class or it must deny the request. Table 6.5 lists the quotas and typical quantities consumed for the major heap consumers in a heap of moderate size.

Scheduling RVM Flushes. The default RVM behavior of flushing transactions as they commit is ideal from the standpoint of persistence, but it is not good at all from that of performance. Performance suffers under this approach because every transaction pays the price of a synchronous disk write. Moreover, there is no opportunity to exploit overwrite behavior, in which transactions closely spaced in time write the same ranges of data. Earlier in this chapter it was observed that overwriting is very common at the level of user transactions. Since most RVM transactions are the direct result of user transactions, it should not be surprising that overwriting is ubiquitous at the RVM level as well.

To make the cost of flush-on-commit concrete, consider the Unix command

Object Class	Quota (MB)	Typical Usage (MB)
File-system object descriptors (fsobjs)	1.5	1.3
Directory and symbolic link contents	N/A	.6
Volume entries (volents)	N/A	.1
Transaction log records	1.0	.1
Hoard entries (hdbes)	1.5	.1

All figures are in megabytes. A few small, miscellaneous heap users are omitted from the table. The heap size in this sample case is slightly less than 5 megabytes, and the corresponding container file usage limit is 24 megabytes. Note that there are no quotas for directory and symbolic link contents, nor for volume entries. Those classes of data are indirectly bounded by the quota on fsobjs, and do not grow out of control in practice.

Table 6.5. Typical Recoverable Heap Quotas and Usage

cp -p dir1/file[0-9] dir2

which copies ten files from one directory to another and preserves each file's last-modified time. Three user transactions are involved per file: a mkfile to make the file skeleton and insert a name for it in dir2, a store to record the file contents, and a utimes to re-write the modify-time attribute. Typically, only one RVM transaction is required for each of the user transactions, although more may be needed if deallocations are necessary to free-up heap space. Therefore, with flush-on-commit, the number of synchronous RVM disk writes to execute this one command would be 30. Unless the sizes of the files were very large, the latency of these writes would dominate the execution time of the command and performance would be noticeably worse than if the copy was performed in a purely local Unix file system.

Venus avoids the performance problems of flush-on-commit by utilizing RVM's no-flush commit option and scheduling log flushes itself. Not flushing on commit has two major benefits. First, transaction commit is asynchronous with respect to logging, so flush latency is never borne directly by a user process. Second, change records representing the same range can be combined, saving buffer space and requiring much less data overall to be written to disk. Thus, in the cp example given above the no-flush approach would write only one copy of dir2's contents to the log while flush-on-commit would write ten. Similarly, no-flush would log only one copy of each file's fsobj while flush-on-commit would log three copies of each. If additional updates to the objects were to occur before a flush was scheduled then the net savings of no-flush would be even greater.

Within RVM, no-flush commit is implemented by buffering a single, *super-transaction* in memory. As additional no-flush transactions commit, new change records are added to the super-transaction's set or existing records are updated as appropriate. Update of an existing change record occurs when the committing transaction has written all or part of the range represented by the record. After its modifications are reflected in the super-transaction's change records, all evidence of the committing transaction as a separate entity is discarded. Its effects have been accounted for entirely by the super-transaction. When an rvm_flush is finally invoked, the super-transaction is written to the log just as if it were a normal transaction. A single commit record representing the super-transaction follows the merged string of change records. The result is that the entire set of no-flush transactions is failure atomic: either their full, combined effects become permanent, or none of their effects do.

No-flush transaction processing in RVM has performance characteristics that are very similar to those of the standard Unix buffer cache. Both offer asynchronous disk writing and reduction of write traffic by merging multiple writes to the same byte ranges. No-flush RVM, however, has one additional property that the buffer cache does not and which makes it superior for many applications. That property is its provision for *bounded persistence*. This means that (a) a consistent state is always recoverable, and (b) the updates that may be lost in event of a crash are bounded in time. The bound, of course, is the maximum length of time between explicit RVM flush invocations. Note that the buffer cache approach cannot similarly bound persistence by flushing (i.e., fsync'ing) at regular intervals, since the buffer cache knows nothing about the dependencies between write operations.

RVM flushes are invoked in Venus by a dedicated LWP, the *RVM-scheduler daemon*. Flushing is synchronous with respect to the daemon, but other LWPs may continue processing and committing transactions while the flush is in progress. The job of the daemon is to wake up every few seconds and initiate a flush when any one of the following conditions are satisfied:

- the super-transaction's *persistence deadline* has been reached.
- the buffer space consumed by the super-transaction exceeds a pre-determined threshold (64 kilobytes by default).
- user request processing has been quiescent for a pre-determined period of time (60 seconds by default), and there is a super-transaction waiting to be flushed.
- a *quit* signal has been received by Venus, instructing it to clean up and terminate gracefully.

The second and fourth conditions are straightforward, and require no further explanation. The first and third conditions, however, are somewhat unusual and are discussed further below.

Persistence Deadlines. To make a bounded persistence guarantee with bound t, Venus must – in principle – initiate an RVM flush no more than t seconds after each transaction commit. A straightforward way of accomplishing that is the following. When a transaction commits, the worker LWP computes the transaction's persistence deadline – the time at which it must be safely on disk

– as t plus the current time. It then compares this value to a global variable representing the persistence deadline of the super-transaction. If the committing transaction's deadline is sooner, then it is installed as the new deadline of the super-transaction. Every time the RVM-scheduling daemon wakes up it compares the current time plus its period to the super-transaction's deadline. If the first quantity exceeds the second, then the daemon invokes a flush. Otherwise it checks the other flush-inducing conditions and either invokes a flush based on one of them or goes back to sleep. Before any flush is invoked, the daemon resets the super-transaction's deadline to infinity so that the next committing transaction will begin the flush countdown anew.

The actual behavior of Venus is very similar to that described above, but it incorporates an important optimization. The optimization is to use a more generous bound than t in computing deadlines for transactions executed in connected mode. The rationale for this is that such transactions are written through to servers at commit time, and hence are persistent regardless of whether or when the originating Venus flushes its new state to disk.[10] If the client should crash before an RVM log flush occurs then its state at recovery will be consistent, but it may not reflect some updates that occurred further than t seconds in the past. Those updates can be recovered, however, simply by fetching the latest copies of the updated objects from the server(s). This *refresh* procedure occurs automatically, either as a side-effect of the first hoard walk following restart, or via the on-demand validation procedure for objects without callback promises.

An assumption made by this optimization is that the relevant servers will be accessible at every post-crash restart. If, in fact, they are, then there is no reason to associate any local persistence deadline at all with connected-mode transactions. While it is indeed likely that a server accessible at crash time will also be accessible at the next restart, there are real cases in which this does not hold. As an example, consider a connected, mobile client which is shut-down uncleanly and next started in a completely different locale, fully-disconnected. To guard against scenarios such as this, Venus computes the persistence deadlines of connected-mode transactions using a large, but not infinite, t-bound. The default values for the connected- and disconnected-mode bounds are 600 and 30 seconds, respectively. It is important to emphasize that with these values the persistence bound guaranteed by Venus is 30 seconds, not 600. The latter value is a bound on the "local visibility" of updates in event of a crash, not the global persistence of the updates themselves.

Load Considerations. The fact that flushes are always performed by a daemon means that, in theory, they should never interfere with user-request

---

[10] Servers also keep their non-volatile state in a combination of RVM segments and UFS container files. They use normal, flush-on-commit transactions when updating meta-data, so a Venus-originated, meta-data update is actually persistent before it commits at Venus.

processing. In practice, however, there are two reasons why flushes can considerably slow the progress of concurrent transaction processing. First, when one LWP blocks while performing disk I/O the entire Unix process is put to sleep. Thus, while the RVM-scheduler daemon is flushing data to the log Venus suffers long delays in servicing new file system requests. The daemon does voluntarily yield to other Venus LWPs in between disk writes, so other processing is not totally locked out, but, nonetheless, the inability to overlap daemon I/O with other LWP activity can be a significant drag on service responsiveness.

The second reason that flushing can interfere with request-processing is a result of economics and disk mechanics. Ideally, we would like to have a separate disk arm actuator to serve each of the different consumers of non-volatile storage at the client. This would mean a separate actuator for each of the following: the RVM log, the RVM recoverable segment, the container file directory, the paging partition, and the "local" partition (which contains things like /tmp and files necessary to boot the machine). Unfortunately, though, most Coda clients have only a single disk with a single head-positioning mechanism. Simultaneous I/O requests for different types of disk data can therefore lead to severe thrashing, as the disk heads are repeatedly pulled from one cylinder to another. Invoking a flush while other disk activity is in progress – be it container file accesses via Venus, paging activity, or whatever – can result in exactly this type of unwanted behavior.

Each of these problems can be "fixed" with existing or soon-to-be-available technology. More modern operating systems than Unix, for example Mach, schedule threads within an address space independently. Thus, the problem of blocking an entire process when one thread performs disk I/O can already be avoided by switching OS platforms. Similarly, inexpensive storage subsystems employing a number of very small, lightweight disks are beginning to come to market. When these subsystems mature, it should be practical to dedicate an actuator to the RVM log and thereby avoid thrashing, even in the case of the most humble client (i.e., a portable).

For Coda to be usable today, though, and on a wide variety of platforms, it must operate within the confines of LWP/Unix and single-actuator disk configurations. This means that Venus must minimize the overlap between flushing and other client activity. The technique it uses is simple, but generally effective. The idea is to maintain a global *idle time* variable, which represents the time since the last user request was completed by Venus (or 0 if a request is in progress). When the RVM-scheduler daemon wakes up and none of the other flush-inducing conditions are satisfied, it checks to see whether the idle time exceeds a threshold and there is a super-transaction waiting to be flushed. If so, it goes ahead and invokes a flush; if not it goes back to sleep. The rationale for this, of course, is that idle time generally exhibits a fair degree of inertia. After a certain period of idleness, the chance that new requests will be submitted in the time it takes to perform a flush is

quite small. An immediate flush in such cases is therefore unlikely to interfere with any other significant client activity, whereas a later flush induced
by deadline or space conditions might well experience contention.

Scheduling RVM Truncates. An RVM log truncation is necessary – and
is performed automatically by the package – at the time a process maps in
its first recoverable region. This ensures that the image copied into virtual
memory reflects all of the stable updates made in the last execution of the
program. In theory, an application can rely exclusively on truncate-at-first-
mapping and not perform any truncations during its normal execution. In
practice, however, this does not occur, as most application instances live
long enough to overflow a log of reasonable size. Even if log space is not
an issue the latency associated with truncating an extremely large log is,
and it leads to the policy of fixing log size and truncating when the limit
is reached. In normal use of the package, "log-full" truncations are invoked
automatically whenever an rvm_end_transaction or rvm_flush call causes the
log-size threshold to be reached. This truncation is performed by a dedicated
LWP internal to the package, so, in theory, it is asynchronous with respect
to the flushing or transaction-committing thread.

Of course, for the same reasons cited in the preceding subsection, an
"asynchronous" truncate can in reality delay the processing of other client
activity substantially. In fact, the potential for delay is actually much greater
with truncation than with flushing, since a typical truncate takes about an
order of magnitude longer than a typical flush. The reason for this disparity
is that a truncate writes – and therefore must seek to – random areas of
the recoverable segment, whereas a flush writes to disk sequentially and thus
avoids most head-positioning costs.

Because of the likelihood that a package-triggered, log-full truncation will
interfere with other client computation, Venus schedules its own truncations
directly. The same daemon which handles RVM flushes is also responsible for
scheduling truncates. The conditions which induce truncation are essentially
a subset of those which induce flushing:

– the size of the log exceeds a pre-determined threshold (256 kilobytes by
  default).
– user request processing has been quiescent for a pre-determined period of
  time (again, 60 seconds by default), and the log is non-empty.

The other two conditions which induce flushing – persistence-deadline expiry
and process shutdown – are motivated by the need to make transactions persistent before impending or anticipated loss of volatile memory. But data that
is already in the log is stable and not affected by the loss of volatile memory,
so there is no need to truncate in response to either of these conditions.

6.4 Other Masking Responsibilities

Transaction logging and data persistence are the most complex emulation-specific requirements for masking disconnection. However, there are two other important responsibilities that Venus must assume while disconnected: access-checking and fid-generation. This section describes what Venus does in support of each.

6.4.1 Access Checking

Protection in Coda is based on the concepts of principals and access rights. Every object logically has an *access vector* associated with it that specifies the rights that each principal known to the system has for that object. As part of its type specification, each transaction requires certain rights to be held by the invoking principal for the objects involved. If the invoker does not have all the necessary rights, then the transaction is illegal and is not accepted by the system. As examples, the store transaction type requires that the invoker have *write* rights for the file in question, and the rename transaction type requires that the invoker have both *delete* rights on the "from-parent" directory and *insert* rights on the "to-parent" directory. Table 6.6 lists the various types of rights that are recognized by the system, along with the privileges they convey.

Type	Privilege
read	principal is allowed to read the attributes of the object, or read its contents if it is a file or symbolic link
write	principal is allowed to change the attributes of the object, or overwrite its contents if it is a file
list	principal is allowed to list the bindings of a directory object
insert	principal is allowed to insert new bindings into a directory object
delete	principal is allowed to delete existing bindings from a directory object
administer	principal is allowed to change the access vector of the object

Table 6.6. Access Right Types and Privileges

The primary responsibility for access checking rests with servers in Coda, since they are the only trusted entities in the system. In connected mode, servers make the necessary access checks for update transactions at transaction commit time and reject any in which the principal's rights are insufficient. The role of Venus in connected mode access-checking is twofold. First, it makes access checks for read-only transactions on its own, using access vector information that it has previously cached. This is necessary to realize the full performance benefits of caching.[11] Second, Venus makes preliminary access checks for update transactions, again using cached access vector information. These checks are preliminary, of course, because the server will re-perform them at commit time. Their utility is in screening out requests that have no hope of succeeding.

It is essential that disconnected operation not compromise the security guarantees of the system. The foremost implication of this is that servers must perform access-checking during reintegration, and refuse to commit logs which contain protection-violating transactions. This is discussed further in Chapter 7. From the client's point of view, however, there are two additional access-checking issues that distinguish disconnected from connected operation.

Authentication. In order to make access checks and commit a transaction, servers require proof of identity from the user. Section 4.2.2 described how this proof is presented. Essentially, the user parlays a secret shared with a trusted authentication server into authentication tokens that are held by Venus. These tokens are then used to establish authenticated RPC connections with servers on the user's behalf. The establishment of such a connection is taken to be prima facie evidence by the server that the user is who he or she claims to be.

A problem arises when a user cannot acquire authentication tokens. This happens when no authentication server is accessible at the time a user logs in or at the time his or her tokens expire and need to be refreshed.[12] The connected mode solution to this problem is to coerce an unauthenticated user's identity to that of the anonymous principal, System:AnyUser. Since this principal's rights are a floor for those of every real principal, this strategy gives the unauthenticated user some file system access – typically the ability to read much of the namespace – but does not compromise security in any way.

The connected mode solution is not acceptable for disconnected operation because even partial disconnection makes it much more likely that a user will be unable to acquire or refresh tokens. Moreover, even if tokens are held when a disconnected transaction is performed, they may be lost or they may expire by the time file server reconnection occurs. This means that there must be a more flexible solution for disconnected operation. The approach taken

---

[11] Access-checking at servers in the read-only case would be pointless anyway, since the only reason to check is to guard against subversion of Venus. But if Venus has been subverted, then all cached data is already visible to the subverter. This illustrates the fact that preventing *unauthorized release* of information is impossible if some nodes are untrusted. Coda's goal is the more realistic one of preventing *unauthorized modification* of data.

[12] To minimize the danger of stolen tokens, they expire after a fixed period (typically 24 hours).

in Coda has two elements. First, Venus makes access checks on disconnected objects with respect to the "real" principal whether they have authentication tokens or not. Second, Venus blocks or *forestalls* reintegration until the user has re-acquired valid tokens. So, in effect, Venus gives the unauthenticated, disconnected user the "benefit of the doubt," and allows them to do locally whatever their authenticated persona could do globally. However, their actions are not made globally visible until it is established that they were indeed "telling the truth" about their identity.

Default Access Rights. In order to perform access checks for a transaction, Venus must have cached the access rights of the invoking principal for the objects involved. This is true regardless of whether the transaction is being executed in connected or disconnected mode. The most straightforward approach to access right caching is to cache the entire access vector along with the status of each file system object. This is impractical in a system of the projected scale of Coda, however, since each access vector may consist of tens of thousands of elements. Hence, Venus caches only a small subset of each access vector, corresponding to the users that have most recently referenced the object at the particular client.[13]

Incomplete caching of access vectors means that misses may occur on vector elements, event though an object is "cached" at a client. In connected mode this is not serious because missing rights may be fetched with only a small time penalty. In disconnected mode, however, an access right miss is much more severe because there is no server to supply the missing information. Fortunately, disconnected access rights misses tend to be rare in practice. This is because if an object is cached and a given user accesses that object disconnected, then it is highly likely that they previously accessed it connected and that their rights are still cached.

There are cases, however, in which disconnected rights misses do occur. Typically, these result from one of two scenarios. In one scenario, a daemon or a "guest user" has accessed an object while connected, but the primary user of the workstation has not. The primary user then happens to access the object during a disconnection. Alternatively, the primary user has accessed an object while connected, but only when they were unauthenticated. In this situation Venus will have cached only the access rights for System:AnyUser, not the (presumably superior) rights of the real principal. If the user then accesses the object disconnected, Venus will not have his or her true rights available.

Venus reduces the pain of disconnected rights misses by using *default rights* in access-checking rather than immediately failing on a miss. Default rights are those that belong to System:AnyUser, and Venus ensures that they are always cached for every object. Using these rights is always conservative, since no real user can have fewer rights than the anonymous principal. This strategy is useful because System:AnyUser normally has at least *read* rights

---

[13] By default, the rights of up to 8 different users may be cached for each object.

for many objects in the system. Hence, a user can read many objects even without his or her real rights. Moreover, if they desperately need to update a "missing rights" object, they can often make a copy of it somewhere where they do have *write* rights and update the data there.

6.4.2 Fid Generation

Each of the object-creating transaction types – mkfile, mkdir, mksymlink – requires a fid to identify the new object. Recall that a fid consists of two components: a 32-bit volume number, and a 64-bit vnode number. Vnode numbers must be unique within a volume for all time. This is ensured by having servers generate fids for the volumes they host and distributing them to Veni in ViceAllocFid RPCs.

Venus allocates fids in advance in order to reduce the cost of creating objects. The first time a fid is needed for a volume, a batch of fids are allocated in a single RPC and the balance are stored in a "pre-allocated fids" data structure associated with the volume. Subsequent allocation requests, whether they occur in connected or disconnected state, can draw fids out of the pre-allocated set until it becomes empty.

The distinction between connected and disconnected processing occurs when the volume's pre-allocated fid set is empty. In the connected case, another ViceAllocFid RPC is simply made to replenish the stash and one of the new batch is used to satisfy the current transaction.

In the disconnected case this option is not available, so a *temporary* fid is generated and used by Venus. A temporary fid is one whose vnode number is drawn from a reserved range that servers do not allocate from. Temporary fids exist only as long as the volume they belong to remains disconnected. They are translated into *permanent* fids during an early step of the reintegration process. Until that time, however, they function as real fids, and indeed are indistinguishable from permanent fids to most of the Venus code. Reserving part of the vnode range for temporary fids is not a serious limitation, since uniqueness needs to be guaranteed only within a <Venus, disconnected session> pair. 2^{32} reserved vnodes per volume (out of 2^{64} total) more than suffices to meet this requirement.

6.5 Mitigating Emulation Failures

Server emulation can fail – making disconnection visible to users and applications – in two significant ways:

– cache misses.
– resource exhaustion.

This and earlier chapters have described the major techniques used by Venus to minimize these failures. This section briefly discusses some additional techniques which can be used to mitigate the effects of these failures even further.

6.5.1 Cache Misses

The default response of Venus to a disconnected cache miss is to return an ETIMEDOUT error to the corresponding system call. This is generally the most useful behavior, as it tends to make the failure immediately visible to the user. Hopefully, he or she can then move on to a different task that requires only objects already in the cache. In the best case, the application is able to mask the failure from the user by substituting some other, available piece of data for the missing object.

There are some situations, however, in which misses are more usefully handled with a *block-and-retry* approach. Block-and-retry requires Venus to suspend its handling of a system call at the outermost level, and retry the call from scratch when connectivity state changes. Block-and-retry tends to be appropriate when both of the following are true: (1) the sufferer of the miss is a batch rather than an interactive task, and (2) the disconnection is involuntary rather than intentional. The first condition means that a human is probably not hanging on the result of the operation. The second implies that the disconnection may end soon, and that no user intervention – such as re-attaching a network cable – is required to make it happen. Thus, simply waiting for reconnection and then continuing may well be the most transparent and user-satisfying approach.

As an example of the utility of block-and-retry, consider the case of a mobile client whose network connection is a low-reliability packet radio link. Such a client may suffer transient disconnections of a few seconds to a few minutes with significant frequency. Now suppose that the user begins a **make** job which compiles and links a good-size application. Such a task may take tens of minutes or more, and thus is likely to encounter one or more periods of disconnection. If Venus uses the reflect-failure approach to miss handling then it's possible that the **make** may have to be watched and restarted several times in order to account for cache misses. With block-and-retry, however, the user can simply put the job in the background and forget about it. If disconnected cache misses do occur then the task will take somewhat longer, but partially-completed work won't need to be discarded and the user won't need to babysit the job.

Venus currently supports block-and-retry cache miss handling at the granularity of a user. A simple utility program is available which allows a user to toggle miss-handling behavior for all of his or her processes between the two approaches. A more useful implementation would allow the choice to be made at the level of individual processes or process-trees. This would allow an application such as **make** to specify block-and-retry for itself and its descendant processes, but not force that behavior for the user's interactive tasks as well. There are no major technical restrictions precluding this enhancement, and it will likely be added at some point in the future.

6.5.2 Resource Exhaustion

It is possible for Venus to effectively exhaust its non-volatile storage while disconnected. The significant instance of this is the quota on container file blocks being used entirely by dirty – and thus not-replaceable – files. The other consumers of disk storage – fsobjs, directory contents, transaction log records, etc – either don't have not-replaceable elements or their quotas are high enough that they never become a constraint before the container file space quota does. When container space is exhausted, attempts to create or extend a file receive an ENOSPC error. The user must then generally wait until reintegration occurs before performing further update transactions. Non-mutating operations can continue when container space is exhausted as long as they reference only cached files. But if a non-mutating operation needs to fetch data from a still-connected server, then it too will receive an ENOSPC error.

In practice, the effects of a growing set of dirty container blocks are felt well before they consume the entire quota. This is because the blocks of other, unmodified files must be evicted as the dirty block count gets larger and larger. Evictions occur in inverse priority order, as described in Chapter 5, so the most valuable objects are retained until the last. Beyond a certain point, however, files which have a significant short-term reference probability will be evicted. As the limit is approached, popular application binaries will be evicted, pretty well guaranteeing that cache misses will soon occur. The effect is that failures which really are a function of resource exhaustion tend to manifest themselves in the same way as predictive failures – i.e., as cache misses.

The simplest way to address resource exhaustion is to increase physical disk capacity. An alternative approach – which is much less expensive in financial terms – is to use compression to make the container space that is available go further. Compression trades off computation time for space, and recent work in both the academic and commercial worlds has shown that the user-visible decrease in performance can be made small [12, 11, 101, 77].

Venus currently offers limited support for container file compression. A user is able to compress the container file of a cached object on demand by supplying its name to a utility program. For example, the command

```
cfs compress /coda/project/coda/src/venus/*.[ch]
```

would compress all of the cached files in the Venus source tree. Typically, on-demand compression is invoked as a disconnected user perceives that container space is getting full and important files are about to be evicted.[14] Decompression may be similarly invoked via the utility program, or it will be performed automatically by Venus the next time the compressed file is specified in an open call.

---

[14] Most users run a monitoring program in its own small window which reports such information.

In its current form, Venus' compression support is suitable only for expert users, and even then it is of marginal use. In order for it to be really useful it must be made fully automatic. Two directions seem most promising in this regard. One approach is to incorporate compression into the data-walk phase of hoard walking. The idea is to establish thresholds for reference inactivity and container file size, and compress files which exceed both thresholds during the data walk. Decompression would be automatic on open as it is currently. In order to avoid unprofitable work, compression could be disabled when the cache already has sufficient free space available. Similarly, decompression could be done in advance of open if free-space suddenly became more plentiful.

An alternative approach is to push compression/decompression into a lower-level of the system than Venus, specifically, into the disk driver or disk controller itself. This appears to be the more useful direction for several reasons. First, it makes it much easier to operate at the block rather than the whole-file level. For large files, whole-file compression and decompression concentrates latency to an unacceptable degree. Second, an in-driver or in-controller implementation makes it feasible to do the compression and decompression in hardware rather than software. Since chips are already available which operate at speeds exceeding typical disk transfer rates [2, 10], this would make it possible to compress and decompress with no performance degradation whatsoever. Finally, Burrows et al [11] have recently shown that compression is particularly effective when combined with a log-structured physical file system (specifically, Rosenblum and Ousterhout's LFS [74]). Since LFS also has major performance advantages over the current physical file system used by Venus, switching container file storage to a compression-capable version of LFS clearly would be the most useful long-term course to take.

7. Reintegration

Reintegration is the process of merging disconnected file activity with the current state at a server. It is initiated by Venus following physical reconnection, and consists of a top-level Venus-to-server RPC plus a variable number of additional RPCs in both directions. Reintegration is performed independently on a per-volume basis, as connectivity changes permit.

This chapter describes the process of reintegration in detail. The description is in three parts. Part one is a step-by-step overview of the algorithm. Parts two and three examine the key issues in greater detail. Part two covers all issues except for certification. Part three is devoted entirely to that particular concern.

7.1 Overview of the Algorithm

Reintegration breaks down cleanly into three stages, which are known as the *prelude*, the *interlude*, and the *postlude*. The prelude encompasses the activity at Venus in between restoration of physical connectivity with a server and the dispatching of a ViceReintegrate RPC request. The interlude represents the handling of the ViceReintegrate RPC at the server. The postlude encompasses the activity at Venus in between receipt of the ViceReintegrate RPC reply and the transition of the local volume state from reintegrating to hoarding. Figure 7.1 illustrates these stages, their major sub-tasks, and the RPC traffic they entail.

7.1.1 Prelude

A volume in the emulating state enters the reintegration prelude when a connectivity change from DOWN to UP is recorded for its custodian. Such a change results from a successful RPC2_Bind exchange initiated by the background probe daemon. Note that many cached volumes may be hosted by the newly-communicating server, in which case all will enter the prelude stage simultaneously.

The prelude can be broken down into two sub-stages. The *early-prelude* consists of several preliminary steps that the volume must go through before

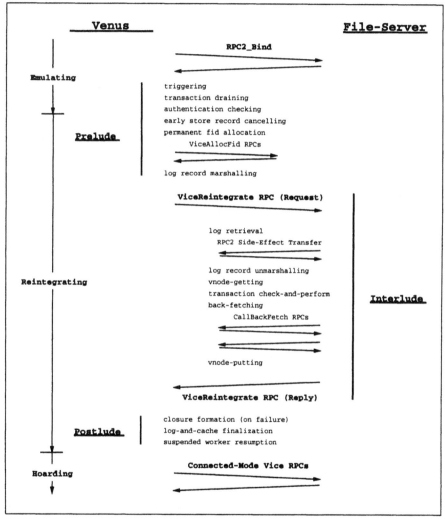

Time moves downward in this diagram. The time-line on the far left shows the state transition points for the volume undergoing reintegration. The other arrows represent message traffic between client and server.

Fig. 7.1. Stages of Reintegration, Major Sub-Tasks, and RPC Traffic

it officially transits from the emulating to the reintegrating state. Those steps are the following:

- **triggering** – the volume remains inactive until one of the following "triggering" events occurs:
  - a worker LWP references any object in the volume while executing a user transaction.
  - the hoard daemon references any object in the volume while performing a hoard walk.
  - the *volume daemon*, one of whose jobs it is to check for pending reintegrations, fires and notices that the volume is in the early-prelude state. (The period of this daemon is 90 seconds by default.)
- **transaction draining** – the LWP which has triggered reintegration must wait until all transactions in progress for the volume have completed. This and the additional step of preventing new transactions from starting are necessary to keep the volume log from changing during the course of the reintegration. Of course, if the volume log is empty – meaning that no disconnected update transactions were performed in the volume – then reintegration is bypassed altogether and the volume transits immediately to the hoarding state.
- **authentication checking** – the triggering LWP checks to make sure that the *volume-log owner* – the user who performed the transactions in the volume log – has valid authentication tokens. Without tokens there is no point in attempting reintegration, since the server will refuse to participate. Therefore, in the token-less case the prelude is exited immediately and the volume remains in the emulating state. Transaction processing continues for the volume as if it were still physically disconnected. Periodically, Venus writes messages of the form "reintegration pending tokens for user <uid>" to the console when reintegration is being forestalled so that the user is aware of the situation.

The second sub-stage of the prelude, the *late-prelude*, follows authentication token verification. It commences with the transition of the volume to reintegrating state and the creation and dispatch of a special *reintegrator* LWP to manage the rest of the reintegration. The triggering LWP is suspended if it is a worker, or it moves on to its next task if it is a daemon. The daemons are programmed to skip over volumes that are being reintegrated so that they do not interfere with reintegrator LWPs. Similarly, new user transactions involving objects in a reintegrating volume continue to be blocked until the reintegration completes. The remaining steps of the late-prelude are the following:

- **early store record cancelling** – the fsobj database is scanned to find files in the volume which are currently open for update. For each such file, the volume log is scanned and any **store** record for the file is cancelled. The need for this "early cancellation" was explained in Section 6.2.3.

- **permanent fid allocation** – the fsobj database is scanned to see whether
  any objects in the volume have temporary fids. Recall that a temporary fid
  is allocated and assigned to an object if it is created disconnected and Venus
  has run out of pre-allocated fids for the volume. If any objects do have
  temporary fids, then Venus makes batch ViceAllocFid RPCs to acquire a
  sufficient quantity of permanent fids. It then replaces each temporary fid
  with a permanent one in all the places where the fid is referenced – fsobjs,
  directory pages, and volume logs.
- **log record marshalling** – an in-memory buffer is allocated and the volume log records are *marshalled* into it. The main purposes of marshalling
  are to convert the data items to a host-independent byte-order and to
  flatten-out linked structures. The stub-generated routines for the corresponding connected-mode RPCs are used to do the marshalling. For example, a mkdir record is marshalled with the ViceMakeDir marshalling routine.
  It is important to note that the contents arguments of store records are
  not copied into this buffer. A separate mechanism is used to transfer that
  data. Hence, the buffer size is roughly the same as the log itself – tens to
  perhaps a few hundred kilobytes.

The prelude comes to an end with the invocation of a ViceReintegrate
RPC. This call is made on an authenticated connection belonging to the
volume-log owner. Its arguments are the volume identifier and a descriptor
which represents the marshalled log-record buffer. The buffer does not go
over the wire in the RPC request packet, but is transferred during the body
of the call via the RPC2 side-effect mechanism.

7.1.2 Interlude

The interlude covers the processing of the ViceReintegrate RPC at the server.
The main task of this stage is the attempted replay of the client's disconnected
update transactions. During the interlude the reintegrator LWP at Venus is
dormant, awaiting the result of the RPC.

The RPC2 multiplexor at the server unmarshalls the ViceReintegrate
request packet and dispatches a Vice worker LWP to handle it. This LWP
performs the bulk of the server-side processing for the reintegration. The
major steps it performs are the following:

- **log retrieval** – the worker is dispatched with the volume identifier and a
  side-effect descriptor as arguments. Its first step is to allocate an in-memory
  buffer large enough to hold the volume log image. The log is then fetched
  from the client by passing the side-effect descriptor and the buffer address
  to an RPC2 library routine.
- **log record unmarshalling** – the buffer is unmarshalled into a sequence of
  log records. As at the client, the stub-generated (un)marshalling routines
  are used for this purpose. The worker now has a volume log representation
  essentially identical to that at the client.

- **vnode-getting** – the volume log is traversed to build a sorted list of all the fids that are involved in any transaction. This list is then used to look up and write-lock the descriptor corresponding to each fid. As noted in Chapter 4, these descriptors are called *vnodes* and are the server-side analog to fsobjs. The locked vnodes are placed on a temporary vnode-list for further manipulation by the worker. Deadlock with other workers performing transactions in the same volume is avoided by acquiring the vnodes in fid-order. All other vnode-lockers are required to do the same, so there is no possibility of wait-for cycles developing.

  The successful lookup of a vnode returns a reference to an in-memory copy of the object. The persistent copies of vnodes are stored in RVM, but they are not accessed directly by the reintegration code.[1] Note that the lookup of a vnode mentioned in the log may fail because the server has no record of it. This can happen for two reasons: (1) the object was created during the partitioning by the client, or (2) it was deleted during the partitioning by the server. Neither of these cases are necessarily fatal to the reintegration, and the worker continues undeterred with the next lookup when failure occurs. The next step of the algorithm will determine whether the lookup failure is fatal or not.

- **transaction check-and-perform** – the volume log records are iterated over, and each transaction is validated for correctness and tentatively performed. Validation consists of making the same checks for each transaction type as are made in connected-mode processing. Four basic types of check are made:

  - **certification** – the history consisting of all connected-partition transactions plus the disconnected-partition prefix up to and including the candidate transaction must be 1SR.
  - **integrity** – the candidate transaction must preserve all standard integrity constraints. For example, the new component name specified in a mkdir transaction must not already be bound in the parent directory.
  - **protection** – the user for whom the reintegration is being performed must have the necessary rights for the given vnodes and candidate transaction type.
  - **resource** – if the candidate transaction requires new disk resources, then there must be sufficient free quota for the volume. In the case of a store transaction, there must also be sufficient space on the container file partition to record the new file contents.

  If validation succeeds, then the transaction is tentatively performed by updating the in-memory copies of vnodes and directory pages (if appropriate). Callback promises to other clients are broken and new version-ids are

---

[1] The copying of vnodes from RVM to an in-memory cache is an artifact of the AFS-2 code that we inherited. That earlier system stored vnodes in Unix files, so it was necessary to explicitly cache active descriptors in memory. With RVM such explicit caching is redundant, and we will eventually eliminate it from our file servers.

installed for updated objects, just as would occur if the transaction was being committed in connected mode.

In the case of a store transaction, the new contents of the file do not appear in its log record. Hence, they must be fetched from the client. Rather than do this fetching as each store record is validated, the server defers all fetches until the check-and-perform loop is complete. In preparation for the later fetch, however, the server does allocate a fresh container file and insert a reference to it in the Vice file's vnode.

If validation fails for any transaction, then the reintegration is aborted at that point. The vnode-putting step is then entered directly with an error-code indicating the cause of the failure.

- **back-fetching** – if validation succeeds for every transaction in the volume log then the *back-fetch* loop is entered. In back-fetching, the worker iterates over the log once more, this time fetching the file contents for each store record encountered. The fetch is made via a special call on the CallBack subsystem, using the server's existing, unauthenticated connection. These CallBackFetch RPCs are serviced at Venus by CallBack Handler LWPs. The fetched data is transferred directly to the container file allocated in the check-and-perform step, without being buffered in server memory.

- **vnode-putting** – the interlude has succeeded if the check-and-perform and back-fetch loops complete without error. In that case the updated vnodes and directory pages are written back to RVM. The write-back of this data occurs within the scope of a single RVM transaction, so the procedure is failure-atomic. That is, either all of the transactions represented by the volume log become permanent at the server or none of them do.

  The interlude has failed if an error occurred in validating some transaction or if something went wrong during a back-fetch. In that case, the new state represented by the in-memory vnodes and directory pages is simply evaporated rather than being written to RVM. Any container files that were allocated (and possibly filled) are similarly discarded.

  A side-effect of vnode-putting, which occurs on success or failure, is the releasing of locks on vnodes. This makes the objects available again to be used in other user transactions.

The interlude concludes with the transmission of the ViceReintegrate reply. The only data in the reply is a return-code indicating whether the interlude succeeded or failed. The reintegrating client is a normal, connected-mode client in the eyes of the server from this point on.

7.1.3 Postlude

The postlude represents clean-up activity at Venus needed before the volume can be returned to the hoarding state. This activity is performed by the reintegrator LWP, which is woken up by the server's reply to the ViceReintegrate RPC. The key steps of the postlude are the following:

- **closure formation** – if the RPC failed then Venus must preserve the effects of the disconnected transactions for manual recovery. The technique it uses is to write a *closure* file in Unix *tape-archive* (tar) format. The closure is written in a local directory accessible only to the volume-log owner. Section 7.2.5 contains more information about closures and the process of recovering data from them.
- **log-and-cache finalization** – if the RPC succeeded then Venus must finalize its local state to effectively commit the disconnected session. Finalization has two steps. First, the log of the reintegrated volume must be truncated and its records returned to the recoverable heap. Second, the dirty fsobjs for the volume must be made clean by resetting their dirty-bits. Both steps are performed within the scope of a single RVM transaction, so there are no recovery complications if the process is interrupted by a crash.

  If the ViceReintegrate RPC failed then Venus must finalize its local state to effectively abort the disconnected session. The initial step of aborting is writing the closure file, as described above. Aborting also entails update of the log and dirty fsobjs, similarly to the commit case. The difference compared to commitment is that dirty fsobjs must be purged rather than be made clean. This follows from the fact that the disconnected transactions were not compatible with those performed at the server; hence, the cached versions of updated objects are not valid. As in the commit case, volume log truncation and fsobj finalization are performed within a single RVM transaction, so crash recovery is not a cause for concern.
- **suspended worker resumption** – all worker LWPs that are waiting to perform transactions involving objects in the volume must be resumed. Suspended workers can result in three ways: (1) a cache miss occurred during emulation for a worker operating in block-and-retry mode, (2) a worker triggered the transition from emulating to reintegrating state while performing a transaction, (3) a worker began a new transaction while the reintegration was in progress. A worker suspended for any of these reasons is made runnable again at this point.

The final two acts of the postlude are the changing of volume state from reintegrating to hoarding, and the retirement of the reintegrator LWP.

7.2 Non-Certification Issues

This and the next section elaborate on key reintegration issues raised in the overview. Section 7.3 covers certification, while this section addresses everything else.

7.2.1 Volume-Log Ownership

A restriction imposed on disconnected operation is that only one user may perform update transactions in any given volume (at any given client). This user is known as the volume-log owner. The owner is not pre-determined, nor is it necessarily the same at different clients or during different disconnected sessions. The overview used the concept of volume-log ownership without explaining why it is necessary or how it is enforced.

The chief motivating factors behind volume-log ownership are protection and the store-record optimization described in Section 6.2.3. Recall that that optimization depends on there being at most one author of disconnected stores for any given file. Volume-log ownership satisfies that requirement trivially.

Protection is also simplified by restricting volume-log updates to a single user. Allowing multiple users to add records to a volume log would complicate protection in two ways. First, it would mean that Venus would have to forestall reintegration until it had authentication tokens for the union of the volume-log writers. A user who refused to refresh his or her tokens could therefore delay the propagation of other users' changes indefinitely. Second, closure preservation would be awkward. Rather than creating a single closure file accessible only to a single user, Venus would either have to make the closure accessible to the set of volume-log writers, or it would have to generate multiple closures, each one containing the data for a particular user's transactions. The former strategy is clearly undesirable from a protection point of view, whereas the latter makes recovery more painful by segregating access to related information.

Volume-log ownership must be enforced by Venus while a volume is in the emulation state. This is achieved in straightforward fashion by associating an owner variable with each log. When the first disconnected update transaction is begun for a volume, its log-owner variable is set to the user performing the transaction. Subsequent update transactions begun by other users before the volume is reintegrated receive a permission-denied error. Read-only transactions can continue to be serviced for all users since they do not require log records to be spooled.

The practical effects of the volume-log ownership restriction are negligible in the prototypical Coda environment. This is because most clients are primary-user workstations, with file accesses by secondary users occurring infrequently. The chances of two users at a workstation contending for disconnected update access to the same volume is therefore very small. In an environment where multi-user access is common the chances for contention would be much higher, and an alternative to the exclusive writer discipline might be appropriate.

7.2.2 Transaction Validation

The validation of each transaction in the interlude's check-and-perform loop consists of four types of checks: certification, integrity, protection, and resource. Certification and resource-checking are necessitated by the fact that connected-partition transactions may have interfered with disconnected activity. The interference detected by certification is conflicting accesses to the same logical data items, while that detected by resource-checking is consumption of limited storage space.

The two other types of checks – integrity and protection – are motivated by security rather than concurrency concerns. Although a reintegration is performed over an authenticated RPC connection, that alone does not mean that the submitted log contains only legitimate transactions. It is possible that a user's authentication tokens were captured by a malicious agent, and that the agent has constructed a phony log. A server cannot prevent the damage that may arise in this case, but it can limit it to the *mutable domain* of the subverted user – i.e., to the set of objects that the subverted user has the right to update. This containment of damage is ensured by making the same protection and integrity checks that would be made in handling connected-mode transactions. Protection checks ensure that an attacker cannot trivially extend the domain of destruction by updating objects inaccessible to the subverted user. Integrity checks ensure that more subtle forms of corruption – typically involving the naming hierarchy – are not successful. For example, the check that a directory being removed is empty prevents an attacker from effectively deleting a protected subtree by removing an ancestor directory for which it has DELETE rights.

7.2.3 Back-Fetching

The current reintegration implementation back-fetches file store contents in batch fashion, as a separate loop following transaction check-and-perform. One can imagine two alternatives to this approach:

- back-fetching within the check-and-perform loop, as each store is successfully validated.
- *in-lining* the data with the volume log, avoiding the need to back-fetch altogether.

The first alternative, incremental back-fetching, is inferior to the current approach because it does unnecessary work in cases where the reintegration is doomed to fail. As an example, consider a case in which many megabytes of data are back-fetched, only to be discarded because the last record in the log is not certifiable.

The second alternative, in-lining, also suffers from doing unnecessary work in the failure case. More importantly, though, it makes unreasonable demands on the server process for buffer space. In a typical reintegration the amount of store data is one to two orders of magnitude larger than the size of the volume log, and a total amount of store data in the tens of megabytes is not unheard of. With in-lining all of this data must be buffered in the server's address space at one time. With the back-fetching approach, however, only a small, fixed amount of space is needed because the data is transferred directly from network buffers to the pre-allocated container files on disk. In addition to the space savings, back-fetching also saves the time cost of one memory-to-memory copy of the data.

Although in-lining is inappropriate as the default technique, it does have an advantage which makes a hybrid strategy attractive. The advantage that in-lining has over back-fetching is that RPC overhead is lower, since only one call is made instead of many. When the reintegration contains many small store transactions, the extra overhead associated with multiple RPCs can be significant. A strategy which would capture the main benefits of both in-lining and back-fetching is to in-line store contents below some threshold size, say 4 or 8 kilobytes, and to back-fetch them above the threshold. It would not be hard to switch to this approach from the current one, and I expect that it will be done in a future version of the system.

A more serious problem with the current back-fetch implementation is that the back-fetch channel is insecure. Servers currently make back-fetch RPCs on the CallBack subsystem using an unauthenticated RPC2 connection. It is therefore simple for an attacker to intercept back-fetch traffic from Venus to server, and, further, to corrupt back-fetched files by substituting bogus packets for those it intercepts. This security hole could be closed with the following, straightforward changes to the implementation:

– Venus makes up a random number of sufficient length and transmits it to the server in the ViceReintegrate request. The Vice RPC2 connection is secure, so no attacker is able to intercept this secret.
– The server uses the secret to establish a secure CallBack connection back to Venus.
– All back-fetch requests are made on the secure CallBack connection. When back-fetching is complete, the connection is torn down.

I have not taken the trouble to make back-fetching secure because our environment is not particularly hostile (and, until now, no one else knew of the hole's existence). I expect that this hole will be closed in a future release of the system.

7.2.4 Atomicity of Reintegration

Reintegration is largely failure-atomic because changes to persistent store are performed within a single, local RVM transaction at both client and server. Specifically, RVM transactions envelop the vnode-putting step at the server and the log-and-cache finalization step at Venus. This feature substantially simplifies the programming of the client and server, as it is not necessary to sort out partially-reintegrated state at either end following a crash. The RVM package takes care of all recovery-related issues.[2]

Although the persistent state changes at each end are failure-atomic, the two sets of changes taken together are not. Figure 7.2 depicts the two sub-tasks that are independently failure-atomic, and illustrates that there is a window of vulnerability between them. If a client crash or communications failure occurs between the start of the interlude phase and the termination of the log-and-cache finalization step, then it's possible that the server will have committed its state change but the client will not have. Although the likelihood of this happening is extremely small in practice, it is not zero. If and when it does occur, the client will retry the reintegration when it next comes into contact with the server. Such retried reintegrations are rather likely to fail, as the current certification protocol is not sophisticated enough to recognize this as a special case.[3]

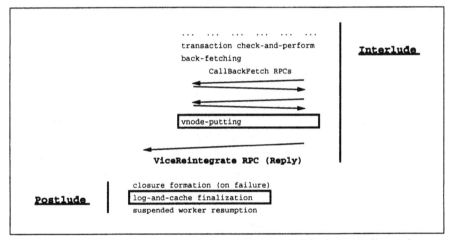

This figure is an enlargement of part of Figure 7.1. The boxes indicate the two sub-tasks – one at the server and one at the client – that are each failure-atomic.

Fig. 7.2. Atomic Sub-Tasks of Reintegration

---

[2] In fact, at the server end some special recovery code is required because container files are kept in the local Unix file system rather than in RVM. A *salvager* thread is responsible for checking all container files at server start-up and de-allocating those created by interrupted transactions. Note, however, that this activity is required even without disconnected operation, as it is just as likely for a connected-mode transaction to be interrupted by a crash as it is for a reintegration. Hence, it is fair to say that no additional recovery mechanism at either client or server is necessitated by disconnected operation.

[3] Various enhancements could be added to make the percentage of unrecognized – and thus falsely rejected – retries very small. Such enhancements have not yet been added because the likelihood of their being needed is itself quite small.

The preceding problem could be eliminated entirely by using a distributed transaction to ensure that Venus and the server commit their new state together. Although the RVM package does not support distributed transactions directly, it would not be hard to layer a commit protocol such as two-phase commit [50, 31] on top of it. I specifically chose not to make that change, however. Involving a client and server in a distributed transaction would violate a fundamental Coda design principle, as it would leave the system dependent on the correct functioning of one client machine in order to provide service to others. This follows from the fact that all distributed commit protocols end up blocking if site or communications failures occur at critical times. It would be possible, therefore, for client failure or disconnection to block a server thread while it was holding locks for many vnodes. These vnodes would be inaccessible to all until the client eventually reconnected. But in the Coda model clients are autonomous, so there is no way to convince them to reconnect promptly or even at all. The inability of servers to limit their vulnerability to client failure or intransigence thus makes the use of distributed commit an infeasible option.

7.2.5 Closures

A closure is the name given to the state saved for recovery from a failed reintegration. Like a closure in the domain of functional languages, a Coda closure is intended to capture the state of a computation.

A Coda closure is represented by a local Unix file and is formed by Venus at the time a reintegration fails. Its pathname encodes the name, mountpoint, and log owner of the volume in question. So, for example, the closure named

`/usr/coda/spool/jjk/p.coda.alphasrc@%coda%project%coda%alpha%src`

corresponds to a failed reintegration by user `jjk` of volume `p.coda.alphasrc` mounted in the namespace at `/coda/project/coda/alpha/src`. Spool directories such as `/usr/coda/spool/jjk` are protected against reading or writing by users other than their owner.

A closure file consists of a sequence of records in Unix tar format. Each record corresponds to a store transaction that appeared in the volume log. The record fields are a pathname, Unix attribute values, and the stored contents of the file. Pathname and attribute values are those which were current for the file at the time of the reintegration. Hence, a tar record may reflect the effect of transactions in addition to the store (for example, a rename or a chmod).

The use of the tar format for closures allows the standard Unix archive utility – also called tar – to be used to recover data. However, to make the task a little easier, a Coda utility program provides some "syntactic sugaring." The utility has options to *examine* and to *replay* all closures of the user who invokes it, or a list of closures specified by their names. The examine and replay functions each check that the volume identified by the closure name is still mounted at the correct place, and then invoke the tar utility with the appropriate arguments. So, for example, user jjk could examine all of his saved closures (at a given client) with the command cfs examine-closure. Then, if he decided that he wanted all of the new values of the closure transactions to be made visible, he could achieve that by issuing the command cfs replay-closure. Alternatively, the closure could just be ignored, or the tar program could be used directly to recover selected file updates.

The initial closure format used was a superset of tar's. It contained record types corresponding to each Coda transaction type, not just stores, and a closure file had a record for each record in the volume log. A separate program was provided to interpret these files for examination and replay purposes. Although this format was more faithful to the idea of disconnected session encapsulation, the added information proved of little use in practice. In fact, more often than not it served to confuse users rather than to aid them in recovery. The current, simplified scheme was adopted as a result.

7.3 Certification

Certification is the sub-task of reintegration responsible for ensuring that a disconnected session was computationally correct. That is, it verifies that the multi-copy history representing the connected and disconnected transactions is equivalent to a one-copy history of the same transactions. In particular, certification determines whether or not the multi-copy history is equivalent to the one-copy history $H_c \cdot H_d$, where H_c and H_d are the connected and disconnected sub-histories respectively. If the two histories are equivalent, then the reintegration succeeds (barring protection or resource or some other class of error). But if the histories are not equivalent, then the reintegration fails and the user must recover the effects of his or her disconnected transactions from a closure file.

Certification checks the equivalence of the two histories incrementally. The basic idea is to consider each transaction in the order specified by the one-copy history, $H_c \cdot H_d$, and determine whether it reads the same values in both cases. If it does, then the prefix of $H_c \cdot H_d$ terminated by the current transaction must be correct, and the check-and-perform loop may continue. But if the current transaction reads different values in the two histories then they cannot be equivalent, and the procedure therefore fails at that point. If the last transaction of $H_c \cdot H_d$ is reached and it passes certification, then it must be true that the entire histories are equivalent.

It is obvious that all H_c transactions read the same values in both histories. This follows from the facts that (a) no H_d transaction precedes any H_c transaction in the one-copy case, and (b) that the relative ordering of H_c transactions is the same in both histories. Consequently, the algorithm can safely skip over the transactions in H_c and begin certification with the first transaction of H_d.

Disconnected transactions can be certified using two different techniques. These are known as *version* and *value* certification. Each has advantages over the other in important respects. Coda uses a combination of the two which exploits the best features of each. The first two subsections below discuss version and value certification separately, and the third explains how and why they are combined. Subsection 7.3.4 covers two additional issues that are pertinent to the certification process, and the final subsection summarizes and comments on the efficacy of the approach.

7.3.1 Version Certification

The principle behind version certification is view equivalence. A transaction which has the same "view" in the multi- and one-copy histories – i.e., which reads every data item in its read set from the same writer – obviously reads the same values in each case. Version certification is implemented by constructing the view of a transaction in each history and comparing the two for equivalence.

The version-ids in a disconnected transaction log record can be used to construct the view of that transaction in the multi-copy history. Recall that new version-ids are installed for updated data item copies when a transaction commits. This is true for both disconnected- and connected-mode commitment. The new version-ids chosen by the system are, in fact, the transaction identifier of the committing transaction. The set of pairs <data item name, logged version-id> is thus an explicit representation of the transaction's view in the multi-copy history.

Similarly, the version-ids associated with the current server state can be used to construct the view of a disconnected transaction in the one-copy history. At the time a given transaction is checked for certifiability, it's clear that the server state reflects the updates of all transactions that precede it in the one-copy history. This follows from the facts that (a) the server state reflects the updates of all transactions in H_c at the start of reintegration, and (b) that every preceding H_d transaction was tentatively performed following its own certification. Hence, the set of pairs <data item name, current server version-id> is an explicit representation of the transaction's view in the one-copy history.

Given the two views, determining equivalence is simply a matter of testing whether the logged and current server version-ids are the same for each data item. If so, then the views are equivalent and the transaction is certifiable. If not, then the views are not equivalent and the transaction is uncertifiable.

7.3.2 Value Certification

Conceptually, value certification is even simpler than version certification. The idea is to compare the values read by a transaction in each history directly rather than comparing the two views. The values read in the multi-copy history are stored in the disconnected transaction log record. The values read in the one-copy history are simply those reflected by the server copies at the time of certification.

The set of histories recognizable by value certification is strictly larger than than recognizable using version-ids. Clearly, any history that is certifiable via view equivalence must be certifiable via value equivalence as well. However, the converse is not true. In particular, value equivalence can be established for many histories in which H_d transactions read data items that undergo identity transformation in H_c. View equivalence cannot be established in these cases because the H_d transactions read the identity-transformed data items from different writers in the multi- and one-copy histories. Figure 7.3 contains an example which illustrates this phenomenon.

Disconnected Partition	Connected Partition
T1: mkfile[d, "foo", f1, u]	T2: mkfile[d, "foo", f2, u]
	T3: rmfile[d, "foo", f2, u]

T1 is value certifiable because it read the same values in its disconnected execution as it would have in the one-copy history T2 · T3 · T1. It is not version certifiable because it read data item d.data[''foo''] from a pre-partitioning transaction (say, T0) in its disconnected execution, but would have read that data item from T3 in the one-copy history.

Fig. 7.3. A History that is Value but not Version Certifiable

Value certification is also able to recognize many more histories than version certification due to practical limitations on version-id granularity. As described in Chapter 2, Coda directory contents and access vectors are logically represented as fixed-size arrays, with each array element an independent data item. Because these arrays are very large – 256^{256} elements in the directory contents case, 2^{32} in the access vector case – it is impractical to associate a version-id with each element. The best that can be done is to represent each array by a single version-id. This means, however, that version certification will fail in many cases in which a transaction's view is really the same in the multi- and one-copy histories. The effect is that of false conflicts, which were identified earlier in Chapter 2. Value certification does not suffer from the same problem because there is no incentive to record old values at granularity coarser than that at which the data is actually used. Figure 7.4 gives a simple example in which value certification would succeed but version certification would fail due to granularity effects.

Disconnected Partition	Connected Partition
T1: mkfile[d, "foo", f, u1]	T2: setrights[d, u2]

T1 is version certifiable if version-ids are maintained at the granularity of individual data items since it reads no item that is written by a connected-partition transaction. It is also obviously value certifiable. However, it is not version certifiable if version-ids are associated with entire objects or with entire access-vector arrays. In that case certification will fail because it will appear that T1 reads data item d.rights[u1] from different transactions in the multi- and one-copy histories. Similar problems arise if version-ids are associated with directory-contents arrays (or entire objects) rather than individual directory entries.

Fig. 7.4. A History that would Fail Version Certification due to Version Granularity

7.3.3 Hybrid Certification

From the preceding subsection it is clear that value certification has significant advantages over version certification. Specifically, value certification is tolerant of identity transformations in the connected sub-history and it is immune to false conflict problems. However, version certification has an advantage over value certification which turns out to be crucial for certain Coda transaction types. That advantage is that version certification has a small, fixed space and time cost per data item.[4] Value certification, in contrast, requires space and time that is proportional to the size of each data item. When data items are small, as in the case of directory entries, for example, the costs of value and version certification are comparable. But when data items are large the cost of value certification becomes exorbitant.

The obvious instance in Coda where value certification is impractical concerns store transactions. Certifying a store by value requires (a) keeping a copy of the file's old contents in its log record at the client (in addition to the file's new contents), (b) transmitting the old contents to the server with the rest of the log record and buffering the old contents at the server, and (c) performing a byte-by-byte comparison of the old contents with the server's current representation of the file. Certifying the store by version, in contrast, requires only 64 bits of client storage and transmission overhead and a 64-bit comparison. Clearly, the latter technique is the only one which is reasonable in the case of stores.

Fortunately, there is no requirement that version or value certification be used at the exclusion of the other. The property that is established by certification is that every read access of every transaction sees the same value in the multi- and one-copy histories. It does not matter whether this is proved for all transactions by version equivalence, or for all transactions by value equivalence, or by any combination of the two. Indeed, it is perfectly legal to

---

[4] The size of a Coda version-id is 64 bits.

mix the techniques at the level of individual data accesses, certifying some accesses of a transaction by version and others by value.

Coda uses a hybrid certification strategy which exploits the advantages of both the version and value approaches. In order to appreciate the Coda hybrid, it is helpful to review the three "pure" certification strategies that have been alluded to: *object-level version certification, data-item-level version certification*, and *value certification*. Table 7.1 lists the advantages and disadvantages of each approach. As the table indicates, only object-level version certification is practical in its pure form. The characterizations of the other two approaches are nonetheless useful, as they establish an availability standard by which any hybrid can be judged.

Strategy	Advantages	Disadvantages
Object-Level Version Certification	space and time efficient.	vulnerable to false conflicts, particularly with respect to directory contents and access-vector entries; unable to take advantage of identity transformations in H_c.
Data-Item-Level Version Certification	not vulnerable to false conflicts.	unable to take advantage of identity transformations in H_c; impractical because space usage per object is proportional to number of logical entries in directory contents and access-vector arrays.
Value Certification	not vulnerable to false conflicts; able to take advantage of identity transformations in H_c; space and time usage is comparable to version certification for small data items.	impractical because space and time usage is exorbitant for large data items (e.g., file contents).

Table 7.1. Comparison of Pure Certification Strategies

Coda Hybrid Specification. The hybrid strategy of Coda is a combination of value and object-level version certification. Table 7.2 identifies the particular mix used for each type of disconnected update transaction. The data items read by a transaction are listed in the table in one of three columns according to whether the item is certified by version, value, or neither. The neither case applies to data items that cannot have been written by a connected partition transaction. This property guarantees that the value actually read by the disconnected transaction is the same as in the one-copy history, $H_c \cdot H_d$. Hence, there is no need to certify that it is true. Two types of data items fall under this exception: fids in any transaction, and any part of an object created by one of the mkobject variants. The former can't be written by connected partition transactions because fids are immutable after object creation. The latter can't be written because an object can only be created once and no data item can be accessed before its object has been created.

Transaction Type	Object-Level Version	Value	Neither
chown[o, u]	o.rights[u], o.owner		o.fid
chmod[o, u]	o.rights[u], o.mode		o.fid
utimes[o, u]	o.rights[u], o.modifytime		o.fid
store[f, u]	f.rights[u], f.modifytime, f.length, f.data[*]		f.fid
link[d, n, f, u]		d.rights[u], d.data[n]	d.fid, f.fid
unlink[d, n, f, u]		d.rights[u], d.data[n]	d.fid, f.fid
rename[$d1$, $n1$, $d2$, $n2$, o, u]		d1.rights[u], d1.data[n1], d2.rights[u], d2.data[n2], o.data[''..'']	d1.fid, d2.fid, o.fid
mkobject[d, n, o, u]		d.rights[u], d.data[n]	d.fid, o.*
rmobject[d, n, o, u]	o.*	d.rights[u], d.data[n]	d.fid

Note that in the rename transaction o.data[''..''] is relevant only when the renamed object is a directory.

Table 7.2. Coda Hybrid Certification Specification

Evaluation. The Coda certification strategy can be evaluated along two dimensions: efficiency and availability.

Efficiency. Certification efficiency can be evaluated with respect to two principal criteria: permanent storage overhead, and the cost of equivalence testing. Two other important criteria, log space and transmission overhead, are directly proportional to the cost of equivalence testing.

The efficiency of the Coda scheme is virtually identical to that of the most efficient pure strategy, object-level version certification. In terms of permanent storage used, Coda is no different than object-level version certification – one version-id per object. This reflects the fact that Coda uses value certification rather than finer-granularity version stamping to avoid false conflicts.

The use of value certification by Coda does not incur significant additional cost in equivalence testing, however. This is because the only types of data items that are certified by value are fids and (per-user) access rights. The size of these types are roughly the same as a version-id; hence, the costs of comparing them during certification are practically identical. In some cases, the Coda scheme must make several comparisons instead of the single one required for version certification, but this cost difference is negligible. Overall, the equivalence testing – and log space and transmission overhead – costs of the Coda approach are indistinguishable from those of pure object-level version certification.

Availability. The availability realized by the Coda scheme is, in practice, very close to that offered by the highest availability pure strategy, value certification. The specific instances where Coda availability is less than pure value certification are the following:

1. chown, chmod, and utimes transactions
   (a) false conflicts with non-chown/chmod/utimes transactions that update the object.
   (b) unrecognized H_c identity transformations (e.g., a series of chown transactions that leave the owner the same as pre-partitioning).
2. store transaction
   (a) false conflicts with the following transaction types: chown, chmod, setrights (when the user is different), link, and unlink.
   (b) unrecognized H_c identity transformations (e.g., a store transaction that rewrites the original file contents, followed by a utimes that rewrites the original modify-time).
3. rmobject transaction
   (a) unrecognized H_c identity transformations (e.g., a mkfile transaction followed by a rmfile of the same file in the directory being removed).

In practice, none of these situations are very important. The most common cases of false conflict and identity transformation involve naming operations, and thus are accounted for by the value certification specified in Table 7.2. Moreover, several of the cases above could be eliminated with minor modification to the system. Specifically, 1(a) and 1(b) could be eliminated by certifying chown, chmod, and utimes by value rather than version, and 2(a) could be eliminated by keeping separate version-ids for each attribute, the access-vector (as a whole), and the data contents (as a whole). Neither of these changes would impact the efficiency of the system significantly. Their net effect would be to add a few dozen bytes to the permanent meta-data of each object, and to increase the cost of equivalence testing by a small constant factor. These enhancements will probably be implemented in a future version of the system, but they are not a high priority and their overall contribution to availability is not likely to be great.[5]

Version-id Maintenance. Part of performing a disconnected transaction following its certification is the installation of new version-ids for the server copies of updated objects. The new version-ids are normally taken to be the *transaction identifier* (transaction-id) of the current transaction. A transaction-id is globally unique, and is assigned by Venus at the time of local transaction commitment. A copy of the transaction-id appears in the disconnected log record.

The perform-time recording of new version-ids serves two purposes. First, it enables correct future connected-mode processing. Recall from Chapter 3 that connected-mode transaction processing relies on object-level version certification for correctness. Object version-ids are used to determine whether cache copies are stale or fresh at the start of a transaction, and whether inter-transaction interference occurred during the transaction's body at the time it tries to commit. Hence, if a reintegrating transaction did not update object version-ids, then a subsequent connected-mode transaction might fail to fetch fresh data or might fail to notice an interfering update in the midst of its execution. In either case, committing the connected-mode transaction would likely be incorrect.

If version certification is being used to certify any disconnected accesses – as it is in Coda – then perform-time version-id update also serves a second purpose. That purpose is ensuring that the one-copy views used to version certify transactions are constructed properly. Consider what would happen otherwise in the (version) certification of transaction T2, where T2 reads an object, o, written by earlier disconnected transaction T1. The multi-copy view would correctly reflect this reads-from relationship, as the version-id of o in T2's log record would be the transaction-id of T1. Without perform-time version-id update, however, the one-copy view constructed for transaction T2 would be in error. The version-id of the server copy of object o would not be that corresponding to T1, but would be that corresponding to the last pre-partitioning transaction to have written the object. The multi- and one-copy views of T2 would therefore not agree, and certification would improperly fail.

Value/Version Complication. Version-id maintenance is complicated somewhat when value and object-level version certification are used in combination. A potential problem arises when a data access is successfully value certified, but object-level version certification of the access would fail as a result of version-id granularity. Figure 7.4 gave one example of this type of

---

[5] Because the system is in regular use by many people, there is considerable administrative cost in changing either communications interfaces or the format of persistent storage. The former requires coordinated release of system software, the latter dumping and restoring large quantities of data. Hence, there is incentive not to make such changes unless the expected benefit is extremely high.

situation, and others which involve partitioned update of different names in the same directory are even more common. The problem occurs if the new version-id installed for the server copy of the object that was value certified is the "normal" one, i.e., the transaction-id of the updating transaction. In that case, the copies of the object at the server and the reintegrating client have the same current version-id, but their contents are not necessarily identical. For example, if the object is a directory, the server copy may contain new bindings that were added by transactions in H_c. If the client goes on to perform transactions on the object – thinking that its copy is identical to the server's – then incorrect behavior may result.

The foregoing problem is avoided by not installing the "normal" new version-id in cases where value certification succeeds but object-level version certification would not. In such cases the server generates a unique *override* version-id and installs it instead. This allows the reintegration process to continue, but guarantees that the client will purge its copy of the object and re-fetch the correct one before using it in future connected-mode transactions.

7.3.4 Other Certification Issues

Two additional issues are pertinent to certification: the handling of counter operations, and the acceptance of partially-certifiable sub-histories.

Counter Operations. Section 2.3.3 explained that treating counters as typed data items rather than generic read/write variables increases availability in Coda. In particular, it means that the increments and decrements of link-count and directory length attributes required by naming operations do not inhibit partitioned execution of those transactions.

In terms of disconnected operation and reintegration, treating counters as typed data items means not certifying increment and decrement operations. Attempting to certify increments and decrements as normal read and write operations would result in failure for many disconnected sub-histories that are, in fact, 1SR. This is true regardless of whether value or version certification is used. Consider the example in Figure 7.5. Value certification of the increment of d.length by T1 would fail because its value at the server at the time of certification would be 3 greater than that "read" in the actual execution. Similarly, version certification would fail because the version-id associated with d.length at the time of certification would differ from that noted by T1 while disconnected.

Not certifying increments and decrements allows legal-looking histories like that illustrated in Figure 7.5 to be reintegrated. But, how can we be sure that such histories are really legal? Stated differently, how can we be certain that the result of reintegrating histories with counter operations yields final states that are equivalent to one-copy executions of the same transactions? The answer to this question follows clearly from two observations.

Disconnected Partition | Connected Partition
T1: mkfile[d, "foo", f1, u] | T2: mkfile[d, "bar", f2, u]

Fig. 7.5. A History that would Fail Certification if Counter Operations were Certified

Consider multi-copy history $H_c \cup H_d$, in which every read access of every transaction in H_d is certifiable. Assume initially that no H_d transaction reads a data item incremented or decremented by a preceding disconnected transaction. (Note that "read" means "true read," not observing a counter's value for purposes of increment or decrement. Thus, it is admissible for several disconnected transactions to have incremented and/or decremented the same counter.) Then, since writes are only dependent on values read and not values observed for increment or decrement, it clearly must be the case that every H_d transaction in the multi-copy history read and wrote the same values as in one-copy execution $H_c \cdot H_d$. The only issue is the final values of data items that were incremented or decremented in the disconnected sub-history. But, because each increment and decrement is indifferent to the initial and final values of the counter, we can produce the final one-copy values simply by summing the increments and decrements of both sub-histories. The Coda algorithm achieves this same effect by performing each increment or decrement "in-line" on the server copies, as transactions are individually certified and replayed.

If transactions can read data items incremented or decremented by preceding disconnected transactions, then it cannot be guaranteed that they read the same values as in one-copy history $H_c \cdot H_d$. Suppose, for example, that disconnected transaction T1 and connected transaction T3 each incremented by 1 a counter whose initial value was 2, and that disconnected transaction T2 read the counter after T1's increment. Then the values read by T2 in the multi- and one-copy histories will be 3 and 4, respectively. Since, in general, we cannot know whether the computation represented by T2 would would write the same values given 3 and 4 as an input, we must conclude that the two histories are not equivalent. Consequently, certification of T2 must fail.

Fortunately, we don't need to do anything special to ensure that disconnected transactions which read counters incremented and/or decremented in both partitions fail to certify. If we re-examine Table 2.3, it's apparent that only one type of transaction can fit this specification: an rmobject that is removing an object whose link-count or length has been incremented/decremented in both partitions. But, from Table 7.2, we also see that data items of an object being removed are certified by version rather than value. Hence, certification of the rmobject is already guaranteed to fail if any update of the object occurred in the connected-partition – regardless of whether it was to a counter or some other component of the object.

Partial Reintegration. The fact that some disconnected transactions in a log are uncertifiable does not mean that all of them are incorrect. Indeed, given a subsequence of uncertifiable transactions Σ_{nc}, it's the case that reintegrating $H_d - \Sigma_{nc}$ yields a final state identical to one-copy execution $H_c \cdot H_d - \Sigma_{nc}$. A strategy of *partial reintegration*, in which only those transactions that fail certification are rejected, is therefore feasible. This would make closures smaller and, presumably, allow users to spend less effort in recovering data from them. Consider the example of Figure 7.6. With an all-or-nothing reintegration strategy, transactions T1, T2, T3, and T4 would all be rejected and a user would need to consider all four for recovery purposes. With partial reintegration, however, T4 would be reintegrated automatically and only T1, T2, and T3 would need to be considered for recovery.

Disconnected Partition	Connected Partition
T1: mkdir[*d1*, *"foo"*, *d2*, *u*]	T5: mkfile[*d1*, *"foo"*, *f1*, *u*]
T2: mkfile[*d2*, *"bar"*, *f2*, *u*]	
T3: store[*f2*, *u*]	
T4: store[*f3*, *u*]	

Transactions T1, T2, and T3 are not certifiable because T1 is in write/write conflict with T5 over d1.data[''foo''] and T2 and T3 are functionally dependent on T1. T4 is certifiable, however, and it could be legally reintegrated.

Fig. 7.6. A History that is Partially Reintegrateable

Despite the added utility of partial reintegration, the current Coda implementation does not employ it in the general case. There are three principal reasons why this is so:

- logs in which any transaction is uncertifiable have been extremely rare in practice.
- it would be awkward to communicate the result of a partially successful reintegration with our current RPC mechanism.
- if one transaction is uncertifiable, it is more likely than usual that other transactions are certifiable only because of incorrect inferences about transactional boundaries. Hence, the policy of failing the whole log gives some protection against incorrect inferences by the Coda model.

Of these three, the first is by far the most important. It has been the case in usage of the system so far that transaction certification simply does not fail very often. Given that fact, there is little incentive to perturb the system to add partial reintegration capability. Chapter 8 comments further on practical experience with the system, including the paucity of failed certifications.[6]

Special Case: Twin Transactions. Although partial reintegration is not generally employed in the current version of Coda, there is one important special case for which it is used. That is the case of *twin transactions*, in which the same transaction is executed in both the connected and disconnected partitions. Figure 7.7 gives the canonical example of this type of situation: an rmobject applied to the same file, directory or symbolic link.

Disconnected Partition	Connected Partition
T1: rmfile[d, *"foo"*, f, u]	T2: rmfile[d, *"foo"*, f, u]

Transaction T1 is not certifiable because the value it read for d.data[''foo''] is not the same as it would be in one-copy history $H_c \cdot H_d$.

Fig. 7.7. Canonical Twin Transaction Example

The normal certification procedure would fail for a twin in the disconnected sub-history and therefore cause the entire reintegration to be aborted. But this would be unnecessarily harsh, as the intent of the uncertifiable transaction has actually been reflected in the system state (albeit by its connected-partition twin). Consequently, the server does not abort the reintegration upon certification failure for a twin. Instead, it skips over the perform step for that transaction and continues on checking and performing the remaining transactions in the log. If it reaches the end without encountering other uncertifiable transactions – except, perhaps more twins – then the reintegration is considered a success. The fact that disconnected twins "failed" and, in the strict sense, were not executed is not reflected back to the user. It is assumed that this information would never be of any practical use.

Detecting twins during certification is straightforward. The defining property is that the new values of the disconnected transaction match the current values of the server copies for all updated data items.[7] Because twin-checking requires comparison of values, it is only practical to perform it when the data

---

[6] In early use of the system, there was in fact one situation that would have benefitted from partial reintegration. Some users enabled a feature that causes the C-shell [40] to write a .history file in their home directory on every logout. This feature allows commands to be conveniently recalled across login sessions. Several times it happened that a user would take his or her portable home and generate a .history file, and also log in and out of a connected client before reintegrating the disconnected session. Then, when the portable was finally reconnected and reintegration attempted, it would fail because the disconnected update of .history could not be certified. Every user to whom this happened disabled the history-saving function in their profile after their first failure.

[7] Under this definition, the "twin" of a disconnected transaction could be a set of connected partition transactions rather than an identical instance of the same

items are small and/or the likelihood of success is high. Servers therefore check for twins only for these transaction types: chown, chmod, utimes, link, unlink, rename, and rmobject. Twin-checking is not performed for store or mkobject transactions, as it is too expensive in the former case and would never succeed in the latter (because a given object cannot be created in more than one partition).

7.3.5 Summary

This subsection summarizes the certification-related aspects of Coda. It does so in two ways. First, it recaps the certification techniques that are used in Coda, and defines precisely the set of histories that are successfully reintegrated. Second, it discusses the efficacy of the approach, explaining why it works well given current system assumptions and why it might not work so well in future incarnations of the system.

The Coda Reintegrateable Histories. The basis for reintegration in Coda is object-level version certification. That technique is a direct extension of the Coda connected-mode concurrency control protocol to disconnected operation.

Using object-level version certification exclusively, however, would result in availability that is unacceptably low. We therefore have modified the approach with a number of supplemental techniques and/or policies. Most of these have been discussed in this chapter, though some were introduced or covered completely in earlier chapters. The five key techniques/policies are the following:

- the use of value rather than version certification for certain data accesses.
- the exploitation of counter semantics in the case of the link-count and directory length attributes.
- the acceptance of weak-consistency for queries.
- the quiet rejection of uncertifiable transactions that have connected-partition twins.
- the application of identity cancellation in disconnected sub-histories.

Figure 7.8 presents the preceding information graphically, in terms of history classes. The box enclosing all of the shaded areas defines the set CR, the *Coda Reintegrateable* histories. The innermost shaded box represents the histories that are recognizable with only object-level version certification, while the other shaded areas represent the contribution to availability of the five supplemental techniques/policies.

The figure also shows the relationship of the set CR to other important history classes. A key point is that two of our extensions – weakly-consistent

---

transaction type. For example, the twin of rename[d, $n1$, d, $n2$, f, u] could be the pair link[d, $n2$, f, u], unlink[d, $n1$, f, u].

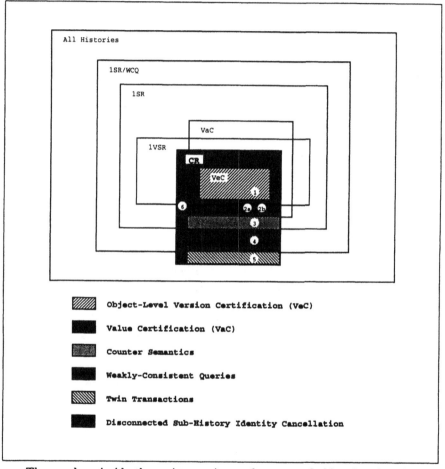

The numbers inside the various regions refer to sample histories given in Figure 7.9.

Fig. 7.8. Set CR: The Coda Reintegrateable Histories

queries and twin transactions – allow some non-1SR histories to be reintegrated. Although this violates the letter of our basic correctness criterion, in both cases the exceptions are well worthwhile. Each class of exception adds considerably to the overall usability of the system, and the departure of each from 1SR is both intuitive and well-defined.

To help make things more concrete, Figure 7.9 gives sample histories illustrating the contribution to availability of each of the five extensions. Each sample history is keyed by number against Figure 7.8 for convenience.

Efficacy of the Approach. Certification has two key advantages that make it extremely effective as the disconnected-partition merge protocol in the current Coda model. First, it is simple and efficient. Transactions can be certified one-by-one, using only information in the transaction log record and the current state of server objects. There are no complex structures to build nor any need to reconsider a transaction after it has been initially validated. As a result, reintegration time is dominated by I/O costs – the cost of moving data from client to server and from server memory to server disk – rather than computation associated with correctness-checking.

The other major advantage of certification is that transaction logging needs to be done only at the disconnected client, not also at the server. This is the key feature which distinguishes certification from other optimistic merge algorithms such as Davidson's optimistic protocol [17]. Not having to log at servers is beneficial for at least two reasons. One, it focuses resource consumption on the nodes that are actually benefitting from disconnected operation, and away from the shared component of the system. Two, given the autonomous nature of clients in the Coda architecture, it would be difficult to bound log growth in any scheme that requires servers to log while partitioned. Since clients are free to disconnect unilaterally and to stay disconnected for arbitrarily long periods, in general a server is always "partitioned" from one or more clients. A server in a log-while-partitioned scheme would therefore be logging continuously, with no clear limit to its log space requirements.

The major disadvantage of certification is that it is highly dependent on the current, inferred transaction specification of Coda. For certification to be acceptable, it must be true that $H_c \cdot H_d$ is a one-copy equivalent history for $H_c \cup H_d$ in most cases in which the multi-copy history has any one-copy equivalent. Otherwise, certification will cause many correct histories to be rejected. With the current Coda model, false rejections by certification are unlikely because update transactions write almost every data item that they read. This means that certification failure is almost always the result of write/write rather than read/write conflict between disconnected and connected partition transactions. In cases of write/write conflict there can be no one-copy equivalent of $H_c \cup H_d$.[8] Consequently, $H_c \cdot H_d$ is almost always a one-copy equivalent for $H_c \cup H_d$ whenever any one exists. Figure 7.10 il-

---

[8] This depends on the standard assumption that there are no blind writes (i.e., that read sets encompass write sets).

1. Object-Level Version Certification

Disconnected Partition	Connected Partition
store[*f1*, *u*]	store[*f2*, *u*]

2. Value Certification

(a) Connected Sub-history Identity Cancellation

Disconnected Partition	Connected Partition
mkfile[*d*, *"foo"*, *f1*, *u*]	mkfile[*d*, *"foo"*, *f2*, *u*]
	rmfile[*d*, *"foo"*, *f2*, *u*]

(b) False Conflict Avoidance

Disconnected Partition	Connected Partition
mkfile[*d*, *"foo"*, *f*, *u1*]	setrights[*d*, *u2*]

3. Counter Semantics

Disconnected Partition	Connected Partition
mkfile[*d*, *"foo"*, *f1*, *u*]	mkfile[*d*, *"bar"*, *f2*, *u*]

4. Weakly-Consistent Queries

Disconnected Partition	Connected Partition
mkfile[*d*, *"foo"*, *f1*, *u*]	mkfile[*d*, *"bar"*, *f2*, *u*]
readdata[*d*, *u*]	readdata[*d*, *u*]

5. Twin Transactions

Disconnected Partition	Connected Partition
rmfile[*d*, *"foo"*, *f*, *u*]	rmfile[*d*, *"foo"*, *f*, *u*]

6. Disconnected Sub-History Identity Cancellation

Disconnected Partition	Connected Partition
mkfile[*d*, *"foo"*, *f1*, *u*]	mkfile[*d*, *"foo"*, *f2*, *u*]
rmfile[*d*, *"foo"*, *f1*, *u*]	

Each history above corresponds to the region in Figure 7.8 bearing the same number.

Fig. 7.9. Histories Illustrating the Availability Contribution of each Reintegration Feature

lustrates one of the few possible cases of certification failure resulting from read/write conflict given the current specification.

Disconnected Partition	Connected Partition
T1: store[f, u]	T2: setrights[f, u]

Transaction T1 is not certifiable because of the read/write conflict with T2 on f.rights[u]. There is no write/write conflict, however, and the execution is 1SR because T1 · T2 is an equivalent one-copy history.

Fig. 7.10. A 1SR History that is not Certifiable due to Read/Write Conflict

As mentioned earlier, a future version of Coda is expected to support explicit, programmer-supplied transactions. In that environment it is unclear whether certification will continue to be an effective reintegration strategy. It will be possible to specify transactions in which many data items that are read are not also written. Hence, the number of situations in which read/write conflict can cause certification to falsely reject 1SR histories will dramatically increase. Figure 7.11 illustrates one simple, 1SR history using explicit transactions that would be falsely rejected by certification. Depending on the actual transactions that are programmed and the patterns of data sharing that occur, the number of false rejections could become intolerable. Consequently, the explicit transaction extension may force a change to a Davidson-style merge algorithm, in which histories from both partitions are used to establish equivalence to one-copy histories other than $H_c \cdot H_d$.

Disconnected Partition	Connected Partition
T1: readdata[f1, u] store[f2, u]	T2: store[f1, u]

This history is 1SR because it is equivalent to the one-copy execution T1 · T2. It is not certifiable, however, because it is not equivalent to the $H_c \cdot H_d$ one-copy execution, T2 · T1.

Fig. 7.11. An Explicit-Transaction History that is 1SR but not Certifiable

8. Evaluation

Disconnected operation in Coda is a reality. It is a feature in daily use by an active and growing user community. This chapter evaluates the system in both qualitative and quantitative terms. The evaluation is preceded by a report on the implementation status and a short description of the testbed environment.

8.1 Implementation Status and Testbed Environment

Implementation Status. Disconnected operation in Coda was implemented over a period of two to three years. All of the features described in this dissertation have been implemented and are, at the time of this writing (early 1993), in daily use. A version of disconnected operation with minimal functionality was demonstrated in October 1990. A more complete version was functional in early 1991 and began to be used regularly by members of the Coda group. By the end of 1991 almost all of the functionality had been implemented, and the user community had expanded to include several non-Coda group "guinea pigs." Several of these new users had no connection to systems research whatsoever. Since mid-1992 implementation work has consisted mainly of performance tuning and bug-fixing. The current user community includes about 15 active and 25 total users, with the main impediment to expansion being the lack of trained support personnel. During 1992 the code was also made available to several sites outside of CMU, and they are now using the system on a limited basis.

The initial hardware platform for both clients and servers was the IBM RT-PC. By the time disconnected operation came into active use our primary platform had switched to the more powerful DECstation line of workstations. In mid-1991 the group acquired several 386-based portable machines, and they were quickly deployed as Coda clients. Our first few portables were Toshiba T5200/100s, which were roughly as powerful as our DECstations but had smaller disk capacity. The Toshibas were soon supplemented by about fifteen IBM PS/2-L40 laptop machines, which were less powerful but considerably lighter – 6 versus 20 pounds. The L40s also had a disk of only 60 megabytes, as compared to 100 megabytes on the Toshibas. The current suite of eight Coda servers are all 5000 series DECstations with about 2 gigabytes of storage each.

Porting Coda to a new machine type is relatively straightforward. Access to kernel source is required, as there is Coda-specific kernel code at both the client and server end. As discussed in Chapter 4, however, the amount of such code is small and it is nearly all machine-independent. The bulk of the effort in porting is simply making sure that the kernel works on the specific piece of hardware and recompiling the Coda client and server code.[1]

Testbed Environment. The testbed hardware consists of the eight Coda servers and the three dozen or so workstations which regularly run a Coda Venus. The testbed volume suite currently numbers about 150. Roughly 25% of the volumes are *user* volumes, meaning that they are assigned to specific users who, initially at least, have sole administrative authority over them. Users are free, of course, to extend access rights to others by changing access-control lists on specific objects in the volume. Approximately 65% of the volumes are *project* volumes, for which administrative rights are assigned collectively to the members of a group. Most of the project volumes are used by the Coda project itself, although there are three or four other groups which have some project volumes. The other 10% of the volumes are *system* volumes, which contain program binaries, libraries, header files, and the like.

To fully understand how we have used Coda, it is necessary to know a little more about the computing environment in the CMU school of computer science (CMU-SCS). Most members of the school have one or more workstations of which they are the primary user. There are also a number of shared, "general purpose" machines which are still used for certain tasks, but most of the computing is performed at primary user workstations. Almost all of the workstations run AFS, and there are about three dozen AFS servers which provide the bulk of the shared storage.[2]

The software environment for CMU-SCS workstations is extremely rich. The facilities staff supports the standard 4.3BSD environment for about 5 or 6 different machine architectures. The environment for each machine type is spread across several system volumes in AFS, and most workstations have symbolic links into the appropriate volumes for the usual system files and directories. In addition, there is a tremendous body of "misc" software which is supported by various individuals and groups. This includes packages such as TeX/LaTeX, the Gnu tools, Scribe, various Lisp systems, MH, RCS, PVM,

---

[1] It should be noted that some of the early ports were not so straightforward, as bugs relating to different machine byte-orders had to be found and new device drivers had to be written. In some cases, the kernel port was going on simultaneously or was not thoroughly debugged, which made our own ports considerably more difficult. Credit belongs to David Steere and Lily Mummert for performing several of the Coda ports, and to members of the Mach group at CMU for assisting in certain cases.

[2] The version of AFS used is AFS-3. All unqualified references to AFS in this chapter should be bound to that version.

Mathematica, and many others. A few packages which are very widely used – for example, the base X11 window system – or which have special licensing requirements – for example, FrameMaker – are administered by the facilities staff rather than by volunteers. All told there are more than 100 misc collections in use, occupying several gigabytes of storage per machine type.

Ideally, to get the greatest degree of real usage, a mirror image of the system areas for all supported machine types would exist in Coda. That would allow a user to run Coda instead of AFS on his or her workstation(s) and still have the same, familiar CMU-SCS environment. Unfortunately, this ideal has so far been unmet. The principal reason is one of manpower. Because the CMU-SCS environment is so rich, maintaining a complete and up-to-date copy of it in Coda would be a large, ongoing task. Performing that task myself would have left too little time for system development and completing this document, and, until quite recently, there was no chance of delegating it to a staff person.

Our solution to this problem has been a compromise that differs by machine type. For our stationary clients, which are DECstations, Sun Sparcstations, and RT-PCs, Coda is currently used for user and project data only. The system portions of the namespace are all supplied via AFS, as for a standard CMU-SCS workstation. Hence, no system-maintenance effort is needed on our part for these machine types. The drawback, of course, is that disconnections from the AFS servers render our clients practically useless. Disconnected operation on these machines is therefore restricted to cases in which AFS servers are accessible but Coda servers are not. Such cases can arise when Coda servers have crashed or are down for maintenance, or when a network partitioning has separated a client from the Coda servers but not those of AFS.[3]

For our mobile clients, which are all Intel X86-based machines, the strategy of relying on AFS for system objects would not be practical. One reason is simply that the disks of the current machines are too small to support reasonably sized caches for both Coda and AFS. Even if that were not the case, however, it would still not be fruitful to rely on AFS because the laptops are almost always used in event of voluntary rather than involuntary disconnection. Hence, the AFS servers would be inaccessible at the same time the Coda servers were. Because of this, we had no real option but to maintain an X86 environment image in Coda. There are two caveats which make this maintenance task bearable. First, we support only the "base system" areas and a small number of the most critical misc packages. A large fraction of the misc software is simply not available from the laptops. Second, we are not

---

[3] In fact, our clients can still operate to some degree when disconnected from the AFS servers because (1) the most critical system objects are maintained in the client's local Unix file system rather than in AFS, and (2) AFS allows cached objects to be read (but not written) during disconnections. The utility of this arrangement, however, is still well below that in which AFS is entirely replaced by Coda.

aggressive in keeping the Coda image up to date with that in AFS. Indeed, the image is generally updated only in response to much inconvenience and persistent nagging from users. Fortunately, despite the two caveats, the process works well enough that computing with the laptops is still quite useful. Indeed, there are many more people wishing to use laptops with Coda than we can accommodate with hardware or support services.

8.2 Qualitative Evaluation

The nature of the testbed environment has meant that we have more experience with voluntary than with involuntary disconnected operation. The most common disconnection scenario has been a user detaching his or her laptop and taking it home to work in the evening or over the weekend. We have also had cases where users have taken their laptops out of town, on business trips and on vacations, and operated disconnected for a week or more.

Although the dependence of our desktop workstations on AFS has limited our experience with involuntary disconnections, it has by no means eliminated it. Particularly during the early stages of development, the Coda servers were quite brittle and subject to fairly frequent crashes. When the crash involved corruption of server meta-data – which was common – repairing the problem could take hours or even days. Hence, there were many opportunities for clients to involuntarily operate disconnected from user and project data. I believe that the insights gained from this experience are largely the same as those that would have been gained had system objects for all machine types been maintained in Coda rather than AFS.

The qualitative evaluation which follows is based on three things: my own experience as a user of the system; conversations with my users and other informal feedback that I've gotten from them over the years; and an anonymous, written survey that I distributed to all users in the spring of 1993. The survey contained approximately 20 "set" questions that involved selecting one out of four or five responses, and 3 "open" questions that allowed users to make whatever comments they wished. The first three subsections below evaluate hoarding, server emulation, and reintegration separately. The final subsection makes some observations which apply to the architecture as a whole.[4]

8.2.1 Hoarding

In our experience, hoarding has substantially improved the usefulness of disconnected operation. Disconnected cache misses have occurred, of course,

---

[4] Throughout this chapter, "we" and "our" are used to denote the set of all Coda users, and to refer to experiences and opinions common to the community at large. "I" and "my" are used for interpretations or conclusions drawn by the author.

and at times they were quite painful, but there is no doubt that both the number and the severity of those misses were dramatically reduced by hoarding. Moreover, this was realized without undue burden on users and without degradation of connected mode performance. In short, the basic premises of hoarding – use of explicit reference information, combination of implicit and explicit information via priorities, active response to disequilibrating events by the cache manager – have been wholly validated by our experience. The rest of this subsection considers the value of the main hoarding mechanisms individually, and then explores some promising directions for improvement.

Value of Specific Mechanisms.

Hoard Profiles. The aggregation of hints into profiles is an exceedingly natural step. If profiles had not been proposed and support for them had not been built into the hoard tool, it's certain that users would have come up with their own ad-hoc profile formulations and support mechanisms. No one, not even the least "system-savvy" of our guinea pigs, has had trouble understanding the concept of a profile or making modifications to pre-existing profiles on their own. And, although there has been occasional direct manipulation of the HDB via the hoard tool the vast majority of user/HDB interactions have been via profiles.

Most users employ about 5-10 profiles at any one time. Typically, this includes one profile representing the user's "personal" data: the contents of his or her root directory, notes and mail directories, etc. Several others cover the applications most commonly run by the user: the window system, editors and text formatters, compilers and development tools, and so forth. A third class of profile typically covers data sets: source code collections, publication and correspondence directories, collections of lecture notes, and so on. A user might keep a dozen or more profiles of this type, but only activate a few at a time (i.e., submit only a subset of them to the local Venus). The number of entries in most profiles is about 5-30, with very few exceeding 50.

Contrary to my expectations, there has been very little direct sharing of profiles. Most of the sharing that has occurred has been indirect; i.e., a user making his or her own copy of a profile and then changing it slightly. There appear to be several explanations for this result:

— early users of the system were not conscientious about placing application profiles in public areas of the namespace.
— as explained earlier, there aren't that many large applications currently available in Coda.
— our users are, for the most part, quite sophisticated. They are used to customizing their environments via files such as .login and .Xdefaults (and, indeed, many cannot resist the temptation to constantly do so).
— most of our users are working independently or on well-partitioned aspects of a few projects. Hence, there is not much opportunity to share data-set profiles.

I expect that in other environments these conditions will not be so pervasive, and, consequently, that the degree of direct profile sharing will be much higher.

Multi-Level Hoard Priorities. The earliest Coda design had only a single level of hoard priority; an object was either "sticky" or it was not. Sticky objects were expected to be in the cache at all times.

Although the sticky approach would have been simpler to implement and easier for users to understand, I am certain that it would have been much less pleasant to use and far less effective in avoiding misses than our multi-level priority scheme. I believe that a sticky scheme would have induced the following, undesirable types of hoarding behavior:

- a tendency to be conservative in specifying hints, to avoid pinning moderately or occasionally interesting objects in the cache.
- a similar tendency to avoid meta-expansion, as an "errant" expansion could pin vast amounts of low-utility data.
- a proliferation of hoard profiles for the same task or data set. For example, we might well have needed "small," "medium," and "large" variants of the TEX/LATEXprofiles to accommodate the needs and resource constraints of different users. And, even with such variety, there would likely have been further customization of public profiles by users in many cases. Similarly, a user might well have maintained profiles for each of his or her papers rather than a single one that encompassed them all.
- micro-management of the hoard database, to account for the facts that profiles would be smaller and more numerous and that the penalty for poor specification would be higher.

The net effect of all this is that much more time and effort would have been demanded by hoarding in a sticky scheme than is the case now. Not only would this have been unpleasant for users, but – precisely because it would have been unpleasant – they would have been less likely to put time and effort into hoarding at all. Disconnected misses would have been more frequent as a result, and the utility of disconnected operation would have been sharply reduced.[5]

One negative aspect of our priority scheme is that the range of hoard priorities is too large. Users are unable to classify objects into anywhere near 1000 equivalence classes, as the current system allows. In fact, they are often

---

[5] An argument besides simplicity which is sometimes used in favor of the sticky approach is that "you know for sure that a sticky object will be in the cache when you disconnect, whereas with priorities you only have increased probability that a hoarded object will be there." That statement is simply not true. Consider a trivial example in which ten objects have been designated sticky and they occupy 90% of the total cache space. Now suppose that all ten are doubled in size by a user at another workstation. How can the local cache manager ensure that all sticky objects are cached? Clearly it cannot. The best it can do is re-fetch an arbitrary subset of the ten, leaving the rest uncached.

confused by such a wide range of choice. Examination of many private and a few shared profiles revealed that, while most contained at least two levels of priority, few contained more than three or four. Moreover, it was also apparent that no user employs more than six or seven distinct levels across all profiles. I therefore believe that future versions of the system should offer a priority range of about 1 - 10 instead of the current 1 - 1000. Such a change would reduce uncertainty felt by some users as well as aid in the standardization of priorities across profiles.

Meta-Expansion. Meta-expansion has proven to be an indispensable feature of hoarding. Virtually all hoard profiles use it to some degree, and some use it exclusively. There are also many cases in which a profile would not even have been created had meta-expansion not been available. The effort in identifying the relevant individual names and maintaining the profile over time would simply have been too great. Indeed, it is quite possible that hoarding would never have reached a threshold level of acceptance if meta-expansion had not been an option.

A somewhat unexpected benefit of meta-expansion is that it allows profiles to be constructed incrementally. That is, a usable profile can almost always be had right away by including a single line of the form "add <rootname> d+," where <rootname> is the directory heading the application or data set of interest. Typically, it is wise also to specify a low priority so that things don't get out of hand if the sub-tree turns out to be very large. Later, as experience with the application or data set increases, the profile can be refined by removing the "root expansion" entry and replacing it with entries expanding its children. Children then known to be uninteresting can be omitted, and variations in priority can be incorporated. This process can be repeated indefinitely, with more and more hoarding effort resulting in better and better approximations of the user's preferences.

Reference Spying. The spy program has been quite useful in deriving and tuning profiles for certain applications. For example, it identified the reason why the X window system would sometimes hang when started from a disconnected workstation. It turns out that X font files are often stored in compressed format, with the X server expected to uncompress them as they are used. If the uncompress binary is not available when this occurs – say, because the client is disconnected and the program is not cached – then the server will hang. Before spy was available, mysterious events such as this would happen in disconnected mode with annoying frequency. Since spy's introduction we have been able to correct such problems on their first occurrence or, in many cases, avoid them altogether.

Periodic Hoard Walking. Background equilibration of the cache is an essential feature of hoarding. Without it there would be inadequate protection against involuntary disconnection. Even when voluntary disconnections are the primary type in an environment, periodic equilibration is still vital from a usability standpoint. First, it guards against a user who inadvertently forgets to demand a hoard walk before disconnecting. Second, it prevents a huge latency hit if and when a walk is demanded. This is very important because voluntary disconnections are often initiated when time is critical – for example, before leaving for the airport or when one is already late for dinner. Psychologically, users find it comforting that their machine is always "mostly current" with the state of the world, and that it can be made "completely current" with very little delay. Indeed, after a short break-in period with the system, users take for granted the fact that they'll be able to operate effectively if either voluntary or involuntary disconnection should occur.

Demand Hoard Walking. Foreground cache equilibration exists solely as an insurance mechanism for voluntary disconnections. The most common scenario for demand walking concerns a user who has been computing at their desktop workstation and is about to detach their laptop and take it home to continue work in the evening. In order to make sure that the latest versions of objects are cached, the user must force a hoard walk. An easy way to do this is to put the line "hoard walk" in one's .logout file. Most users, however, seem to like the reassurance of issuing the command manually, and internalize it as part of their standard shutdown procedure. In any case, the requirement for demand walking before voluntary disconnection cannot be eliminated since, for reasons enumerated in Chapter 5, the background walk period cannot be set too close to 0. This bit of non-transparency has not been a source of complaint from our users, but it could conceivably be a problem for a less sophisticated user community.

Directions for Improvement.

Reporting and Monitoring. A real weakness of the current implementation is that users cannot get an accurate picture of the cache state at their workstations. The hoard program will list the current HDB contents on demand, but its output is unstructured and generally not very helpful. There is no way, for example, to verify that every object mentioned in a hoard profile is cached, or to find out how close to eviction a particular object may be. Similarly, there is no reporting of entries that have been meta-expanded, nor of those that are inhibited from expansion for space or other reasons. No feedback is given on whether hinted objects are being referenced or not, and no useful information whatsoever is reported for cached objects that have not been hinted. Users must take on faith that their hints have been accurate and complete, and that the cache manager is "doing the right thing" in preparing for disconnection. A suite of tools or extensions to Venus which clearly reported cache state would go a long ways towards lessening user anxiety and improving the level of hoarding proficiency.

A related problem is that all communication between user and cache manager is one-way: users request actions of the cache manager and the cache manager obliges. With the two forms of information gathering that users currently have, reference spying and HDB listing, the cache manager is a passive entity. It merely reports information that it is specifically asked for and it makes no interpretations of its own. The only active role the cache manager takes in hoarding is the prescribed merging of reference and hint information (and, of course, the pre-fetching and name expansion accompanying equilibration). Although this often suffices to yield good disconnected results, it's clear that in many cases – particularly with less skillful users – a more active, interpretive cache manager could do even better.

There are a number of techniques that could be explored in turning Venus into a true *hoarding assistant*. Some are straightforward, while others border on becoming full-blown expert systems. One technique likely to be both simple and useful is the long-term correlation of reference and hint information. For example, if it were discovered that a hinted object hadn't been referenced in a very long time, Venus could either remove the hint or mark it as one that should be queried in an interactive reporting session with the user. Similarly, an unhinted object found to be referenced occasionally over a long period could become hinted automatically or be marked for user questioning. The design and evaluation of hoarding techniques such as this one is a rich and largely unexplored area. Further exploration will be conducted by another Coda student, who has proposed to make this and other issues relating to hoarding the topic of her thesis work.

Extending the Profile Concept to Venus. A design decision was made early on that hoard profiles should be strictly an application-level concept – i.e., not visible to Venus. The primary factors driving this choice were simplicity and a belief that sharing would be enhanced if profiles were ordinary files. I also didn't want to preempt other useful forms of hint generation and organization that might be discovered along the way.

Although these factors all remain valid, it's clear to me now that there should be some, optional means of conveying profile associations to Venus. Having such information recorded in Venus could be exploited in at least two ways:

– it would allow many important conditional utility relationships to be enforced. For example, it would be possible to enforce something like, "files A and B have hoard priority x on their own, but have priority $100\,x$ jointly."
– it would aid in the more sophisticated forms of reporting and monitoring alluded to earlier. For example, it would cleanly support queries like, "give me a status report for profile x."

The interface changes to make these things possible should be straightforward. Of course, the code to implement the new functionality is likely to be much more complex.

Other Specification Enhancements. Usage experience has revealed two more specification enhancements that would be worth implementing. First, although meta-expansion has proven to be extremely useful so far, there are many sensible expansions that cannot be expressed in the current specification language. For instance, it is impossible to say, "I want all children of directory foo, except for any named core." As another example, it is impossible to ask for just those children which contain the substring "coda" in their names. To accommodate expansions such as these, the language would have to be extended to accept regular expressions for *include* and *exclude* directives. These directives would then need to be applied by Venus during meta-expansion instead of the "include-all" directive that is implicitly applied now. The implementation of these changes should not take a great deal of effort.

The second enhancement concerns the normalization of priorities in hoard profiles. Profile writers currently assign priorities according to their own preferences and intuitions. For "personal" profiles, this is obviously the appropriate thing to do. For "group" or "public" profiles, however, it can create problems because everyone's conventions are not likely to be the same. Moreover, even if people basically agree on the intra-profile assignment of priorities, there are still likely to be differences in inter-profile preferences. For example, user A may consider the TEX/LATEX profile to be twice as important as the Mathematica profile while user B may feel just the opposite. Under such conditions it is impossible to assign priorities that will satisfy everyone. This phenomenon is probably at least as important in explaining why we have had so little profile sharing as are those cited earlier.

I propose to rationalize priority assignment through two simple steps. The first is to issue a policy recommendation advising profile writers to assign priorities based on a set list of criteria (e.g., use value 10 for the "essential" objects, 5 for the "useful" objects, 1 for the "discretionary" objects, and interpolate values for classes in between). The second step is to add a *scale* parameter to the hoard tool, which will have a range of 0 to 1. When supplied along with a hoard profile, the parameter will be used to weight every priority in the profile. Taken together, these two steps should allow profiles to be shared much more widely than is the case now, without imposing a global ordering of tasks and data sets.

Graphical User Interface. A general problem with the current system is that communication between users and Veni is line and text oriented. This is inefficient and often frustrating, given that the volume of data is sometimes high and that there is structure – the directory hierarchy – which is not being utilized.

A very useful exercise would be the layering of graphical interfaces on top of our tools. For example, it would be much more convenient to specify a hoard profile by clicking on nodes in a window displaying part of the file system tree than by typing pathnames into an editor. When the next generation of tools is created the importance of graphical interfaces is likely to be even greater. Consider, for example, the reporting of a profile's coverage in the cache via a graph in which cached objects are colored and uncached objects are not versus flat listings of each class of object. Indeed, I believe that for hoarding and disconnected operation to make it into the "mainstream," for them to be really accessible to non-expert users, a well-designed graphical facade will be required.

8.2.2 Server Emulation

The qualitative evaluation of server emulation centers on three issues: transparency, cache misses, and performance.

Transparency. Server emulation by Venus has been quite successful at making disconnected operation transparent to users. Many involuntary disconnections have not been noticed at all, and for those that have the usual indication has been only a pause of a few seconds in the user's foreground task at reintegration time. Even with voluntary disconnections – which cannot be totally transparent since, by definition, the user deliberately detaches from and reattaches to the network – the smoothness of the transition has generally caused the user's awareness of disconnection to fade very quickly.

The high degree of transparency is directly attributable to our use of a single client agent to support both connected and disconnected operation. If, like FACE, we had used a design with separate agents and local data stores for connected and disconnected operation, then every transition between the two modes would have been visible to users. Such transitions would – in many cases – have entailed the substitution of different versions of the same logical objects. It is hard to believe that our users – who, for the most part, are quite sophisticated and able to cope with unusual system events – would have been willing to use a system with that property.

Cache Misses. Many disconnected sessions experienced by our users – including many sessions of extended duration – involved no cache misses whatsoever. I attribute this to two primary factors. First, as noted in the preceding subsection, hoarding has been a generally effective technique for our user population. Second, most of our disconnections were of the voluntary variety, and users typically embarked on those sessions with well-formed notions of the tasks they wanted to work on. For example, they took their laptop home with the intent of editing a particular paper or working on a particular software module; they did not normally disconnect with the thought of choosing among dozens of distinct tasks.

When disconnected misses did occur, they often were not fatal to the session. In most such cases the user was able to switch to another task for which the required objects were cached. Indeed, it was often possible for a user to "fall-back" on different tasks two or three times before they gave up and terminated the session. Although this is a result I expected, it was still quite a relief to observe it in practice. It confirmed my belief that hoarding need not be 100% effective in order for the system to be useful.

Our experience with disconnected misses highlighted something else that I long suspected, that evaluating hoarding – and disconnected operation in general – according to conventional caching metrics is not very useful. The obvious way to evaluate different hoarding schemes or different users' hoarding abilities is to take reference traces from connected operation scenarios and simulate their disconnected execution given initial cache contents corresponding to the different schemes/users. The scheme/user which consistently encounters the fewest misses is then "the winner." Unfortunately, this approach is almost worthless in practice. While it's true that a miss-free disconnected run of a given reference stream is always preferable to every run of the same stream that encounters misses, the preferability of two runs involving some misses is only loosely correlated to hit ratio. As discussed earlier, this is partly due to the fact that disconnected miss penalties are generally not constant. But it is also due to the fact that the "fall-back utilities" of the two cache contents are not captured by hit ratios. That is, if the simulated activity was really being performed disconnected, the user would likely search for another task to fall-back on following a miss rather than continuing with the references contained in the trace. How useful that fall-back effort would be is orthogonal to the overall hit ratio of the simulation and, indeed, to any conventional metric.

A final point to make here is that our users have made no real use of the "block-and-retry" option for handling disconnected misses. Users have invariably relied on the default "reflect-failure" behavior instead. This is almost certainly due to the fact that all of our involuntary disconnections have occurred in the context of networks with high mean-time-to-repair (MTTR). As discussed in Subsection 6.5.1, I believe that in networks with low MTTRs block-and-retry will be a valuable and commonly used option.

Performance. An early concern was whether performance – particularly latency – would suffer as a result of adding disconnected support. The primary basis for this concern was the decision to place Venus' meta-data in RVM. As explained in Section 6.3, earlier versions of Coda had achieved good performance in part by keeping meta-data in UFS files and making updates asynchronously. This strategy could not be continued with disconnected operation because it could not bound data loss in event of process failure. Hence, there was no choice but to switch to RVM or something else which could guarantee reasonable persistence.

The initial performance of Coda with RVM was indeed pretty poor. The amount of disk activity was significantly higher than before, with much of it being synchronous. The situation was worse during disconnected than connected operation because log flushes were more frequent, but even during connected operation it was still quite bad. This result can largely be traced to two factors:

– RVM was being developed concurrently with disconnected operation and it had yet to be tuned. In particular, two key features, known as the *intra-transaction* and *inter-transaction* optimizations [87], had yet to be implemented. The intra-transaction optimization coalesces log records for overlapping and adjacent modify ranges in the same transaction, while the inter-transaction optimization does the same for no-flush transactions that have yet to be flushed to disk. The effect of these optimizations is to reduce – substantially in the case of Venus – the amount of data that must be written to disk.

– Venus did not schedule RVM flushes and truncates to take advantage of user idle time. Flushes were performed as soon as the persistence deadline was reached or the buffer size exceeded its threshold, and truncates were initiated as soon as log size reached a certain point. Very often these events occurred right in the midst of new user requests.

The performance of Venus improved dramatically once the RVM optimizations were implemented and flush and truncate scheduling were revised to exploit idle periods. Latency is now comparable to AFS-3 on the same hardware and it is no longer a serious concern of our users. Subsection 8.3.2 reports on controlled experiments which confirm this claim.

8.2.3 Reintegration

The qualitative evaluation of reintegration centers on two issues: performance and failures.

Performance. The latency of reintegration has not been a limiting factor in our experience. Most reintegrations have taken less than a minute to complete, with the majority having been in the range of 5-20 seconds. Moreover, many reintegrations have been triggered by background Venus activity rather than new user requests, so the perceived latency has often been nil. Subsection 8.3.3 reports empirically on reintegration latencies in our environment.

Something which we have not experienced but consider a potential problem is "reintegration storms." Storms could arise when many clients try to reintegrate with the same server at about the same time. This could occur, for instance, following recovery of a down server or repair of a major network artery. The result could be serious overloading of the server and greatly increased reintegration times. I believe that we've not observed this phenomenon yet because our client population is too small and because most of our disconnections have been voluntary rather than the result of failures. I do, however, have two ideas on how the problem should be addressed if/when we start to encounter it:

– have a server return a "busy" result once it reaches a threshold level of reintegration activity. Clients will back-off different amounts of time according to whether their reintegration was triggered by foreground or background activity, then retry. The back-off amounts in the foreground case will be relatively short and those in the background case will be relatively long.

- break logs into independent parts and reintegrate the parts separately. Of course, only the parts corresponding to foreground triggering should be reintegrated immediately; reintegration of the other parts should be delayed until the storm is over.

The second technique is also important for the extension of Coda to "weakly-connected" environments, and is discussed further in the future work section of Chapter 10.

Detected Failures. Failed reintegrations have been very rare in our experience with Coda. The majority of failures that have occurred have been due to bugs in the implementation rather than to uncertifiable volume logs. I believe that this mostly reflects the low degree of write-sharing intrinsic to our environment. There is no doubt, however, that it also reflects certain behavioral adjustments on the part of our users. The most significant such adjustments were the tendencies to favor indirect over direct forms of sharing, and to avoid synchronization actions when one was disconnected. So, for example, if two users were working on the same paper or software module, they would be much more likely to each make their own copy and work on it than they would to make incremental updates to the original object. Moreover, the "installation" of a changed copy would likely be delayed until a user was certain he or she was connected. Of course, this basic pattern of sharing is the dominant one found in any Unix environment. The observation here is that it appeared to be even more common among our users than is otherwise the case.

Although detected failures have been rare, recovering from those that have occurred has been painful. Our approach of forming closures and storing them at clients has several problems:

- there may not be enough free space at the client to store the closure. This is particularly true in the case of laptops, on which disk space is already precious.[6]
- the recovery process is tied to a particular client. This can be annoying if a user ever uses more than one machine.
- interpreting closures and recovering data from them requires at least an intermediate level of system expertise. Moreover, even for expert users it can be difficult to determine exactly why some reintegrations failed.

The first two limitations could be addressed by "migrating" closures to servers rather than keeping them at clients. That strategy was, in fact, part of the original design for disconnected operation, and it continues to look like a worthwhile option.

---

[6] The way such cases are handled now is inelegant: the volume in question is essentially "frozen" at the disconnected client while the user copies out any changes that they wish to preserve. The user must issue an explicit "unfreeze" command when he or she is finished, allowing Venus to go ahead and purge the non-reintegrateable state.

I believe that the third problem can be addressed through a combination of techniques that (a) reduce the number of failures that must be handled manually, and (b) simplify the handling of those that remain. Failure handling can be automated via two related techniques. The first of these is the automatic re-execution of rejected transactions by Venus. This is precisely the approach advocated by Davidson in her seminal work on optimistic replication in databases [17], and it will be feasible to use it in Coda once the proposed explicit transaction extensions are completed. Automatic re-execution would be appropriate in many cases involving the make program, for example.

The second technique for automating failure recovery is like re-execution, but it makes use of application-specific knowledge. An *application specific resolver* (ASR) [48] is a piece of code that knows how to merge divergent replicas of objects associated with a particular application. As a practical example of this approach, consider a calendar management application. The ASR in this case might merge appointment database copies by selecting all non-conflicting appointments and, for those time slots with conflicts, choosing one arbitrarily and sending mail to the rejected party(s). ASR support is also expected to be incorporated into Coda as part of the explicit transaction extensions.

A pair of techniques also come to mind for simplifying recovery from failures that cannot be fully automated. The first is just to provide more context for the user and to employ better user interface technology in the repair tools than we do now. For example, it would be quite helpful if the tool had a "side-by-side comparison" mode, in which directory-like listings of closures and the corresponding server state were presented and the user could "select" the copy of a file he or she wanted merely by clicking a mouse button.

The second recovery-simplifying technique is to employ ASR technology for the purpose of partial automation. Consider, for example, the case of two users who have both edited a document or program source file. An "interactive ASR" could be employed in this case which pops up side-by-side windows containing the two versions and highlights the sections which differ. The user could then quickly perform the merge by cutting and pasting. Similarly, a more useful version of the calendar management ASR might begin with a view of the appointment schedule merged with respect to all non-conflicting time slots, then prompt the user to choose between the alternatives for each slot that conflicts.

Undetected Failures. An interesting question is, how many testbed reintegrations succeeded that "shouldn't have?" In other words, how often were logs certifiable with respect to the transaction boundaries inferred by the system when, in fact, they were not certifiable with respect to the "true" boundaries in the minds of the programmers and users?

Unfortunately, it is impossible to give a solid answer to this question. We simply don't know what the true boundaries were in every case, nor even in which cases the inferred boundaries were wrong. Indeed, if the system had known the true boundaries we certainly would have had it reject those cases which were truly uncertifiable!

However, I strongly suspect that there were very few instances of "undetected failure" in our usage. The reasons are essentially those that resulted in low rates of detected failure: intrinsically low degrees of sharing in the environment, and behavioral adjustments that made sharing during disconnected periods even less likely than usual. Of course, the sharing referred to here is read/write rather than write/write, but the same principles apply.

8.2.4 General Observations

Optimistic Replication. The decision to use optimistic rather than pessimistic replica control was undoubtedly the most fundamental one in the design of Coda. Having used the system for more than two years now, I remain convinced that the decision was the correct one for our type of environment.

Any pessimistic protocol must, one way or another, allocate the rights to access objects disconnected to particular clients. This allocation involves an unpleasant compromise between availability and ease of use. The less involved are users in the allocation process, the greater is the responsibility that falls to the system and, consequently, the worse are the allocation decisions. Bad allocation decisions translate directly into lowered availability; a disconnected client either does not have a copy of a critical object, or it has a copy but it cannot use it because it was not allocated the necessary rights. On the other hand, the more involved are users in the allocation process, the less transparent and convenient to use does the system become.

The optimistic replication approach avoids the need to make allocation decisions altogether. Our users have never been faced with the situation in which they are disconnected and have an object cached, but they cannot access it because of insufficient replica control rights. Similarly, they have never had to formally "grab control" of an object in anticipation of disconnection, nor have they had to "wrest control" from another client that had held rights they didn't really need. The absence of these situations has been a powerful factor in making the system effective and pleasant to use.

Of course, there is an advantage of pessimistic over optimistic replica control, which is that reintegration failures never have to be dealt with. Our experience indicates that, in a Unix file system environment, this advantage is not worth much because there simply are very few failed reintegrations. The amount and nature of sharing in the workload make reintegration failures unlikely, and users adopt work habits that reduce their likelihood even further. In effect, the necessary degree of cross-partition synchronization is achieved voluntarily, rather than being enforced by a pessimistic algorithm.

Herlihy [37] once gave the following motivation for optimistic concurrency control, which applies equally well to optimistic replica control:

...[optimistic replica control] is based on the premise that it is more effective to apologize than to ask permission.

In our environment, the cases in which one would wrongfully be told "no" when asking permission vastly outnumber those in which a "no" would be justified. Hence, we have found it far better to suffer the occasional indignity of making an apology than the frequent penalty of a wrongful denial.

Security. There have been no detected violations of security in our use of Coda, and I strongly suspect that there have been no undetected violations either. The friendliness of our testbed environment is undoubtedly one important explanation for this. However, I believe that the Coda implementation would do well security-wise even under much more hostile conditions.

The basis for this belief is the faithful emulation of the AFS security model. Coda servers demand to see a user's credentials on every client request, including reintegration. Credentials can be stolen, but this requires subversion of a client or a network-based attack. Network attacks can be thwarted through the use of (optional) message encryption, and the danger of stolen credentials is limited by associating fixed lifetimes with them. Access-control lists further limit the damage due to credential theft by confining it to areas of the namespace legitimately accessible to the subverted principal. Disconnected operation provides no back-doors that can be used to circumvent these controls.[7]

AFS has provided good security at large-scale and under circumstances that are traditionally somewhat hostile. Indeed, I know of no other distributed file system in widespread use that provides better security with a comparable level of functionality. This strongly suggests that security would not be a factor limiting Coda's deployment beyond our testbed environment.

Public Workstations. The undergraduate computing facilities at CMU include a number of public workstation clusters. Although it was never a primary goal to support disconnected operation in that domain, it was something that I hoped would be possible and which influenced Coda's early design to some degree.

Our experience with disconnected operation has convinced me that it is simply not well suited to public access conditions. The key problem is essentially one of security. Without disconnected operation, it's the case that when a user leaves a public workstation his or her data is all safely at servers and he or she is totally independent of the given client. This allows careful users to flush their authentication tokens and their sensitive data from the cache when they depart, and to similarly "scrub" the workstation clean when

---

[7] Subsection 7.2.3 described a security hole that does, in fact, exist in the current implementation: the back-fetching of data during reintegration over an insecure channel. However, that subsection also described a simple means of closing the hole.

they arrive. But with disconnected operation, scrubbing is not necessarily an option. The departing user cannot scrub if he or she has dirty objects in the cache, waiting to be reintegrated. The need to leave valid authentication tokens with the cache manager is particularly worrying, as that exposes the user to arbitrary damage. And even if damage does not arise due to security breach, the departing user still must worry that a future user will scrub the machine and thereby lose his or her pending updates.

The other major factor that makes disconnected operation unsuited to public workstations is the latency associated with hoarding. Loading a cache with one's full "hoardable set" can take many minutes. Although this is done in the background, it can still slow a client machine down considerably. Moreover, if a user intends to use a machine for only a few tens of minutes or an hour – as is often the case with public machines – then the effort is likely to be a total waste. It is only when the cost of hoarding can be amortized over a long usage period that it becomes a worthwhile exercise.

8.3 Quantitative Evaluation

The preceding sections reported that users can effectively operate disconnected from a shared file store. Indeed, most users are enthusiastic about doing so. Those facts alone suffice to prove the thesis stated in Chapter 1 of this document. However, it is also important to characterize the parameters of disconnected operation – to identify the ranges over which it is effective and to quantify the costs involved. To that end, this section quantitatively addresses four key questions concerning disconnected operation:

1. how much client storage is required to satisfy disconnections of varying duration?
2. what is the effect on file system performance of disconnected operation support?
3. how long does it take to reintegrate typical disconnected sessions?
4. how likely are write/write conflicts across clients?

Several different experiments were conducted and the results analyzed to answer these questions. The results in each case and the methodology behind each experiment are given in the four subsections that follow.

8.3.1 Client Storage Requirements

Clients require non-volatile storage in order to support serious disconnected operation. The amount of storage required is a function of many factors: the type of activity the user is engaged in, the frequency with which he or she changes tasks, the duration of each disconnection, the effectiveness of hoarding, and the sensitivity of the user to disconnected cache misses.

The consumption of non-volatile storage during a disconnection can be divided into three classes:

- *cache in use* – space managed by Venus which has been directly used to satisfy disconnected file requests. This includes fsobjs, container files, and directory and symbolic link contents that have been read or written, as well as the volume log records recording the history of disconnected update transactions.
- *cache in reserve* – space managed by Venus which has not been directly used to satisfy disconnected file requests. This includes fsobjs, container files, and directory and symbolic link contents that are cached but have not been referenced, plus space for the hoard database.
- *other system overhead* – space not managed by Venus, but which is necessary for the client to function. This includes the kernel image and boot files, the cache manager binary, other files needed to bring up the machine (e.g., password and host name files), devices, directories for temporary objects (e.g., /tmp), and paging space. All of these space consumers are supported by a local Unix file system mounted at boot time.

The last of these classes is easy to characterize and plan for. Although the amount of paging space needed may grow somewhat over time, the total overhead requirement is fairly static for a given user and machine type. On our L40s roughly 25 megabytes has been allocated for this purpose, and that amount has almost always proved sufficient for disconnections lasting upwards of a week.

The first two classes – space used and space held in reserve by Venus – are the interesting ones. From our use of the L40s, it's clear that about 35 megabytes ($= 60 - 25$) is sufficient for both classes for many disconnections lasting one to several days. However, it's also true that 35 megabytes has been a little too small for some shorter disconnections (e.g., a day in duration), and clearly insufficient for some longer ones (e.g., a week in duration).

To obtain a better understanding of client storage requirements, I simulated the disconnected mode execution of a number of file reference traces taken from workstations in our environment. The simulator reported the amounts of cache resources in use for each trace at regular intervals of simulated time. From these figures we therefore have a clear view of how one of the two remaining client storage classes – cache space used – changes over time. The other storage class – cache space held in reserve – is a topic for future work and is not characterized by this analysis. Subsection 8.3.1 below gives details of the traces and the simulation technique, while Subsection 8.3.1 reports the key results.

Methodology. The file reference traces used in the analysis were collected by Lily Mummert [61]. She began an extensive tracing project at CMU in the fall of 1990 which has continued to the present day. Approximately twenty-five Unix workstations have run tracing kernels and reported data for at least part of that period. The total amount of trace data archived so far exceeds 150 gigabytes and consists of several thousand individual traces. The traces are at the level of Unix system calls and contain data on all of the file system types supported by a given machine: Coda, AFS, NFS, and UFS (4.3BSD/FFS). Each trace record includes copies of all relevant system call arguments. Traced workstations by default record all file system calls except read and write. Read/write tracing can be enabled as an option, as can name resolution tracing.

Ten traces were selected for analysis from the period of February to October 1991. The selected traces consist of two groups of five each. The first group is denoted the "Work-Day" set and the second the "Full-Week" set. The Work-Day traces are each 12 hours long and cover a typical working day for the workstation's primary user. The types of activity engaged in in each case were software development, document preparation, electronic mail, and other tasks typical of academic computing users. The traces were carefully screened to ensure that the primary users were active on the given days. The Full-Week traces are each 168 hours long. They too were screened to make sure that they covered active seven-day periods for the workstation users. Table 8.1 lists the vital statistics of each selected trace.[8]

Writing and validating a simulator that precisely models the complex caching behavior of Venus would be quite difficult. That difficulty was avoided by modifying Venus to act as its own simulator. When running in simulator mode, Venus is driven by trace records rather than by messages from the kernel. Code to perform I/O on container files is stubbed out in simulator mode, and RVM requests are directed to a special area of virtual memory rather than to a real recoverable segment. Code to perform network I/O by the probe and other daemons is also stubbed out. Network I/O for purposes of fetching or writing back objects is not explicitly disabled because every volume is always in the emulating state. Hence, those code branches are avoided indirectly. Trace objects from outside the Coda namespace are converted to Coda objects by a function which maps each AFS volume or UFS or NFS file system to its own Coda volume.

Two additional aspects of simulator mode are significant. First, since the purpose of the simulation is to measure the extent of resource usage, object replacement must be disabled. Thus when a resource limit is encountered, say for container blocks or log records, the limit is transparently raised instead of replacing an object or signalling a resource exhaustion condition. Second, Venus must transparently "load" a pre-existing object into the cache the first time it is referenced. This is because the trace does not contain a snapshot of

---

[8] The post-processing package that accompanies the traces allows filtering based on arbitrary begin and end times (as well as other criteria). Hence, it was not necessary to find traces that were exactly 12 or 168 hours in duration, or whose active periods coincided with the actual start time of the trace. Trace sub-periods were extracted by supplying the corresponding filter specification to the post-processing routines.

Trace Identifier	Name	Machine Type	Simulation Start	Trace Records
Work-Day #1	brahms	IBM RT-PC	25-Mar-91, 11:00	195289
Work-Day #2	holst	DECstation 3100	22-Feb-91, 09:15	348589
Work-Day #3	ives	DECstation 3100	05-Mar-91, 08:45	134497
Work-Day #4	mozart	DECstation 3100	11-Mar-91, 11:45	238626
Work-Day #5	verdi	DECstation 3100	21-Feb-91, 12:00	294211
Full-Week #1	concord	Sun 4/330	26-Jul-91, 11:41	3948544
Full-Week #2	holst	DECstation 3100	18-Aug-91, 23:21	3492335
Full-Week #3	ives	DECstation 3100	03-May-91, 12:15	4129775
Full-Week #4	messiaen	DECstation 3100	27-Sep-91, 00:15	1613911
Full-Week #5	purcell	DECstation 3100	21-Aug-91, 14:47	2173191

These traces were selected from over 1700 collected during February-October 1991. The selection process was simplified tremendously by a set of summary statistics for each trace, computed and archived by Lily Mummert. The summaries allowed traces with substantial idle periods to be filtered out immediately, and identified the points at which users began working seriously. The "Trace Records" column refers to the number of records in each trace during the simulated period (i.e., between simulation-start and simulation-start plus 12 or 168 hours).

Table 8.1. Vital Statistics for the Work-Day and Full-Week Traces

the workstation's initial state and, in the case of the distributed file system types, there is no way to recreate a "fetch" that was made during the real execution by the workstation cache manager.

Results.

Optimized Cache Space Usage. Figure 8.1 shows the *high-water mark* of cache space usage for the Work-Day and Full-Week traces as a function of time. The high-water mark is simply the maximum cache space in use at the current and all previous points in the simulation. The high-water mark therefore never declines, although the current cache space in use may (due to the deletion of objects). Sub-figures (a) and (b) plot the high-water marks of each trace in the Work-Day and Full-Week sets, respectively.

The curves in Figure 8.1 indicate that cache space usage tends to grow rapidly at the start, but that it tapers off dramatically in short order. For example, most of the Work-Day traces had reached 80% of their 12-hour high-water marks within a few hours of their start. Similarly, all but one of the Full-Week traces had reached a substantial fraction of their 7-day high-water marks by the end of the second day. Note that it was not the case that the workstations simply became idle after the first parts of the traces; the

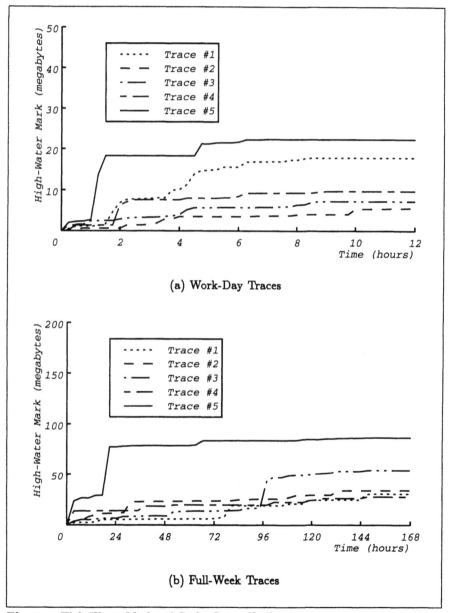

Fig. 8.1. High-Water Marks of Cache Space Used

traces were carefully selected to ensure that users were active right through to the end of the simulated periods.

The phenomenon exhibited by the traces is, of course, that of *working sets*. The early rise in cache space usage represents the first references to objects in the user's working set. Subsequent slower growth reflects the fact that most working set objects are already in the cache and only the occasional new reference or extension of a cached object requires any additional space. The final phase of working set evolution results in a near-flattening of the high-water mark curve. This indicates that almost all of the new space required is balanced by truncation or deletion of objects already cached and in the working set. The only substantial increase in high-water mark likely to occur after this point corresponds to turnover of the tasks that compose the working set. For example, if the user begins work on a new component of a software development, then that may result in a surge of the high-water mark. In the traces that I simulated there is only one significant instance of this effect – Full-Week trace #3 showing a rise of 30 megabytes around the 96 hour mark. Apart from that one case, the task composition of working sets appears to have been pretty static.

The levels of the curves in Figure 8.1 are very encouraging for disconnected operation. The most expansive of the Work-Day traces peaked out at below 25 megabytes, with the median of the traces peaking at around 10. For the Full-Week traces, the maximum level reached was under 100 megabytes and the median was under 50. Subtracting even the largest of these figures from the disk capacity of today's typical desktop workstation leaves hundreds of megabytes to cover cache reserve requirements and system overhead. The fact that the latter is satisfiable in 25-50 megabytes means that one to several hundred megabytes should almost always be available to support cache reserve. Although we do not yet have scientific evidence concerning cache reserve requirements, intuition suggests that this should be plenty for most week-long disconnections.

The cache space usage results are also encouraging for disconnected operation on today's typical laptop machines, although to a lesser degree than in the desktop case. A laptop such as an L40 can satisfy system overhead and the median work-day amount for cache usage with 20-25 megabytes left over for cache reserve. This suggests – and it is confirmed by our actual usage experience – that a user moderately proficient at hoarding can survive many one-day disconnections with no or only a few cache misses. Satisfying system overhead plus the maximum work-day amount for cache usage leaves only 5-10 megabytes of storage for cache reserve, however. This suggests – and it is again confirmed by our experience – that some one-day disconnections can only be "survived" if the user is an extremely proficient hoarder or is tolerant of a fair number of cache misses. For disconnections of a week's duration, the amount of reserve space in the median case is around zero and it is well into the negative range for the maximum case. This means that a machine such as an L40 cannot support all or perhaps even the majority of one-week disconnections without a substantial number of misses. Again, this is consistent with our usage experience. Fortunately, laptops with larger disks than the L40 are already on the market, and machines with disks the size of today's desktop workstations are already in view. For that generation of machine the problem of limited cache reserve is unlikely to be serious for disconnection durations of a week or even more.

Unoptimized Cache Space Usage. The results of Figure 8.1 reflect simulations performed with the cache optimizations of Chapter 6 enabled. Two of those optimizations have to do with transaction cancellation: they reclaim space whenever a transaction overwrites an earlier one or when a set of transactions constitute an identity subsequence. The third optimization saves space by keeping a reference to a container file in a store record rather than a copy of the new file contents.

In order to understand how much space these optimizations save in practice, the simulator was augmented to report cache usage statistics with the optimizations turned off as well as on. Figure 8.2 compares the high-water marks of the traces with optimizations enabled and disabled. Sub-figure (a) covers the Work-Day set and sub-figure (b) the Full-Week set. Each curve represents the median values of the five corresponding individual traces.

The differences between the curves in each case are substantial. After an initial period in which the two curves increase more or less together, the unoptimized curves continue to increase while the optimized curves taper off. For the Work-Day traces, the unoptimized total has grown to nearly twice that of the optimized case by the 12-hour mark. The trend continues unabated with the Full-Week traces, with the unoptimized total being more than 5 times that of the optimized case at the end of the week. This equates to a difference of more than 145 megabytes. The slopes of the two lines indicate that the difference would increase even further over periods of greater length.

Table 8.2 shows that the differences for certain individual traces are even more striking. That table lists the unoptimized and optimized totals for each trace at its termination (i.e., after 12 or 168 hours). In addition, each total is broken down into its two constituents: container space and RVM space. The greatest savings tend to be realized in container space, although the RVM space savings are also substantial in most cases. The far right column shows the ratio of unoptimized to optimized total space usage. The maximum ratio for the Work-Day traces is 3.1, indicating that more than three times the amount of space would have been needed without the optimizations. The maximum ratio for the Full-Week traces is an astonishing 28.9, which corresponds to a difference of more than 850 megabytes.[9]

---

[9] Out of curiosity, Full-Week trace #1 trace was examined to see what activity was accounting for all of the reclaimable space. It turned out that the user of this workstation was building the Standard ML compiler and associated tools. Each build would re-write a few files whose total size was several megabytes. Over the course of the week more than 100 iterations of this cycle were performed.

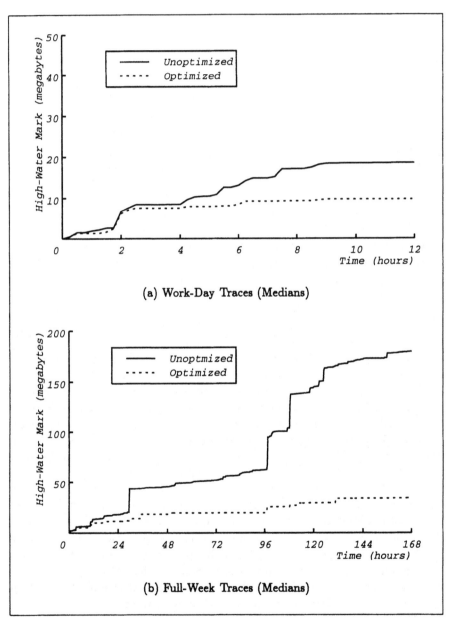

(a) Work-Day Traces (Medians)

(b) Full-Week Traces (Medians)

Fig. 8.2. Optimized versus Unoptimized Cache Space High-Water Marks

Trace	Container Space		RVM Space		Total Space		
	Unopt	Opt	Unopt	Opt	Unopt	Opt	Ratio
Work-Day #1	34.6	15.2	2.9	2.7	37.5	17.8	2.1
Work-Day #2	14.9	4.0	2.3	1.5	17.2	5.5	3.1
Work-Day #3	7.9	5.8	1.6	1.4	9.5	7.2	1.3
Work-Day #4	16.7	8.2	1.9	1.5	18.6	9.7	1.9
Work-Day #5	59.2	21.3	1.2	1.1	60.4	22.3	2.7
Full-Week #1	872.6	25.9	11.7	4.8	884.3	30.6	28.9
Full-Week #2	90.7	28.3	13.3	5.9	104.0	34.2	3.0
Full-Week #3	119.9	45.0	46.2	9.1	165.9	54.0	3.1
Full-Week #4	222.1	23.9	5.5	3.9	227.5	27.7	8.2
Full-Week #5	170.8	79.0	9.1	7.7	179.8	86.5	2.1

The figures in the "Unopt" and "Opt" columns are in megabytes.

Table 8.2. Optimized versus Unoptimized High-Water Marks at Simulation End

The results of Figure 8.2 and Table 8.2 confirmed what I intuitively believed – that the cancellation and store record optimizations are essential for managing space at a disconnected client. The degree of their importance was something of a surprise, however. Subsection 8.3.3 later in this chapter reports that the cancellation optimizations are equally important for keeping the time cost of reintegration low.

8.3.2 Task Latency

A workstation user's main criterion for judging file system performance is latency. What he or she cares about most is how long it takes for common file system tasks to be performed. Disconnected operation raises two questions regarding latency. First, how does the latency of a task executed in disconnected mode compare with that of the same task executed while the workstation is connected? Second, how does the latency of a task executed in a disconnected-capable system compare with that of the same task in a system without support for disconnected operation? Both of these questions are addressed in this subsection.

Methodology. Task latency was evaluated by comparing the execution times of two well-defined tasks under a variety of conditions. The first of these tasks is the Andrew benchmark [39], which has been widely used to compare file system performance in the past. The benchmark operates on a collection of files constituting the source code of a simple Unix application. Its input is a subtree of 70 files totalling 200 kilobytes in size. There are five distinct phases in the benchmark: *MakeDir*, which constructs a target subtree that is identical in structure to the source subtree; *Copy*, which copies every file from the source subtree to the target subtree; *ScanDir*, which recursively traverses the target subtree and examines the status of every file in it;

ReadAll, which scans every byte of every file in the target subtree twice; and *Make*, which compiles and links all the files in the target subtree. The second of the tasks is the compilation and linking of the current version of Venus. This is comparable to the *Make* phase of the Andrew benchmark, but the application being built in this case is roughly an order of magnitude larger.

Each of the tasks was executed and measured in four file system configurations: connected-mode Coda, disconnected-mode Coda, AFS-3, and the local Unix file system. The client machine was the same in every case: a DECstation 5000/200 with 32 megabytes of memory and a 1.8 gigabyte hard disk. The server in the Coda configurations was an identical machine, and in the AFS-3 case it was a Sun 4/65 with comparable memory and disk space. Client and servers were connected by a 10 megabit/second ethernet. The local file system at the client was the 4.3BSD fast file system (FFS). In the connected-mode Coda and AFS-3 cases, the client cache was warmed with the initial set of files prior to the first iteration of each task.

Results. The results of executing the Andrew benchmark and Venus make tasks in the various configurations are summarized in Table 8.3. The first number in each column is the average time out of three trials. The figures in parentheses are standard deviations.

Task	Disconnected Coda	Connected Coda	AFS-3	Unix 4.3BSD
Andrew Benchmark	114 (4)	140 (3)	122 (3)	95 (3)
MakeDir	1 (0)	5 (1)	5 (0)	2 (0)
Copy	13 (1)	31 (0)	18 (2)	10 (2)
ScanDir	10 (0)	11 (0)	11 (0)	9 (1)
ReadAll	25 (3)	23 (1)	23 (1)	16 (1)
Make	65 (1)	71 (3)	65 (4)	58 (1)
Venus Make	1319 (11)	1389 (18)	1361 (14)	1182 (5)

This data was obtained with a DECstation 5000/200 client. The servers in the Coda and AFS-3 configurations were a DECstation 5000/200 and a Sun 4/65, respectively. The first number of each pair is the mean of three trials. The second number is the standard deviation. All times are in seconds.

Table 8.3. Task Latency

Disconnected- versus Connected-Mode Coda. Table 8.3 shows that disconnected mode has noticeably lower latency than connected mode for both of the tasks. This is consistent with users' subjective view of the system on a wide variety of other file-intensive tasks.

Although this result may seem surprising at first, there is a simple explanation for it. The reason is that the disconnected client must only update its local state for each mutating transaction, whereas the connected client must additionally update the state of the server. Although there is some write-behind which allows overlapping of server communication with subsequent file operations, there is a synchronous component of every update transaction that cannot be avoided. The effect of synchronous server communication can be clearly seen by examining the sub-task results of the Andrew benchmark. They show that all of the difference between disconnected and connected mode Coda is accounted for by the *MakeDir*, *Copy*, and *Make* phases of the benchmark. Those are precisely the phases that involve server communication. The *ScanDir* and *ReadAll* phases do not require any server communication, and their times are virtually identical in the two cases.

The performance disadvantage of connected mode could be reduced considerably by employing true copy-back of updates instead of the largely write-through protocol that Coda uses now. True copy-back would allow many redundant stores and cancelable directory operations to be absorbed locally, without server communication. In addition, it would allow Venus to schedule write-backs at times of low client load rather than have them contend with later requests in the same bursts of activity. True copy-back in connected mode is very likely to be implemented at some point in the future.[10]

Coda versus AFS-3 and UFS. Table 8.3 indicates that Coda performance is competitive with that of AFS-3. Disconnected mode Coda is somewhat faster than AFS-3 and connected mode Coda is somewhat slower. This is solid evidence that disconnected operation can be supported without sacrificing the main-line performance of a distributed file system.

Disconnected mode Coda is faster than AFS-3 for the same reason that it is faster than connected mode Coda – it doesn't write results back to servers. The more interesting comparison is connected mode Coda versus AFS-3. Why is connected mode Coda any slower? There are, in fact, several reasons:

- RPC overhead is higher in Coda than in AFS-3. This is partially due to the fact that the Coda Venus is a user-level process (and thus data must be copied more times and more context switches must be made than in the AFS-3 case), and partially because AFS-3 is a commercial product and its subsystem has been tuned and updated over the years to incorporate new RPC technology. In contrast, Coda's RPC package is largely unchanged from its initial design and implementation in AFS-2 7 years ago.
- request processing in general is faster in AFS-3 than in Coda because the AFS-3 cache manager is in the kernel and the Coda cache manager is not.

---

[10] Anecdotally, users have been known to achieve copy-back manually, by intentionally disconnecting their workstations before performing file-intensive tasks (such as large compiles) and then reconnecting when the task is finished. If users are willing to go to this much trouble then, clearly, the absence of copy-back is a real deficiency of the system.

– the server replication protocol used in Coda requires that meta-data changes be committed to stable storage before the server replies to a client's RPC [86]. Consequently, every update-class RPC requires at least one synchronous disk write in Coda. In AFS-3 the server is free to perform most disk writes asynchronously, and therefore can usually return to the client with less delay than is possible in Coda.

The combination of these three factors likely accounts for all of the discrepancy between the connected mode Coda and the AFS-3 results.[11]

Table 8.3 also indicates that Coda has higher latency than the local Unix file system. Comparing the average of the two Coda figures with the UFS result for each task shows that Coda is approximately 25% slower for the Andrew benchmark and 13% slower for the Venus make. While these are not ideal results, they do not indicate that Coda is tremendously slower than UFS. Indeed, since most real tasks are less file system intensive than these two, the perceived degradation of Coda is more like 10 than 20 percent. When true copy-back is added to connected mode and some additional performance tuning is completed, the degradation of Coda should be even less; probably 5-10% for file system intensive tasks and effectively 0 for most others. This is undoubtedly a reasonable price to pay for the benefits of distribution and availability that are offered by Coda.

8.3.3 Reintegration Latency

Reintegration latency is proportional to the "net" amount of update activity performed at the disconnected client. That is, it is a function of the update activity that remains after all cancellation optimizations have been taken. In our use of the system, most one-day disconnections have resulted in reintegration times of a minute or less, and longer disconnections in reintegration times of at most several minutes. This subsection reports on experiments that were conducted to characterize reintegration times and the effect of the cancellation optimizations in more precise terms.

Methodology. Reintegration latency was evaluated by performing specific tasks at a disconnected client and then reconnecting and measuring the time to reintegrate. In addition to the elapsed time, statistics concerning the number of log records reintegrated and the number of bytes back-fetched were also collected.

Two sets of tasks were used in the experiments. The first set consisted of the two tasks used in the task latency evaluation: the Andrew benchmark and the Venus make. The second set of tasks was the "replay" of the traces

---

[11] A fourth factor which may have some weight is that the servers in the Coda and AFS-3 tests were not identical (DECstation 5000/200 in the Coda tests, Sun 4/65 in the AFS-3 tests). The processing and I/O capabilities of these machines are believed to be quite similar, but even modest differences could account for some of the observed variation.

that were simulated in the cache space usage experiments. This was arranged by modifying the simulator to output two new files at the termination of each run. The *skeleton* file contains a list of commands which can be used to construct the start-of-trace skeleton of the portions of the namespace mutated during the simulation. The *replay* file contains a list of commands which can be used to re-perform the mutating transactions of the trace in any area which has been initialized with the skeleton. Each "trace-replay" experiment was conducted as follows: (1) from a connected client, create a skeleton in a scratch area of the Coda namespace; (2) disconnect the client and perform the replay; (3) reconnect the client and observe the reintegration. The reintegration measured by this procedure is identical to that which would have followed disconnected execution of the high-level tasks contained in the trace. All experiments were run at times when the client and server were lightly loaded, but no attempt was made to exclude other activity entirely.

In order to quantify the effect of the cancellation optimizations on reintegration, statistics were also collected concerning the number of log records that would have been reintegrated and the number of bytes that would have been back-fetched had the optimizations been disabled. In the cases of the Andrew benchmark and Venus make experiments, these figures were extracted directly from Venus at the termination of each reintegration. For the trace-replay experiments these figures were derived from the existing set of statistics output by the simulator.

Results.

Optimized Reintegration Latency. Table 8.4 reports the latency, log record, and back-fetch figures for the reintegration experiments. Latency is reported separately for each of the three reintegration phases – prelude, interlude, postlude – as well as in total. The apportionment of latency between the three phases varied slightly from experiment to experiment, but on average the proportions were about 10, 80, 10 for prelude, interlude, and postlude, respectively. Figure 8.3 shows the total latency information in graphical form.

The results of Table 8.4 and Figure 8.3 confirm that typical one-day disconnections in our environment take a minute or less to reintegrate. The Andrew benchmark, Venus make, and four of the five Work-Day trace-replay experiments all reintegrated in under 40 seconds. The fifth Work-Day trace-replay experiment took only slightly more than a minute to reintegrate.

The results of the seven-day reintegration experiments are mostly consistent with our qualitative observations as well. Four of the five Full-Week trace-replay experiments reintegrated in under five minutes, with three completing in three minutes or less. The other trace-replay experiment is an outlier; it required a good 20 minutes to reintegrate. It turns out that the user of that workstation had spent most of the trace period conducting file system experiments himself. His experiments consisted of growing and shrinking large sub-trees over and over again. Although it is not surprising that this replay took longer than the others, the magnitude of the difference is puzzling.

Task	Log Record Total	Back-Fetch Total	Latency Pre-lude	Latency Inter-lude	Latency Post-lude	Total	
Andrew Benchmark	203	1.2	1.8	7.5	.8	10	(1)
Venus Make	146	10.3	1.4	36.2	.4	38	(1)
Work-Day #1 Replay	1422	4.9	6.5	54.7	10.7	72	(5)
Work-Day #2 Replay	316	.9	1.9	9.8	1.7	14	(1)
Work-Day #3 Replay	212	.8	1.0	6.2	.9	8	(0)
Work-Day #4 Replay	873	1.3	2.9	23.2	5.9	32	(3)
Work-Day #5 Replay	99	4.0	.9	20.5	.5	22	(2)
Full-Week #1 Replay	1802	15.9	15.2	138.8	21.9	176	(3)
Full-Week #2 Replay	1664	17.5	16.2	129.1	15.0	160	(2)
Full-Week #3 Replay	7199	23.7	152.6	881.3	183.0	1217	(12)
Full-Week #4 Replay	1159	15.1	5.1	77.4	7.0	90	(1)
Full-Week #5 Replay	2676	35.8	28.2	212.8	31.7	273	(9)

This data was obtained with a DECstation 5000/200 client and server. The Back-Fetch figures are in megabytes. Latency figures are in seconds. Each latency number is the mean of three trials. The numbers in parentheses in the "Latency Total" column are standard deviations. Standard deviations for the individual phases are omitted for space reasons.

Table 8.4. Reintegration Latency with Log Optimizations Enabled

One would expect reintegration latency to be directly proportional to the number of log records and the amount of data back-fetched. To test this hypothesis, I performed regression analysis on the figures in Table 8.4. A simple linear regression did not yield a very good fit. Non-linear regression, however, yielded excellent results. A fit of the number of log records, the square of that quantity, and the amount of data back-fetched had an R^2 value of .999. The regression coefficients were .026 for the number of log records, .0000186 for its square, and 2.535 for the number of megabytes back-fetched. The first of these implies a direct overhead per log record of 26 milliseconds. This seems about right, given that many records will require at least one disk access at the server during the interlude phase. The third coefficient implies a rate of about 400 kilobytes/second for bulk data transfer. This too seems about right, given that the maximum transfer rate between 2 DECstation 5000/200s on an ethernet that we've observed is 476 kilobytes/second.[12]

The presence of the quadratic term implies that there are supra-linear steps in our implementation. An inspection of the code following these experiments immediately revealed two places where, indeed, quadratic algorithms

---

[12] This rate has been observed transferring large files via FTP. Rates for smaller files are lower due to various fixed overheads.

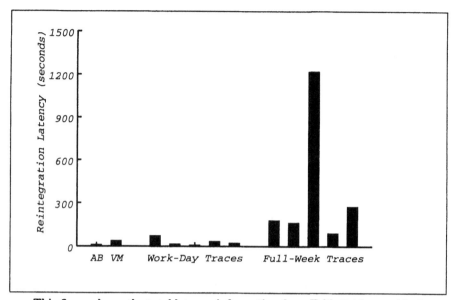

This figure shows the total latency information from Table 8.4 in graphical form. The bar labeled "AB" represents the Andrew Benchmark experiment and that labeled "VM" the Venus Make.

Fig. 8.3. Reintegration Latency with Log Optimizations Enabled

were being used: sorting vnodes into fid-order at the server, and replacing temporary fids with real ones at the client. It's likely that other supra-linear steps exist in our code as well. Given these facts, it's clear why the Full-Week #3 trace-replay experiment took so much longer than the others. At the ranges of log size associated with the other experiments, the quadratic steps did not dominate the total reintegration time. But at the number of log records associated with the Full-Week #3 trace-replay experiment, the quadratic steps account for nearly 80% of the total. An important piece of future engineering work is to reduce the complexity of the quadratic steps so that large logs don't take unbearably long to reintegrate.[13]

It is worth making two additional points about reintegration latency here. First, because reintegration is often triggered by a daemon rather than a user request, perceived latency is often nil. That is, reintegrations often occur entirely in the background and do not delay user computation at all. Second, the trace-replay experiments reflect activity that was originally performed in a number of volumes. For the Work-Day traces 5-10 volumes were typically involved, and for the Full-Week traces the number was typically 10-15.

---

[13] It should be possible to eliminate quadratic effects altogether in the implementation. If the stricture on acquiring vnodes in fid-order is retained, then we will not be able to do better than $O(n \log n)$. But if an alternative deadlock avoidance scheme is adopted (or a deadlock detection scheme used instead), then we may be able to make the entire procedure linear.

For logistical reasons, the replay experiments were each performed within a single Coda volume. Hence, there was only one reintegration for each experiment. Following an actual disconnected execution of the trace activity, though, there would have been a number of smaller reintegrations instead of one large one. If the reintegrated volumes were spread over different servers, a significant amount of parallelism could have been realized. The total latency might therefore have been much smaller, perhaps by a factor of three or four.

Unoptimized Reintegration Latency. The results of Table 8.4 reflect experiments performed with the cancellation optimizations of Chapter 6 enabled. Earlier in this chapter it was shown that the optimizations are tremendously important in reducing space requirements at clients. Using the preceding regression results and the statistics collected for each experiment regarding unoptimized log records and data back-fetched, we can estimate the benefits due to the optimizations in reducing reintegration latency as well.

Table 8.5 gives unoptimized and optimized figures for log records, back-fetch amounts, and total latency for each of the twelve experiments. For the log record and back-fetch quantities, the unoptimized figures are those reported by Venus following the reintegration (in the cases of the Andrew benchmark and Venus make experiments) or by the trace simulator (in the cases of the trace-replay experiments). The unoptimized total latency figures are computed from the corresponding log record and back-fetch total numbers using the regression coefficients given earlier; i.e., .026 for the number of log records, .0000186 for its square, and 2.535 for the number of megabytes back-fetched. The far right column shows the ratio of unoptimized to optimized total latency.

The time savings due to the cancellation optimizations reported in Table 8.5 are enormous. The figures indicate that without the optimizations, reintegration of the trace-replay experiments would have averaged 10 times longer than actually occurred for the Work-Day set, and 160 times longer for the Full-Week set. Reintegrating the unoptimized replay of Full-Week trace #3 would have taken more than 6 days, or nearly as long as the period of disconnection! Obviously, much of the extra time is due to the fact that the unoptimized log record totals are well into the range at which the quadratic steps of our implementation dominate. When our code is made more efficient the savings will not be as great. They will not be inconsequential by any means, however. Even if the quadratic term is ignored in projecting unoptimized latency – implying that we can reduce the time of the quadratic steps to zero – the ratios of unoptimized to optimized latency are still pronounced: 4.5 and 7.6 on average for the Work-Day and Full-Week trace-replay sets, respectively.

8.3.4 Cross-Client Write-Sharing

In the qualitative evaluation section it was reported that very few failed reintegrations had occurred in our experience. This means that partitioned

Task	Log Record Total		Back-Fetch Total		Latency		
	Unopt	Opt	Unopt	Opt	Unopt	Opt	Ratio
Andrew Benchmark	211	203	1.5	1.2	10	10	1.0
Venus Make	156	146	19.5	10.3	54	38	1.4
Work-Day #1 Replay	2422	1422	19.1	4.9	221	72	3.1
Work-Day #2 Replay	4093	316	10.9	.9	446	14	31.9
Work-Day #3 Replay	842	212	2.1	.8	41	8	5.1
Work-Day #4 Replay	2439	873	8.5	1.3	196	32	6.1
Work-Day #5 Replay	545	99	40.9	4.0	123	22	5.6
Full-Week #1 Replay	33923	1802	846.9	15.9	24433	176	138.8
Full-Week #2 Replay	36855	1664	62.4	17.5	26381	160	164.9
Full-Week #3 Replay	175392	7199	75.0	23.7	576930	1217	474.1
Full-Week #4 Replay	8519	1159	199.1	15.1	2076	90	23.1
Full-Week #5 Replay	8873	2676	92.7	35.8	1930	273	7.1

This data is from the same set of experiments as Table 8.4. Back-Fetch figures are in megabytes and latencies in seconds. The reported latencies are the means of three trials. Standard deviations are omitted for space reasons.

Table 8.5. Optimized versus Unoptimized Reintegration Latency

write/write conflicts did not occur very often and, by implication, that cross-client write-sharing is rare in our environment.

A low degree of write-sharing is a long-held assumption of Unix environments, and, indeed, it was a major factor in the decision to use optimistic rather than pessimistic replica control in Coda. However, there are other phenomena besides infrequent write-sharing that could explain the low rate of reintegration failure that we experienced:

- most of our users are quite knowledgeable about the system. As noted earlier, many adjusted their activity somewhat to avoid conflicting updates. The same might not be true in other environments, particularly where less savvy users predominate.
- our user community is still rather small. It's possible that as the number of users increases the rate of write-sharing may as well.
- most of our disconnections were 1-2 days or less, with only a small number lasting more than a week. If it were true that write-sharing increases rapidly over intervals beyond a few days, then longer duration disconnections would be much more susceptible to reintegration failure.

To allay concerns over these possibilities, I collected data on write-sharing from the AFS servers in the CMU-SCS environment. These servers are the primary data repository for most members of the department – some 300 faculty, graduate students, and staff personnel. The usage profile of these individuals includes a significant amount of collaborative activity. Moreover, the observed activity involved no disconnected operation, so there was no possibility that users were "acting conservatively." Finally, the collection spanned a very long period (more than 12 months), so it was possible to observe sharing rates over time. Hence, the data corrects for each of the potential objections concerning our testbed environment, and the degree of write-sharing it contains should thus be an excellent indicator of the likelihood of reintegration failure under more realistic conditions.

Methodology. Write-sharing was measured by having servers compare the identity of the current and previous updaters for every object of every mutating operation that they processed. If the updaters or *authors* of an object were different, then a sharing event was counted. If the authors were the same then a non-sharing event was counted. If multiple objects were involved then counters were incremented multiple times. Event counts were kept on a volume basis, with separate totals for plain files and for directories.[14] The definition of a "mutating operation" here is the same as an updating Coda transaction: store, chown, rename, etc.

Events were also classified according to the time interval separating the current and previous update. Six ranges were defined: less than one minute, one to ten minutes, ten to sixty minutes, one hour to one day, one day to one week, and greater than one week. Thus, each volume had 24 counters associated with it – 6 each for: files-same-author, files-different-author, directories-same-author, directories-different-author. The counters were logged and reset once a day by each server, and the data was later collected and entered into a database by an agent process.

Since the current versus previous author comparisons were made on the basis of users and not machines, the sharing measured was really cross-user rather than cross-client. The distinction is not very important for our purposes, since most clients were used only by a single individual and most individuals did not normally use more than one machine at a time. But in environments where multi-user machines are common and/or where users commonly employ several machines simultaneously, the implications of the two types of sharing for partitioned operation could be different.

Results.

Write-Sharing by Time Interval. Table 8.6 presents the write-sharing observations over a period of twelve months. The data is classified using the same volume types introduced earlier in this chapter: user, project, and system. On average, a project volume has about 2600 files and 280 directories, and a system volume has about 1600 files and 130 directories. User volumes tend to be smaller, averaging about 200 files and 18 directories, because users often place much of their data in their project volumes. Note again that this classification is strictly informal; for example, users can and typically do share some data in their user volumes simply by setting access-control lists appropriately.

---
[14] Symbolic links were considered to be plain files for these purposes.

However, the classification does capture the typical usage characteristics of most volumes pretty well.

Table 8.6 shows that over 99% of all modifications were by the previous writer, and that the chances of two different users modifying the same object less than a day apart is at most 0.72%. Interestingly, the highest degree of write-sharing is found on system volumes rather than project volumes, as one might expect. I conjecture that a significant fraction of system file and directory sharing arises from modifications by operators, who change shift periodically. If system files and directories are excluded, the absence of write-sharing is even more striking: more than 99.7% of all mutations are by the previous writer, and the chances of two different users modifying the same object within a week are less than 0.2%.

These results are highly encouraging from the point of view of extending disconnected operation to environments larger than our testbed. The low incidence of write-sharing implies that partitioned write/write conflicts – and hence failed reintegrations – would not be common if our user community were to expand by at least one order of magnitude. Moreover, since users tend to share among small groups rather than randomly among the population as a whole, it seems likely that the same result would hold even at much larger scale.

The Table 8.6 data also indicates that conflict likelihood does not increase dramatically with time. Considering just the user and project volume types, the probability of write-sharing a file increases only from 0.21% to 0.25% when the interval goes from one week to infinity. For directories the increase is greater, 0.15% to 0.30%, but still not very dramatic. Based on this evidence, it appears unlikely that reintegration failure rates would be very high even for very long disconnection durations.

Further Modeling and Simulation. The preceding data is highly suggestive that write-sharing will not limit the extension of disconnected operation along either the dimension of scale or disconnection duration. However, it does not answer questions of the form, "If I work disconnected in my user volume for X hours, what is the probability that reintegration will fail?" Of course, the answer to this would depend on the particular user, but it would still be nice to characterize the situation for an "average" person.

A good deal of effort was expended in model-building and further analyzing the AFS write-sharing data to try to answer questions such as the one above. The basic approach was to simulate a system of clients and servers in which clients disconnected and reconnected according to various connectivity assumptions. When to make an update and from which client would be determined by probabilities derived from the AFS data. The simulator would attempt reintegration upon each reconnection event and, having noted the disconnected client's updates as well as those made by connected clients, determine whether the reintegration succeeded or not. Aggregated over many clients and many simulation runs, this data ought to provide a picture of failure likelihood for combinations of disconnection duration and volume type.

Unfortunately, it turned out that the AFS write-sharing data lacked too much detail to get meaningful results from this approach. In particular, I found the AFS data to be inadequate in the following respects:

- the directory sharing information is at the level of entire directories rather than individual entries.
- the data contains no information concerning the inter-object clustering of write-sharing events. So, for example, although we may be able to deduce that 10 write-sharing events should occur for objects in a given volume in a given time period, we have no way of knowing whether they should involve 10 different objects all at about the same time or the same object at times spaced throughout the interval.
- the data contains no information concerning the dispersal of write-sharing events across clients. So, for example, there is no way of knowing whether 10 write-sharing events should involve clients A and B only or clients A, B, ... K.

The information missing in each of these cases is critical to accurately simulating update behavior. Of course, "informed" assumptions could be made about the missing information and/or the missing quantities could be parameterized. Indeed, these techniques were used in some very extensive analysis. However, it eventually became clear that the results were quite sensitive to the parameter values chosen, even over ranges that were "intuitively reasonable." Specifically, it was possible to generate failure rates from 0 to around 50% using parameters that were at least somewhat plausible. As a result, the analysis was finally abandoned.

The modeling and simulation approach could be resurrected by collecting more detailed write-sharing information than that which we currently have. Perhaps this will actually be done at some point in the future. There are two issues that cast doubt on the usefulness of such an exercise, however. First, a key property of the original collection was that it perturbed the existing system software only very slightly. This fact was crucial in convincing the system administrator that he should allow us to perform the collection. Collecting the more detailed sharing information would result in much more extensive changes and quite possibly a significant performance hit. It's doubtful whether our (or any other) system administrator would allow a collection under those circumstances. Second, the existing evidence – both from our usage experience and from the earlier collection results – is already quite strong in support of low reintegration failure rates. The chance that further analysis would contradict the results we already have appears to be small. Given that there would be considerable cost in performing that analysis, it seems to make more sense to test the hypothesis directly – by deploying the system more widely – than to test it indirectly via modeling and simulation.

Type of Volume	Number of Volumes	Type of Object	Total Mutations	Same Author	Different Author					
					< 1 min	< 10 min	< 1 hour	< 1 day	< 1 week	Total
User	529	Files	3287135	99.87%	.04%	.05%	.06%	.09%	.09%	.13%
		Directories	4132066	99.80%	.04%	.07%	.10%	.15%	.16%	.20%
Project	108	Files	4437311	99.66%	.17%	.25%	.26%	.28%	.30%	.34%
		Directories	5391224	99.63%	.00%	.01%	.03%	.09%	.15%	.37%
System	398	Files	5526700	99.17%	.06%	.18%	.42%	.72%	.78%	.83%
		Directories	4338507	99.54%	.02%	.05%	.08%	.27%	.34%	.46%
All	1035	Files	13251146	99.55%	.09%	.17%	.27%	.41%	.44%	.45%
		Directories	13861797	99.68%	.02%	.04%	.06%	.16%	.21%	.32%

This data was obtained between June 1990 and May 1991 from 13 AFS servers in the cs.cmu.edu cell. The column entitled "Same Author" gives the percentage of mutations in which the user performing the mutation was the same as the one performing the immediately preceding mutation on the same file or directory. The remaining mutations contribute to the columns headed by "Different Author."

Table 8.6. Write-Sharing in AFS

9. Related Work

Coda was the first file system to exploit caching for purposes of performance and high availability. No other system has been implemented to date which duplicates this key property of Coda.

This chapter summarizes other work related to disconnected file service. The first section reports on other file systems that have offered, or have claimed to offer, some form of disconnected operation. The second section discusses additional work related to some of the key mechanisms that are used to provide disconnected file service in Coda.

9.1 Systems

There has been little other direct work in the area of disconnected file service. Only one other implemented file system has had disconnected operation as its primary goal: the FACE file system developed by a group of researchers at Princeton. Two other systems – AFS and Cedar – have supported a very limited, read-only form of disconnected file service. A fourth system has been designed by Tait and Duchamp at Columbia which offers some disconnected support and bears some similarity to Coda, but it is so far unimplemented. A fifth file system, Ficus, has claimed to support disconnected operation, but its structuring as a peer-to-peer rather than a client/server system makes this claim inaccurate. These systems are discussed further in the subsections that follow.

9.1.1 FACE

FACE [4, 15] is the only other implemented file system to have had disconnected operation as an explicit goal. FACE differs from disconnected operation in Coda in at least two significant respects. First, it does not integrate disconnected file service support with caching. A FACE client maintains a separate *stash*, which contains copies of objects that are used when the client is disconnected. A client process called the *bookkeeper* is in charge of fetching objects into the stash and periodically re-validating their currency with the server. Objects are made stashable and unstashable via stash and unstash system calls, respectively. When the client is connected, it uses copies of objects supplied by the local cache manager, which is the in-kernel NFS agent in the FACE prototype. The VFS layer in the kernel switches between the cache and stash copies of an object depending on whether its server is currently accessible or not.

As mentioned earlier, FACE's segregated approach is inferior to the integrated approach employed in Coda in at least three important ways. First, without integration, there is no real transparency. FACE switches between the cache and stash copies of objects automatically, but the versions are not guaranteed to be the same. So, for example, a user could be reading the current version of a file from the cache in connected mode, and then be switched to an out-of-date version in the stash when disconnection occurs. Second, the segregated approach makes poor utilization of client storage resources; copies of the same object may be kept in both the cache and the stash. This waste of space reduces performance in connected mode and availability in disconnected mode. Third, the segregated approach cannot easily take advantage of reference information to identify objects that would be useful to stash; in FACE, only those objects that were specifically stashed can be used while disconnected.

The FACE designers observed that stashing could be combined with caching, but simply making the observation misses the point entirely. The point is that absent integration with caching, disconnected file service is just too awkward and painful for the user. Without integration, users might as well deal with disconnections by manually shuffling files between a local file system and the shared data repository. The value-added by stashing alone is simply not that great. The real value of disconnected operation is apparent only when it is supplied transparently – and transparency demands full integration with caching.

The other major difference between FACE and Coda is that the FACE design and implementation were far from complete. The only parts that they seem to have implemented were the redirection of disconnected requests to stash copies of objects, and enough of the bookkeeper to accept stash and unstash calls and to periodically re-fetch fresh copies of stashable objects. They discussed some possible tools and strategies for identifying files that would be useful to stash, which roughly correspond to Coda's hoard profiles and spy facility. However, there is no indication that any tools or other support mechanisms were ever implemented. Similarly, they noted the need to log disconnected operations at the client and to have a means for reintegration, but neither issue was addressed in their prototype. The absence of logging – and indeed any support for persistence of stash meta-data – meant that a FACE client could not continue operating if it was restarted while disconnected. Reintegration in the FACE prototype consisted simply of timestamp comparison of conflicting updates and (silent) retention of the "most recent" one.

Not surprisingly, the FACE prototype appears to have had little real use. No mention of any user community is made in the literature, and the only indication that the prototype was ever used are some measurements which reported the overhead in redirecting requests to stash copies. The absence of real usage information makes it impossible to compare FACE with Coda in terms of usability, performance, or secondary design choices.

9.1.2 AFS and Cedar

Two file systems that have seen serious use, AFS [85, 39, 83] and Cedar [90, 28], support limited disconnected operation as a side-effect of their basic structure. Both systems cache data in persistent storage at clients; entire files in the case of Cedar, and large chunks in the case of AFS.[1] Hence, it is straightforward for the cache manager in each system to allow processes to read cached data while the client is disconnected. In AFS the utility of this feature is somewhat reduced, because it is possible to miss on important pieces of a partially-cached file.

Read-only disconnected operation is obviously better than none at all, but it is a far cry from the read/write capability that is supported in Coda. Because only reading is allowed, there is no notion of logging or of reintegration in either system. Moreover, there are no mechanisms for supplying hints to the cache manager about what objects would be useful to have cached at the time of disconnection. The user must be satisfied with whatever the standard LRU policy has kept in the cache.

Finally, it should be noted that, although the disconnected service capabilities of these two systems are very limited, disconnected operation was not a significant design goal of either one.

9.1.3 Tait and Duchamp

Tait and Duchamp (TAD) [20, 98, 97, 96] have recently described a design for a file service that is specifically targeted at mobile clients. Their design has a fair bit in common with Coda's: both systems cache data in non-volatile storage at clients; both exploit server replication and disconnected operation for availability; and both manage replicas optimistically (at least in part). At present there is no published information on an implementation of the TAD design, so it is difficult to know whether differences between the two systems are significant or not.[2]

The most obvious design difference between Coda and TAD is the latter's use of "variable consistency" semantics. They split the traditional Unix read

---

[1] AFS-1 and AFS-2 used whole-file caching; AFS-3 and AFS-4 cache in 64 kilobyte chunks.

[2] Through private communication, it's recently been disclosed that a prototype implementation of the TAD design now exists. However, there's no information on how complete the implementation is, nor of any usage experience with it.

call into two alternatives: loose_read and strict_read. Essentially, the former returns the value of the nearest copy of the object and the latter the most recent in the current partition. There is no explicit separation of the write call into loose and strict variants, but since updates are almost always preceded by reads there is a de facto division along those lines.

The ability to operate disconnected in the TAD design depends on whether processes use the loose or strict form of the interface. Loose reads and subsequent writes are allowed on objects in the client cache, as is true for all operations in Coda. Conflicting updates can occur because of this, and the system detects such conflicts using a simple version stamping scheme. The TAD design literature is vague about how one would recover from conflicts, however. It mentions that messages would be sent to clients, but gives no indication how they would translate into user-level actions. Similarly, there is no discussion of directory update handling. In particular, it is not clear whether partitioned update of distinct names in the same directory would be handled automatically – as is the case in Coda, or whether such activity would require manual resolution.

The permissibility of strict operations while disconnected is more complicated. To perform such an operation disconnected the client must hold a *currency token* (CT) for the object, which is roughly equivalent to a callback promise in Coda. Without a CT, a strict read (and any subsequent write) is refused, even though the client has a copy of the object in its cache. A disconnected client holding a CT knows that its cache copy was the latest in the partition at time of disconnection, and that at that point no other client in the partition had expressed an interest in writing the object. Holding a CT does not mean, however, that no other client can read or write the object while the CT holder is disconnected. The disconnected client's CT can be unilaterally revoked by a server, allowing other clients to access the object. Holding a CT, therefore, just increases the probability that a disconnected read or write will not conflict with activity at other clients. A final point is that all strict operations at a disconnected client are refused after a restart, since CTs are kept in volatile store.

It is not clear that the separation of the read call into loose and strict variants is a useful one. The intent appears to be to offer a choice between true Unix semantics – the strict interface – and a more available approximation – the loose interface. TAD's strict interface, however, does not guarantee true Unix semantics; it merely increases the probability that they will be supplied. The extent of that increase varies with workload and connectivity parameters, and is not yet well understood. The Coda experience – using a real implementation of optimistic file service – is that behavior akin to TAD's loose mode is acceptable for the majority of applications. For applications that do require stronger semantics, the explicit transaction extension to Coda proposed in Section 10.2 seems more useful than the strict interface of TAD. Explicit transactions add semantic power well beyond that which is achievable in non-distributed Unix systems. Strict reads, on the other hand, can at best provide true Unix semantics. Those semantics are still too weak, however, for many applications for which we might expect to use strict read – for example, the make program. Since strict reads also imply lower availability than the Coda approach, it is hard to see what their comparative advantage would be.[3]

The other major difference between the TAD design and Coda is in the area of hoarding. The Coda philosophy is that both implicit and explicit information have roles in avoiding disconnected misses. This is reflected in the implementation, where hints are solicited and made use of by the cache manager. Tait and Duchamp, on the other hand, eschew explicit hints in favor of more exotic implicit information strategies. In [96] they describe an algorithm that maintains graphs of file accesses made by defunct processes, and matches them to the patterns of currently executing programs. When a sufficiently good initial match is detected, the cache manager pre-fetches objects named in the matched tree that are not already cached. So, in cases where some objects are not already cached and a disconnection occurs after the pre-fetching is completed, the algorithm serves to increase availability.

The TAD algorithm is a useful technique to be sure, but by itself it does not constitute an acceptable hoarding strategy. A major limitation is that the "hints" it generates come too close to the time objects are needed to provide much protection against disconnection. (Indeed, the greatest benefit of the algorithm appears to be in reducing latency in connected operation.) Moreover, many important tasks do not involve large sets of objects; for example, the editing of a plain text or program source file. There is no reason, however, why Tait and Duchamp's technique cannot be incorporated into the Coda hoarding framework, increasing the overall power of the system. In fact, deriving additional techniques along these lines and incorporating them into Coda is one aspect of the future work discussed in Section 10.2.

9.1.4 Ficus

Ficus [34, 33] is a distributed file system in which nodes are structured as peers rather than being firmly divided into clients and servers. Ficus objects are organized into volumes, as in AFS and Coda, and a volume may be replicated across any number of nodes. Ficus and Coda are both in some sense descendants of Locus [69], as each takes an optimistic approach to the management of partitioned replicas. The two differ fundamentally in that

---

[3] The TAD designers also claim that their design would perform very well in failure-free mode, because it delays the write-back of updates much longer than is typical. Indeed, delayed write-back can be quite effective in distributed file systems, as demonstrated by Sprite [64] several years back. It is not at all clear, though, that delayed write-back in a replicated or disconnected-capable environment requires the loose/strict interface changes to be effective. The issues appear to be completely orthogonal.

Ficus continues with the peer orientation of Locus, whereas Coda marries optimistic replication to the client/server, caching-dominated architecture of AFS.

For objects belonging to volumes that it hosts, a Ficus node accesses the local copies. This is relatively efficient. Updates are propagated to other storage sites by having them "pull" new data over at convenient times. There is no notion of caching in Ficus, however. If a node does not store the volume of a referenced object, then it must remotely access the copy of an actual storage site. Optimistic replica control permits a process to read or write an object as long as it can reach at least one copy. Partitioned, conflicting write accesses are detected by a version vector scheme [67], and a part logging, part inferencing algorithm is used to automatically reconcile partitioned updates to distinct entries of directories.

A recent paper by Heidemann et al [36] incorrectly implies that Ficus supports disconnected operation. This would mean that a Ficus node that is not a first-class storage site for some volume – and which is partitioned from all such sites – could continue operating by accessing local, second-class copies of that volume's objects. But Ficus has no notion of second-class replicas; a node either contains a first-class replica or it must get service from another node which does. Hence, all "disconnected accesses" in Ficus necessarily fail. What Heidemann et al really reported on was access from *isolated first-class nodes*: nodes which store a first-class copy of an object and which are partitioned from all of their cohorts. This is not disconnected operation, but rather a sub-case of general, first-class partitioned operation.

Although in theory the Ficus approach can provide as high a level of service in the face of failures and voluntary detachments as can true disconnected operation, in practice there are at least two factors which strongly favor the latter. First is the fact that replica placement is much more flexible and adaptive with second- than with first-class replication. With Coda, a second-class or cache copy is created transparently, as a side-effect of actual reference. In Ficus, establishment of a first-class replica at a node is a heavyweight, administrative operation. The same light versus heavyweight distinction is also true for discarding a replica. In general, these differences make the set of objects cached at a disconnecting client more useful for continued operation than the set of first-class objects resident at a newly isolated Ficus node (given identical disk capacities). In addition, caching offers improved performance in failure-free operation vis à vis the Ficus approach by reducing the need to read data from other hosts.

The second – and even more crucial – advantage of disconnected operation in Coda over the Ficus replication approach is scalability. Three sub-issues point to much greater scaling potential with the Coda design:

- *protocol overhead* – the overhead in time and space of replication protocols is typically much lower for second- than for first-class replicas. For example, second-class replicas can be updated by invalidation and later re-fetch by only those sites which actually reference the object again. First-class replicas, on the other hand, must eventually see the effects of all updates, even if their copies are never actually used. Similarly, each Ficus replica requires storage for version information proportional to n (the number of replicas), whereas each Coda replica requires only a small constant amount.

– *security* – the explicit division of hosts in Coda into clients and servers greatly reduces the set of machines that a user must trust. Essentially, he or she need only trust the first-class replication sites – i.e., the servers. In Ficus, a user need only trust first-class sites as well, but that set includes *every* site which stores a given volume. This may be fine in an environment consisting of a few dozen users, where everyone knows everyone else, but it is untenable in an environment of even moderate scale.

– *autonomy* – in a large-scale environment consisting of personal workstations, it is essential that users be able to treat their machines as truly personal computers, with no obligations to other hosts. Again, the design of Coda supports this property because of the client/server separation, while Ficus does not because of its flat, peer structure. As a simple illustration, consider what would happen if a laptop host were dropped on the floor, destroying its disk. In Coda, no other client would be aware of the laptop's disappearance or its eventual reincarnation with a clean disk. In Ficus, however, other common storage sites would try indefinitely to contact the failed host, in the normal process of garbage collecting meta-data related to directory updates. So while the laptop was down, garbage would pile up at all of the other common storage sites. An administrative action eventually would be needed to permanently remove the laptop from the replication suite or to reflect its reappearance with a clean disk.

It is important to emphasize that first-class replication per se is not non-scalable, only the exclusive reliance on it. As noted earlier and explained fully in [86], Coda also supports first-class replication, but it does so while retaining the client/server model. Disconnected operation is a complementary mechanism which reaps further availability benefits while remaining within a scalable framework.

9.2 Mechanisms

In addition to the preceding systems, there has been other work related to specific aspects of the Coda design for disconnected operation. That work is discussed in the following subsections.

9.2.1 Replica Control

The foundational work on optimistic replica control is due to Davidson [16, 17]. She presented an algorithm in which peer sites in a database system log transactions while partitioned from one another, and reconcile their state via a merge algorithm executed at partitioning heal. The merge algorithm uses a graph formalism, the *precedence graph*, and it involves exchanging the new values of certain transactions and undo/redo of certain others. She also gave a proof that the protocol satisfies one-copy serializability (viewed at instants where the replication sites are not partitioned).

The replica control strategy of Coda can be seen as an asymmetric variant of Davidson's basic approach. The asymmetry is manifested in two significant ways. First, logging is performed only at one of the sites in a merge pair – the client. Servers do not log to support disconnected operation.[4] The absence of a server log means that a precedence graph cannot be built during the merge. Instead, the hybrid certification algorithm described in Section 7.3 is used to identify conflicting transaction subsequences. The other manifestation of asymmetry concerns the restoration of mutual consistency. The Coda merge process makes only the server state consistent with the global history covering the two partitions. Client state is updated to reflect partitioned server activity lazily, by the method of invalidation and re-fetch on demand.

Coda's lighter-weight, asymmetric approach is made possible by two environmental features: the client/server architecture, and the specifics of the inferred transaction model. The client/server dichotomy means that there is already an inferior/superior relationship between replication sites. That relationship is exploited by the policy of always choosing the inferior's transaction for undo when some undo is necessary, which in turn eliminates one of the two motivations for logging at servers (i.e., the capability to undo a transaction). The other motivation for logging at servers is to discriminate between harmful and benign read/write conflicts. But with the Coda inferred transaction specification there are very few cases of benign read/write conflict. That is, in almost all cases where partitioned transactions are in read/write conflict, they are also in write/write conflict. Consequently, certification – which does not require a server log but views all read/write conflicts as harmful – can be used without unnecessarily forcing undo in very many cases.

9.2.2 Pre-Fetching and Hoarding

All other work in the area of file pre-fetching has been done with the goal of latency reduction rather than availability in mind. A range of techniques have been described which accept access hints from running programs or derive them from reference pattern observations. These hints are then used to pre-fetch data into secondary or primary storage at the client before it is referenced, so that the cost of network and/or disk I/O can be avoided. Examples of this type of work can be found in [68, 47, 32, 66]. While these

---

[4] Coda servers do log transactions to support server replication [49], but that is orthogonal to disconnected operation. Server logs have no role in the reintegration process.

techniques can be quite useful in improving the performance of connected operation, they (so far) can do little for disconnected operation. This is because, as explained earlier in the discussion of the TAD pre-fetching technique, the hints become known to the system far too late to provide much protection against disconnection.

Though largely unrelated to other pre-fetching work, hoarding in Coda has been influenced by a local CMU facility known as SUP [91]. SUP stands for "Software Upgrade Protocol," and is a set of programs that allow collections of files to be kept loosely synchronized with a central repository.[5] A SUP control file specifies the remote host serving as the collection repository, the root for the collection in the repository's local file system, and the root at the local host. One or more "list" files are also associated with a SUP collection, which identify different subsets of the files that can be selected. A client synchronizes its copy of the collection by executing the SUP front-end program with the appropriate control file as an argument. Typically, this is set up to be done once a day by a background daemon process.

Experience with SUP provided several insights that were valuable in the design of hoarding. First, it offered proof that many tasks could be usefully characterized without excessive detail or continued user attention. This indicated that the basic strategy of soliciting reference hints was feasible. Second, it revealed that the key to success was abstraction based on the existing, hierarchical structure of the namespace. This indicated that meta-expansion was an essential feature to provide. Third, it showed that control information could be simply and effectively shared, amortizing the community-wide cost of task characterization. This lent further support to the basic strategy, and in addition it emphasized that a user-level representation of hints – such as hoard profiles – was also necessary.

Indeed, it is possible to view the hoarding subsystem in Coda as the essence of SUP, extended in four important ways:

- *unification of the namespaces at client and server.* This, of course, is the key advantage of any distributed file system: absent failures, users are able to share data with the same ease as in a centralized system. Changes are made visible to other clients as soon as is feasible, rather than at the next SUP synchronization event.
- *maintenance of callback and name expansion state.* This makes synchronization complexity a function of remote update activity and connectivity changes, rather than the number of objects in the collection. The practical effect is that hoard walks can be reasonably conducted with high frequency – at least one every few minutes, while scalability concerns limit SUP synchronizations to at most a few per client per day.
- *combination of hint information with reference knowledge.* Neither a pure hint- nor a pure reference-based scheme yields local data sets as useful for

---

[5] The purpose and functioning of SUP is very similar to that of the BSD rdist facility.

disconnected operation as does Coda's combined approach. Reference information identifies useful objects that were overlooked in hint generation, and hints identify critical objects that may not have been used recently.

— *mapping of the entire set of useful objects onto an arbitrary amount of disk space.* Prioritization identifies the currently most useful subset of objects, and adjusts that subset automatically in response to local and remote events. SUP imposes an all-or-nothing requirement at the granularity of collections, and has little means for automatic adjustment.

These differences make hoarding much more scalable, transparent, and flexible than SUP, but do not sacrifice its basic simplicity.

9.2.3 Log Optimizations

The log record cancellation optimizations of Section 6.2.2 bear surface similarity to the *log transformation* techniques of Blaustein et al [8, 9]. Both generate shorter, equivalent versions of logs that arise in the context of partitioned transaction processing. The two are fundamentally different, however, in that the Coda optimizations are *intra-site* – they operate on the log of a single host, whereas Blaustein et al's are *inter-site* – they operate on the concatenation of logs from two merging hosts. The Coda optimizations address both space conservation at partitioned sites and reduction of merge effort, while the inter-site techniques address only the latter. Many differences in detail also arise out of the intra- versus inter-site distinction. The techniques, in fact, can be considered complementary; a system which logs at both merging sites could employ the intra- and inter-site optimizations in combination.

9.2.4 Recovery in Physical File Systems

Coda guarantees persistence of client data by storing all of Venus' meta-data in RVM. As explained in Section 6.3, RVM ensures recoverability by recording all changes in a write-ahead log and executing a standard redo algorithm upon restart. The technique of logging file system meta-data updates is not new; in the last few years it has been employed in Episode [14], IBM JFS [13], and Cedar [35]. Rosenblum and Ousterhout have taken the idea to its extreme with their Log Structured File System (LFS) [74], which maintains both regular and meta-data strictly in log format.

Two aspects of the Coda approach distinguish it from these other systems. The first is structural: logging and recovery in Coda is done at the user-level, via a general-purpose package. The others perform these functions in the kernel, using tailored algorithms. With the Coda structure it is a simple matter to add new types of meta-data or new invariants, since the recovery algorithm is oblivious to all such changes. With the other systems it is not clear that extensibility is so easily achieved.

The other unique aspect of the Coda approach is the use of server state to minimize local log flushes. In connected mode, Venus knows that servers have stably performed meta-data changes corresponding to local update transactions, and consequently it sets log flush deadlines far into the future. This provides greater opportunity for absorbing overwrites in main memory and for scheduling flushes during user idle periods. If a client crash should occur there is high probability that servers will be available at restart to refresh Venus' state with the most recent updates. But when Venus makes disconnected updates the same is not true, so log flushes occur with much higher frequency. Performance suffers somewhat because of this, but persistence is maintained at an acceptable level. None of the other meta-data logging file systems have taken this variable-flush optimization, presumably because they are strictly non-distributed or because their logging interface does not make it convenient.

10. Conclusions

Client disconnection is an increasingly important phenomenon in distributed computing. Its importance is being driven by two major trends: the expanding scale of such systems, and the proliferation of powerful mobile clients. The former increases the likelihood of involuntary disconnection, since large networks are more prone to failures than are small ones. The latter introduces voluntary disconnections to wired network environments, and increases the likelihood of involuntary disconnection in those that employ wireless technologies. The combined effect of these factors is to make disconnected operation an ever more valuable capability.

In this dissertation I have described a system which supports disconnected operation for a key distributed service: general purpose file management. The architecture revolves around the idea that disconnected file service support should be integrated into the client cache manager. Integration permits a high degree of transparency; in many cases, it is possible to mask disconnection entirely from users and applications. It also makes effective use of scarce local resources, and facilitates the use of reference information in preparing for disconnected sessions.

Coda is the first system to convincingly demonstrate that disconnected file service is practical. The system has been deployed within a moderately-sized user community for a period of almost two years. User response generally has been very positive. The system has been quite usable, although there are aspects of it that clearly could stand improvement. No real usage experience has ever been reported for any other system claiming to support disconnected file service.

10.1 Contributions

The thesis stated in Chapter 1 posited that disconnected file service could be supported effectively using caching. Further, it hypothesized that the increased availability could be realized without large sacrifice of other important distributed file system properties, such as transparency, performance, scalability, or security. The top-level contributions of this work are the following:

– recognition of the facts that disconnections are an increasingly serious problem, and that traditional, server-based techniques for addressing it are inadequate.

– demonstration of the thesis, via design, implementation, and evaluation of a complete system.

– a very usable platform, from which further research into distributed and mobile computing issues can be conducted.

At the next level of detail, specific contributions can be cited in four distinct areas:

1. *architecture*
   – a unified framework for addressing voluntary and involuntary disconnections, and for integrating mobile computers into traditional distributed computing environments.
   – the placement of Unix file access into a formal framework that permits reasoning about correctness and availability, and informal proofs that the system's replica control protocol does meet the standard of correctness.

2. *implementation*
   – an algorithm for cache management that combines reference and hint information, and adapts efficiently to local and remote stimuli.
   – demonstration that operation logging is a viable technique for replica control, even at very resource-poor clients such as laptops.
   – specification of two classes of log optimization – overwrite and identity cancellation – which have general applicability to transactional environments.
   – evidence that persistent meta-data can be managed effectively using a lightweight, user-level transaction mechanism.

3. *qualitative validation*
   – proof that user assistance in working-set prediction can be usefully employed.
   – proof that disconnected file service can be supported without sacrificing the security properties demanded by large, untrusted distributed computing environements.

4. *quantitative validation*
   – analysis of the client storage requirements for disconnected file access over time, based on real workstation traces.
   – evidence that reintegration latency is not a serious impediment to typical disconnected file access for disconnection durations of at least a week.
   – measurements from a large, distributed Unix environment which confirm that cross-client write-sharing is rare (and, thus, that optimistic replication is a viable technique).

10.2 Future Work

A number of minor enhancements to the Coda implementation of disconnected operation have been suggested in this dissertation. For example, Chapter 7 pointed out that in-lining small files in back-fetching would improve
reintegration performance. Similarly, value rather than version certification
of attribute-setting operations would eliminate some false reintegration failures, without adding appreciably to overhead costs. A third example is the use
of process-group information in reference spying for hoarding, which would
filter out unwanted noise in some cases.

Beyond the set of minor enhancements, there are three major extensions
to my work that are worth exploring immediately: weakly-connected support,
improved hoarding, and explicit transaction support. Work is, in fact, already
underway in each of these areas by other Coda group members. The rest of
this section discusses that work in slightly more detail.

Weakly-Connected Operation. The current Coda implementation views connectivity as a binary variable: a client is either connected (with respect to a
given area of the namespace) or it is disconnected. In reality, however, there
are many intermediate points on the spectrum between these two extremes.
For example, a mobile client may have a 9600 baud modem or packet radio
link that can be used to connect to servers when its normal LAN connection
is down.

In an earlier paper [45] we termed such forms of network connection *weak
connectivity*. A connection may be weak along one or more of the following
dimensions: bandwidth, latency, reliability. Weak connections are particularly
important for mobile clients, as they are likely to be taken to places where
traditional – high bandwidth, low latency, high reliability – networks are not
available.

Lily Mummert [60] has been investigating ways in which weak connections
can be exploited in Coda. The key benefits appear to be in two areas. First,
a weak connection can be used to service cache misses that might otherwise
have impeded computation. This can be enormously beneficial, particularly
when the missed objects are small and can be fetched with little delay. Second,
a weak connection can be used to "trickle" updates back from client to server,
effectively reintegrating "in parts" rather than "in toto" as is the case now.
This can prevent a client from exhausting its cache space prematurely, and
can also avoid some reintegration failures that would arise in waiting for
full connectivity to be restored. It also can make updates visible to others
earlier in time, which is beneficial even when reintegration failure would not
otherwise result.

Improved Hoarding Tools and Analysis. Chapter 8 reported that hoarding has
been useful in reducing the number and severity of disconnected cache misses.
However, it also noted a number of deficiencies in the current implementation.

These deficiencies are serious enough that non-expert users have been unable to realize many of the benefits of hoarding.

Maria Ebling [21] has recently begun work aimed at improving the effectiveness of hoarding. She plans to focus on two main techniques. The first is making the concept of a task more prominent in the system. Instead of the loose organization implied by hoard profiles, Ebling's tasks will impose structure on the cache that better matches the work patterns of users. Tasks will allow feedback to be given at a much more intuitive level, and may provide a framework in which the system can generate hints automatically (for example, using algorithms like Tait and Duchamp's [96]). The other technique she plans to explore is the use of more distant reference information in making pre-fetch decisions. Her hypothesis is that keeping a small amount of state about objects that have departed the cache will prove useful in later decisions about how to use freshly available space.

A key component of Ebling's work will be the investigation of new metrics for evaluating the benefits of hoarding. My work has exposed the fact that cache hit ratio – the standard for normal cache evaluation – is largely inapplicable to the domain of hoarding. What is needed are metrics which approximate the utility to the user of cache contents, but which are feasible to compute. Such metrics are needed to evaluate the effectiveness of new tools and hoarding techniques, and also to understand the marginal utility of increasing the cache resources at clients.

Explicit Transaction Support. A recurrent theme of this dissertation is that file system interfaces in general – and the Unix interface in particular – are too weak to take full advantage of disconnected operation. The fundamental problem is that the system does not know the mapping of data accesses to computations. In a non-partitionable system, such as a single Unix host, this results in classic concurrency control failures; i.e., unwanted interleavings of operations on shared data. File system users traditionally have not made a big deal over this, primarily because the level of sharing is low enough that such failures are rare.

With partitioned operation, however, the opaqueness of the data access to computation mappings is much more serious. The replica control protocol used by the system is bound to embody assumptions about the mappings that are sometimes wrong. For example, any protocol which forbids partitioned read/write conflicts is implicitly assuming that the accesses in each partition belong to a single computation. When that assumption is wrong availability suffers. The current Coda protocol, on the other hand, embodies the much more liberal assumption that most data accesses are independent of one another. When it is wrong, correctness may suffer as inconsistent states may be seen by partitioned computations.

The work recently proposed by Qi Lu [53] to make computation boundaries explicit in the Unix interface will eliminate the preceding types of problem. For disconnected operation in Coda specifically, it will have two major benefits. First, it will eliminate cases in which incorrect disconnected computations are mistakenly reintegrated. Successful reintegration will truly mean that the computation is 1SR with respect to all other committed transactions in the system. Second, it will permit the automatic re-execution of many disconnected transactions that do fail reintegration. This should greatly reduce the manual repair burden, and thus make the system much more accessible to non-expert users. A third benefit of Lu's work, which is orthogonal to disconnected operation and Coda in general, is that unwanted interleavings between computations in the same partition will also be prevented.

10.3 Final Remarks

Distributed computing involves an endless struggle between the states of *autonomy* and *interdependence*. Autonomy is valued because it gives users control over their resources and insulates them from problems that befall others. Interdependence is not of value by itself, but is the inevitable consequence of sharing – a capability which is highly valued. Modern computing environments have tended to maximize sharing potential – and thus interdependence – with attendant sacrifice of client autonomy. This sacrifice has often been acceptable, as disconnections have not been prevalent in many environments. However, as argued in this dissertation, conditions are changing in ways that make disconnections much more likely: namely, increasing system scale and the proliferation of mobile computers. Under these new conditions, the sacrifice of autonomy may be very painful indeed.

Disconnected operation is a means of reclaiming autonomy without trading too much back in the way of sharing capability. At its most effective, disconnected operation provides the best of both worlds. When the system is without failure or voluntary disconnection, disconnected support should be unobtrusive and the degree and convenience of sharing should be unaffected. Under conditions of failure or voluntary disconnection, however, the emphasis should be on autonomy. The ability of a user to get work done while disconnected should not be less than if the user were at an unnetworked personal computer. Within that constraint, of course, the ease and transparency of sharing should be as great as possible.

My work has shown that disconnected operation can be profitably applied to general purpose file management, and that a much better balance between autonomy and interdependence than that found elsewhere can be realized for this important service. The techniques for supporting disconnected file service described in this dissertation can and should be applied to other distributed file systems. The prerequisites are few and they have other sound motivations supporting them: a true client/server architecture; non-volatile storage at clients; server- rather than client-based cache coherence. The advantages of disconnected file service are so compelling that its support will – in my opinion

– be a standard feature of all widely-used operating environments of the future.

Bibliography

1. M. Accetta, R. Baron, W. Bolosky, D. Golub, R. Rashid, A. Tevanian, and M. Young. Mach: A new kernel foundation for Unix development. In *Proceedings of the Summer Usenix Conference*, June 1986.
2. Advanced Hardware Architectures, Inc. *AHA3210 Data Compression Coprocessor IC Product Brief.*
3. S.V. Adve and M.D. Hill. Weak ordering – a new definition. In *Proceedings of the Seventeenth Annual International Symposium on Computer Architecture*, May 1990.
4. R. Alonso, D. Barbara, and L. Cova. Using stashing to increase node autonomy in distributed file systems. In *Proceedings of the Ninth Symposium on Reliable Distributed Systems*, October 1990.
5. M. Baker, J. Hartman, M. Kupfer, K. Shirriff, and J. Ousterhout. Measurements of a distributed file system. In *Proceedings of the Thirteenth ACM Symposium on Operating Systems Principles*, October 1991.
6. P.A. Bernstein, V. Hadzilacos, and N. Goodman. *Concurrency Control and Recovery in Database Systems*. Addison-Wesley, 1987.
7. A. Birrell. Autonomy or independence in distributed systems? (position paper). In *Proceedings of the 1988 ACM SIGOPS European Workshop*, September 1988.
8. B. Blaustein, H. Garcia-Molina, D. Ries, R. Chilenskas, and C. Kaufman. Maintaining replicated databases even in the presence of network partitions. In *Proceedings of the IEEE EASCON Conference*, September 1983.
9. B. Blaustein and C. Kaufman. Updating replicated data during communications failures. In *Proceedings of the Eleventh International Conference on Very Large Databases*, August 1985.
10. S. Bunton and G. Borriello. Practical dictionary management for hardware data compression. *Communications of the ACM*, 35(1), January 1992.
11. M. Burrows, C. Jerian, B. Lampson, and T. Mann. On-line data compression in a log-structured file system. Technical Report 85, Digital Systems Research Center, 1992.
12. V. Cate and T. Gross. Combining the concepts of compression and caching for a two-level file system. In *Proceedings of the Fourth ACM Symposium on Architectural Support for Programming Languages and Operating Systems*, April 1991.
13. A. Chang, M.F. Mergen, R.K. Rader, J.A. Roberts, and S.L. Porter. Evolution of storage facilities in AIX version 3 for RISC System/6000 processors. *IBM Journal of Research and Development*, 34(1), January 1990.
14. S. Chutani, O.T. Anderson, M.L. Kazar, B.W. Leverett, W.A. Mason, and R.N. Sidebotham. The Episode file system. In *Proceedings of the Winter Usenix Conference*, January 1992.

15. L.L. Cova. *Resource Management in Federated Computing Environments.* PhD thesis, Princeton University, October 1990.

16. S.B. Davidson. *An Optimistic Protocol for Partitioned Distributed Database Systems.* PhD thesis, Princeton University, October 1982.

17. S.B. Davidson. Optimism and consistency in partitioned distributed database systems. *ACM Transactions on Database Systems,* 9(3), September 1984.

18. S.B. Davidson, H. Garcia-Molina, and D. Skeen. Consistency in partitioned networks. *ACM Computing Surveys,* 17(3), September 1985.

19. P.J. Denning. The working set model for program behavior. *Communications of the ACM,* 11(5), May 1968.

20. D. Duchamp and C. Tait. An interface to support lazy replicated file service. In *Proceedings of the Second Workshop on the Management of Replicated Data,* November 1992.

21. M.R. Ebling. Evaluating and improving the effectiveness of hoarding. Thesis proposal, Carnegie Mellon University School of Computer Science, April 1993.

22. J.L. Eppinger, L.B. Mummert, and A.Z. Spector, editors. *Camelot and Avalon: A Distributed Transaction Facility.* Morgan Kaufmann, 1991.

23. R.A. Floyd. Directory reference patterns in a Unix environment. Technical Report 179, University of Rochester Computer Science Department, 1986.

24. R.A. Floyd. Short-term file reference patterns in a Unix environment. Technical Report 177, University of Rochester Computer Science Department, 1986.

25. R.A. Floyd. *Transparency in Distributed File Systems.* PhD thesis, University of Rochester, January 1989.

26. H. Garcia-Molina and G. Wiederhold. Read-only transactions in a distributed database. *ACM Transactions on Database Systems,* 7(2), June 1982.

27. D.K. Gifford. Weighted voting for replicated data. In *Proceedings of the Seventh ACM Symposium on Operating Systems Principles,* August 1979.

28. D.K. Gifford, R.M. Needham, and M.D. Schroeder. The Cedar file system. *Communications of the ACM,* 31(3), March 1988.

29. D. Golub, R. Dean, A. Forin, and R. Rashid. Unix as an application program. In *Proceedings of the Summer Usenix Conference,* June 1990.

30. C.G. Gray and D.R. Cheriton. Leases: An efficient fault-tolerant mechanism for distributed file cache consistency. In *Proceedings of the Twelfth ACM Symposium on Operating Systems Principles,* December 1989.

31. J.N. Gray. Notes on database operating systems. In *Operating Systems: An Advanced Course, Lecture Notes in Computer Science.* Springer-Verlag, 1978.

32. A.S. Grimshaw and E.C. Loyot Jr. Elfs: Object-oriented extensible file systems. Technical Report TR-91-14, University of Virginia Department of Computer Science, July 1991.

33. R.G. Guy. *Ficus: A Very Large Scale Reliable Distributed File System.* PhD thesis, University of California, Los Angeles, June 1991.

34. R.G. Guy, J.S. Heidemann, W. Mak, T.W. Page, G.J. Popek, and D. Rothmeier. Implementation of the Ficus replicated file system. In *Proceedings of the Summer Usenix Conference,* June 1990.

35. R. Hagmann. Reimplementing the Cedar file system using logging and group commit. In *Proceedings of the Eleventh ACM Symposium on Operating Systems Principles,* November 1987.

36. J.S. Heidemann, T.W. Page, R.G. Guy, and G.J. Popek. Primarily disconnected operation: Experience with Ficus. In *Proceedings of the Second Workshop on the Management of Replicated Data,* November 1992.

37. M.P. Herlihy. Optimistic concurrency control for abstract data types. In *Proceedings of the Fifth Annual Symposium on Principles of Distributed Computing,* August 1986.

38. A. Hisgen, A. Birrell, T. Mann, M. Schroeder, and G. Swart. Availability and consistency tradeoffs in the Echo distributed file system. In *Proceedings of the Second Workshop on Workstation Operating Systems (WWOS-II)*, September 1989.

39. J.H. Howard, M.L. Kazar, S.G. Menees, D.A. Nichols, M. Satyanarayanan, R.N. Sidebotham, and M.J. West. Scale and performance in a distributed file system. *ACM Transactions on Computer Systems*, 6(1), February 1988.

40. W. Joy. An introduction to the C shell. In *Unix User's Manual Supplementary Documents, 4.3 Berkeley Software Distribution*. University of California, Berkeley, 1986.

41. M.L. Kazar. Synchronizing and caching issues in the Andrew file system. In *Winter Usenix Conference Proceedings*, February 1988.

42. M.L. Kazar, B.W. Leverett, O.T. Anderson, V. Apostilides, B.A. Bottos, S. Chutani, C.F. Everhart, W.A. Mason, S. Tu, and E.R. Zayas. Decorum file system architectural overview. In *Proceedings of the Summer Usenix Conference*, June 1990.

43. J.J. Kistler. Increasing file system availability through second-class replication. In *Proceedings of the Workshop on Management of Replicated Data*, November 1990.

44. J.J. Kistler and M. Satyanarayanan. Transparent disconnected operation for fault-tolerance. *Operating Systems Review*, 25(1), January 1991.

45. J.J. Kistler and M. Satyanarayanan. Disconnected operation in the Coda file system. *ACM Transactions on Computer Systems*, 10(1), February 1992.

46. S.R. Kleiman. Vnodes: An architecture for multiple file system types in Sun Unix. In *Summer Usenix Conference Proceedings*, June 1986.

47. K. Korner. Intelligent caching for remote file service. In *Proceedings of the Tenth International Conference on Distributed Computing Systems*, May 1990.

48. P. Kumar. Supporting Optimistic Replication in a Distributed File System. Thesis proposal, Carnegie Mellon University School of Computer Science, December 1991.

49. P. Kumar and M. Satyanarayanan. Log-based directory resolution in the Coda file system. In *Proceedings of the Second International Conference on Parallel and Distributed Information Systems*, January 1993.

50. B. Lampson and H. Sturgis. Crash recovery in a distributed data storage system. Technical report, Computer Science Laboratory, Xerox Palo Alto Research Center, 1976.

51. S.J. Leffler, M.K. McKusick, M.J. Karels, and J.S. Quarterman. *The Design and Implementation of the 4.3 BSD Unix Operating System*. Addison-Wesley, 1989.

52. E. Levy and A. Silberschatz. Distributed file systems: Concepts and examples. *Computing Surveys*, 22(4), December 1990.

53. Q. Lu. Isolation-only transactions in distributed Unix file systems. Thesis proposal, Carnegie Mellon University School of Computer Science, May 1993.

54. J.H. Maloney and A.P. Black. File sessions: A technique and its application to the Unix file system. In *Proceedings of the Third International Conference on Data Engineering*, February 1987.

55. K. Marzullo and F. Schmuck. Supplying high availability with a standard network file system. Technical Report 87-888, Cornell University Department of Computer Science, 1987.

56. H.H. Mashburn. *RVM User Manual*. Carnegie Mellon University School of Computer Science, 1.1 edition, June 1992.

57. M.K. McKusick. A fast file system for Unix. *ACM Transactions on Computer Systems*, 2(3), August 1984.

58. M.K. McKusick and T.J. Kowalski. Fsck – the Unix file system check program. In *Unix System Manager's Manual, 4.3 Berkeley Software Distribution*. University of California, Berkeley, 1986.

59. S.J. Mullender, G. van Rossum, A.S. Tanenbaum, R. van Renesse, and H. van Staveren. Amoeba: A distributed operating system for the 1990s. *Computer*, 23(5), May 1990.

60. L. Mummert. Exploiting weak connectivity in a distributed file system. Thesis proposal, Carnegie Mellon University School of Computer Science, December 1992.

61. L. Mummert and M. Satyanarayanan. Efficient and portable file reference tracing in a distributed workstation environment. Carnegie Mellon University School of Computer Science, manuscript in preparation, 1993.

62. R.M Needham and M.D. Schroeder. Using encryption for authentication in large networks of computers. *Communications of the ACM*, 21(12), December 1978.

63. B.J. Nelson. *Remote Procedure Call*. PhD thesis, Carnegie Mellon University, 1981.

64. M.N. Nelson, B.B. Welch, and J.K. Ousterhout. Caching in the Sprite network file system. *ACM Transactions on Computer Systems*, 6(1), February 1988.

65. J. Ousterhout, H. Da Costa, D. Harrison, J. Kunze, M. Kupfer, and J. Thompson. A trace-driven analysis of the Unix 4.2 BSD file system. In *Proceedings of the Tenth ACM Symposium on Operating Systems Principles*, December 1985.

66. M.L. Palmer and S.B. Zdonik. Fido: A cache that learns to fetch. Technical Report CS-91-15, Brown University Department of Computer Science, February 1991.

67. D.S. Parker Jr., G.J. Popek, G. Rudisin, A. Stoughton, B.J. Walker, E. Walton, J.M. Chow, D. Edwards, S. Kiser, and C. Kline. Detection of mutual inconsistency in distributed systems. *IEEE Transactions on Software Engineering*, SE-9(3), May 1983.

68. R.H. Patterson, G.A. Gibson, and M. Satyanarayanan. A status report on research in transparent informed prefetching. *Operating Systems Review*, 27(2), April 1993.

69. G.J. Popek and B.J. Walker. *The LOCUS Distributed System Architecture*. MIT Press, 1985.

70. J. Postel. User datagram protocol. Technical Report RFC-768, SRI Network Information Center, 1980.

71. J. Postel. Internet protocol. Technical Report RFC-791, SRI Network Information Center, 1981.

72. T.D.M. Purdin. Fault tolerance in file systems with easily removable media. Technical Report CS-88-132, Colorado State University Department of Computer Science, October 1988.

73. T.D.M. Purdin, R.D. Schlichting, and G.R. Andrews. A file replication facility for Berkeley Unix. *Software Practice and Experience*, 17(12), December 1987.

74. M. Rosenblum and J.K. Ousterhout. The design and implementation of a log-structured file system. *ACM Transactions on Computer Systems*, 10(1), February 1992.

75. D.S.H. Rosenthal. Evolving the vnode interface. In *Proceedings of the Summer Usenix Conference*, June 1990.

76. M. Rozier, V. Abrossimov, F. Armand, I. Boule, M. Gien, M. Guillemont, F. Herrmann, P. Leonard, S. Langlois, and W. Neuhauser. The Chorus distributed operating system. *Computing Systems*, 1(4), 1988.

77. Salient Software, Inc. *AutoDoubler User Manual*, 1992.

78. R. Sandberg, D. Goldberg, S. Kleiman, D. Walsh, and B. Lyon. Design and implementation of the Sun network filesystem. In *Summer Usenix Conference Proceedings*, June 1985.

79. M. Satyanarayanan. A study of file sizes and functional lifetimes. In *Proceedings of the Eighth ACM Symposium on Operating Systems Principles*, December 1981.

80. M. Satyanarayanan. RPC2 user manual. Technical Report CMU-ITC-038, Carnegie Mellon University, Information Technology Center, 1986.

81. M. Satyanarayanan. Integrating security in a large distributed system. *ACM Transactions on Computer Systems*, 7(3), August 1989.

82. M. Satyanarayanan. A survey of distributed file systems. In *Annual Review of Computer Science*. Annual Reviews, Inc, 1989. Also available as Tech. Rep. CMU-CS-89-116, Carnegie Mellon University School of Computer Science, February, 1989.

83. M. Satyanarayanan. Scalable, secure, and highly available distributed file access. *Computer*, 23(5), May 1990.

84. M. Satyanarayanan. The influence of scale on distributed file system design. *IEEE Transactions on Software Engineering*, 18(1), January 1992.

85. M. Satyanarayanan, J.H. Howard, D.N. Nichols, R.N. Sidebotham, A.Z. Spector, and M.J. West. The ITC distributed file system: Principles and design. In *Proceedings of the Tenth ACM Symposium on Operating Systems Principles*, December 1985.

86. M. Satyanarayanan, J.J. Kistler, P. Kumar, M.E. Okasaki, E.H. Siegel, and D.C. Steere. Coda: A highly available file system for a distributed workstation environment. *IEEE Transactions on Computers*, 39(4), April 1990.

87. M. Satyanarayanan, H.H. Mashburn, P. Kumar, D.C. Steere, and J.J. Kistler. Lightweight recoverable virtual memory. Technical Report CMU-CS-93-143, Carnegie Mellon University School of Computer Science, April 1993.

88. M. Schroeder. Autonomy or independence in distributed systems? (position paper). In *Proceedings of the 1988 ACM SIGOPS European Workshop*, September 1988.

89. M.D. Schroeder, A.D. Birrell, M. Burrows, H. Murray, R.M. Needham, T.L. Rodeheffer, E.H. Satterthwaite, and C.P. Thacker. Autonet: A high-speed, self-configuring local area network using point-to-point links. Technical Report 59, Digital Systems Research Center, April 1990.

90. M.D. Schroeder, D.K. Gifford, and R.M. Needham. A caching file system for a programmer's workstation. In *Proceedings of the Tenth ACM Symposium on Operating Systems Principles*, December 1985.

91. S.A. Shafer. *The SUP Software Upgrade Protocol User Manual*. Carnegie Mellon University School of Computer Science, August 1990.

92. R.N. Sidebotham. Volumes: The Andrew file system data structuring primitive. In *European Unix User Group Conference Proceedings*, August 1986. Also available as Tech. Rep. CMU-ITC-053, Carnegie Mellon University, Information Technology Center.

93. A.J. Smith. Long term file reference patterns and their applications to file migration algorithms. *IEEE Transactions on Software Engineering*, 4(7), July 1981.

94. D.C. Steere, J.J. Kistler, and M. Satyanarayanan. Efficient user-level file cache management on the Sun vnode interface. In *Proceedings of the Summer Usenix Conference*, June 1990.

95. L. Svobodova. File servers for network-based distributed systems. *Computing Surveys*, 16(4), December 1984.

96. C. Tait and D. Duchamp. Detection and exploitation of file working sets. In *Proceedings of the Eleventh International Conference on Distributed Computing Systems*, May 1991.

97. C. Tait and D. Duchamp. Service interface and replica consistency algorithm for mobile file system clients. In *Proceedings of the First International Conference on Parallel and Distributed Information Systems*, December 1991.

98. C. Tait and D. Duchamp. An efficient variable consistency replicated file service. In *Proceedings of the Usenix File Systems Workshop*, May 1992.

99. G.M. Tomlinson, D. Keeffe, I.C. Wand, and A.J. Wellings. The PULSE distributed file system. *Software Practice and Experience*, 15(11), November 1985.

100. Laptop, notebook and palmtop computers. in USA Today, June 23, 1992.

101. D.L. Whiting and R.A. Monsour. Data compression breaks through to disk memory technology. *Computer Technology Review*, Spring 1991.

102. E.R. Zayas and C.F. Everhart. Design and specification of the cellular Andrew environment. Technical Report CMU-ITC-070, Carnegie Mellon University, Information Technology Center, 1988.

Index

Lecture Notes in Computer Science

For information about Vols. 1–949

please contact your bookseller or Springer-Verlag